MODERN
MYSTERY
WRITERS

Writers of English: Lives and Works

MODERN
MYSTERY
WRITERS

Edited and with an Introduction by

Harold Bloom

CHELSEA HOUSE PUBLISHERS
New York   Philadelphia

Jacket illustration: Hand-colored photograph by J.K. Potter (courtesy of J.K. Potter).

CHELSEA HOUSE PUBLISHERS

Editorial Director Richard Rennert
Executive Managing Editor Karyn Gullen Browne
Copy Chief Robin James
Picture Editor Adrian G. Allen
Creative Director Robert Mitchell
Art Director Joan Ferrigno
Production Manager Sallye Scott

Writers of English: Lives and Works

Senior Editor S. T. Joshi
Series Design Rae Grant

Staff for MODERN MYSTERY WRITERS

Assistant Editor Mary Sisson
Research Peter Cannon, Stefan Dziemianowicz, Robert Green
Picture Researcher Ellen Dudley

© 1995 by Chelsea House Publishers, a division of Main Line Book Co.

Introduction © 1995 by Harold Bloom

First Printing

1 3 5 7 9 8 6 4 2

Library of Congress Cataloging-in-Publication Data

Modern mystery writers / edited and with an introduction by Harold Bloom.
    p.   cm.—(Writers of English)
    Includes bibliographical references.
    ISBN 0-7910-2375-3.—ISBN 0-7910-2376-1 (pbk.)
    1. Detective and mystery stories, English—History and criticism. 2. Detective and mystery stories, American—History and criticism. 3. Detective and mystery stories—Bio-bibliography. I. Bloom, Harold. II. Series.
PR830.D4M63 1994
823'.087209—dc20   94-5888
                                                                            CIP

◈ Contents

▣ User's Guide

THIS VOLUME PROVIDES biographical, critical, and bibliographical information on the thirteen most significant modern mystery writers. Each chapter consists of three parts: a biography of the author; a selection of brief critical extracts about the author; and a bibliography of the author's published books.

The biography supplies a detailed outline of the important events in the author's life, including his or her major writings. The critical extracts are taken from a wide array of books and periodicals, from the author's lifetime to the present, and range in content from biographical to critical to historical. The extracts are arranged in chronological order by date of writing or publication, and a full bibliographical citation is provided at the end of each extract. Editorial additions or deletions are indicated within carets.

The author bibliographies list every separate publication—including books, pamphlets, broadsides, collaborations, and works edited or translated by the author—for works published in the author's lifetime; selected important posthumous publications are also listed. Titles are those of the first edition; variant titles are supplied within carets. In selected instances dates of revised editions are given where these are significant. Pseudonymous works are listed; but not the pseudonyms under which these works were published. Periodicals edited by the author are listed only when the author has written most or all of the contents. Titles enclosed in square brackets are of doubtful authenticity. All works by the author, whether in English or in other languages, have been listed; English translations of foreign-language works are not listed unless the author has done the translation.

The Life of the Author
Harold Bloom

NIETZSCHE, WITH EXULTANT ANGUISH, famously proclaimed that God was dead. Whatever the consequences of this for the ethical life, its ultimate literary effect certainly would have surprised the author Nietzsche. His French disciples, Foucault most prominent among them, developed the Nietzschean proclamation into the dogma that all authors, God included, were dead. The death of the author, which is no more than a Parisian trope, another metaphor for fashion's setting of skirt-lengths, is now accepted as literal truth by most of our current apostles of what should be called French Nietzsche, to distinguish it from the merely original Nietzsche. We also have French Freud or Lacan, which has little to do with the actual thought of Sigmund Freud, and even French Joyce, which interprets *Finnegans Wake* as the major work of Jacques Derrida. But all this is as nothing compared to the final triumph of the doctrine of the death of the author: French Shakespeare. That delicious absurdity is given us by the New Historicism, which blends Foucault and California fruit juice to give us the Word that Renaissance "social energies," and not William Shakespeare, composed *Hamlet* and *King Lear*. It seems a proper moment to murmur "enough" and to return to a study of the life of the author.

Sometimes it troubles me that there are so few masterpieces in the vast ocean of literary biography that stretches between James Boswell's great *Life* of Dr. Samuel Johnson and the late Richard Ellmann's wonderful *Oscar Wilde*. Literary biography is a crucial genre, and clearly a difficult one in which to excel. The actual nature of the lives of the poets seems to have little effect upon the quality of their biographies. Everything happened to Lord Byron and nothing at all to Wallace Stevens, and yet their biographers seem equally daunted by them. But even inadequate biographies of strong writers, or of weak ones, are of immense use. I have never read a literary biography from which I have not profited, a statement I cannot make about any other genre whatsoever. And when it comes to figures who are central to us—Dante, Shakespeare, Cervantes, Montaigne, Goethe, Whitman, Tolstoi, Freud, Joyce, Kafka among them—we reach out eagerly for every scrap that the biographers have gleaned. Concerning Dante and Shakespeare we know much too little, yet when we come to Goethe and Freud, where we seem to know more than everything, we still want to know more. The death of the author, despite our current resentniks, clearly was only a momentary fad. Something vital in every authentic lover of literature responds to Emerson's battle-cry sentence: "There is no history, only biography." Beyond that there is a deeper truth, difficult to come at and requiring a lifetime to understand, which is that there is no literature, only autobiography, however mediated, however veiled, however transformed. The events of Shakespeare's life included the composition of *Hamlet,* and that act of writing was itself a crucial act of living, though we do not yet know altogether how to read so doubled an act. When an author takes up a more overtly autobiographical stance, as so many do in their youth, again we still do not know precisely how to accommodate the vexed relation between life and work. T. S. Eliot, meditating upon James Joyce, made a classic statement as to such accommodation:

> We want to know who are the originals of his characters, and what were the origins of his episodes, so that we may unravel the web of memory and invention and discover how far and in what ways the crude material has been transformed.

When a writer is not even covertly autobiographical, the web of memory and invention is still there, but so subtly woven that we may never unravel it. And yet we want deeply never to stop trying, and not merely because we are curious, but because each of us is caught in her own network of memory and invention. We do not always recall our inventions, and long before we age we cease to be certain of the extent to which we have invented our memories. Perhaps one motive for reading is our need to unravel our own webs. If our masters could make, from their lives, what we read, then we can be moved by them to ask: What have we made or lived in relation to what we have read? The answers may be sad, or confused, but the question is likely, implicitly, to go on being asked as long as we read. In Freudian terms, we are asking: What is it that we have repressed? What have we forgotten, unconsciously but purposively: What is it that we flee? Art, literature necessarily included, is regression in the service of the ego, according to a famous Freudian formula. I doubt the Freudian wisdom here, but indubitably it is profoundly suggestive. When we read, something in us keeps asking the equivalent of the Freudian questions: From what or whom is the author in flight, and to what earlier stages in her life is she returning, and why?

Reading, whether as an art or a pastime, has been damaged by the visual media, television in particular, and might be in some danger of extinction in the age of the computer, except that the psychic need for it continues to endure, presumably because it alone can assuage a central loneliness in elitist society. Despite all sophisticated or resentful denials, the reading of imaginative literature remains a quest to overcome the isolation of the individual consciousness. We can read for information, or entertainment, or for love of the language, but in the end we seek, in the author, the person whom we have not found, whether in ourselves or in others. In that quest, there always are elements at once aggressive and defensive, so that reading, even in childhood, is rarely free of hidden anxieties. And yet it remains one of the few activities not contaminated by an entropy of spirit. We read in hope, because we lack companionship, and the author can become the object of the most idealistic elements in our search for the wit and inventiveness we so desperately require. We read biography, not as a supplement to reading the author, but as a second, fresh attempt to understand what always seems to evade us in the work, our drive towards a kind of identity with the author.

This will-to-identity, though recently much deprecated, is a prime basis for the experience of sublimity in reading. *Hamlet* retains its unique position in the Western canon not because most readers and playgoers identify themselves with the prince, who clearly is beyond them, but rather because they find themselves again in the power of the language that represents him with such immediacy and force. Yet we know that neither language nor social energy created Hamlet. Our curiosity about Shakespeare is endless, and never will be appeased. That curiosity itself is a value, and cannot be separated from the value of *Hamlet* the tragedy, or Hamlet the literary character. It provokes us that Shakespeare the man seems so unknowable, at once everyone and no one as Borges shrewdly observes. Critics keep telling us otherwise, yet something valid in us keeps believing that we would know Hamlet better if Shakespeare's life were as fully known as the lives of Goethe and Freud, Byron and Oscar Wilde, or best of all, Dr. Samuel Johnson. Shakespeare never will have his Boswell, and Dante never will have his Richard Ellmann. How much one would give for a detailed and candid *Life of Dante* by Petrarch, or an outspoken memoir of Shakespeare by Ben Jonson! Or, in the age just past, how superb would be rival studies of one another by Hemingway and Scott Fitzgerald! But the list is endless: think of *Oscar Wilde* by Lord Alfred Douglas, or a joint biography of Shelley by Mary Godwin, Emilia Viviani, and Jane Williams. More than our insatiable desire for scandal would be satisfied. The literary rivals and the lovers of the great writers possessed perspectives we will never enjoy, and without those perspectives we dwell in some poverty in regard to the writers with whom we ourselves never can be done.

There is a sense in which imaginative literature *is* perspectivism, so that the reader is likely to be overwhelmed by the work's difficulty unless its multiple perspectives are mastered. Literary biography matters most because it is a storehouse of perspectives, frequently far surpassing any that are grasped by the particular biographer. There are relations between authors' lives and their works of kinds we have yet to discover, because our analytical instruments are not yet advanced enough to perform the necessary labor. Perhaps a novel, poem, or play is not so much a regression in the service of the ego, as it is an amalgam of *all* the Freudian mechanisms of defense, all working together for the apotheosis of the ego. Freud valued art highly, but thought that the aesthetic enterprise was no rival for psychoanalysis, unlike religion and philosophy. Clearly Freud was mistaken; his own anxieties about his indebtedness to Shakespeare helped produce the weirdness of his joining in the lunacy that argued for the Earl of Oxford as the author of Shakespeare's plays. It was Shakespeare, and not "the poets," who was there before Freud arrived at his depth psychology, and it is Shakespeare who is there still, well out ahead of psychoanalysis. We see what Freud would not see, that psychoanalysis is Shakespeare prosified and systematized. Freud is part of literature, not of "science," and the biography of Freud has the same relations to psychoanalysis as the biography of Shakespeare has to *Hamlet* and *King Lear*, if only we knew more of the life of Shakespeare.

Western literature, particularly since Shakespeare, is marked by the representation of internalized change in its characters. A literature of the ever-growing inner self is in itself a large form of biography, even though this is the biography of imaginary beings, from Hamlet to the sometimes nameless protagonists of Kafka and Beckett. Skeptics might want to argue that all literary biography concerns imaginary beings, since authors make themselves up, and every biographer gives us a creation curiously different from the same author as seen by the writer of a rival *Life*. Boswell's Johnson is not quite anyone else's Johnson, though it is now very difficult for us to disentangle the great Doctor from his gifted Scottish friend and follower. The life of the author is not merely a metaphor or a fiction, as is "the Death of the Author," but it always does contain metaphorical or fictive elements. Those elements are a part of the value of literary biography, but not the largest or the crucial part, which is the separation of the mask from the man or woman who hid behind it. James Joyce and Samuel Beckett, master and sometime disciple, were both of them enigmatic personalities, and their biographers have not, as yet, fully expounded the mystery of these contrasting natures. Beckett seems very nearly to have been a secular saint: personally disinterested, heroic in the French Resistance, as humane a person ever to have composed major fictions and dramas. Joyce, self-obsessed even as Beckett was preternaturally selfless, was the Milton of the twentieth century. Beckett was perhaps the least egoistic post-Joycean, post-Proustian, post-Kafkan of writers. Does that illuminate the problematical nature of his work, or does it simply constitute another problem? Whatever the cause, the question matters. The only death of the author that is other than literal, and that matters, is the fate only of weak writers. The strong, who become canonical, never die, which is what the canon truly is about. To be read forever is the Life of the Author.

✦ Introduction

THE MYSTERY WRITER Elizabeth Mackintosh, who wrote her most successful books under the pen name of Josephine Tey, had an extraordinary sense of history, whether of her native Scotland or of England in the tumult of the Wars of the Roses. Tey's mysteries are likely to prove as ephemeral as those of her contemporaries: Nicholas Blake (the poet C. Day Lewis), Michael Innes (the scholar J. I. M. Stewart), and Margaret Millar (the best of this group). Yet there is an exception by Tey: *The Daughter of Time*, a rehabilitation of King Richard III, the first of Shakespeare's great hero-villains. "Truth is the daughter of time," the ironical proverb that is Tey's epigraph, stands little chance of prevailing in the case of Richard III, where the truth is inevitably less interesting than Shakespeare's fascinating and frightening monster. Tey's *The Daughter of Time* evidently will survive as a useful if ineffectual corrective to Shakespeare's history play, which accepted the Tudor myth of Richard's wickedness in contrast to the supposed goodness of Henry VII, the grandfather of Elizabeth I, in whose reign Shakespeare wrote his dramatic version of the Wars of the Roses.

Tey's Inspector Grant, the hero of her mysteries, is immobilized all through *The Daughter of Time*, gradually mending his broken leg in a hospital. He becomes obsessed with a portrait of Richard III by an unknown artist contemporary with the hunchback king, who supposedly had been responsible for the murder of his two little nephews in the Tower of London. Yet the haunted eyes of the portrait do not suggest a villain to Grant's shrewdly experienced seeing. Instead he beholds "someone too conscientious," who had influenced English history quite profoundly, despite a reign of only two years. The mystery that the crippled Scotland Yard detective sets out to solve can be resolved only by the initial intuition that began his quest for the authentic, historic Richard III. This is the intuition of a superior sensibility by another such sensibility, in defiance of time and its misrepresentations. Free-ranging in spirit though confined in body, Grant employs intermediaries to bring him the information he requires, until the perfect assistant appears in a young American. This amateur historian, Brent Carradine, gradually helps Grant to a persuasive synthesis that absolves the maligned Richard III, and clears up the mystery of the young princes, who were slain at the orders of the usurper, Henry VII.

Rereading Tey's *The Daughter of Time* after many years, I reflect upon how neatly the old mystery is cleared up by Grant (as it also is by some modern historians), yet how little difference the truth makes against Shakespeare's poetic power. Whether Shakespeare himself dared to have any doubts concerning Tudor historiography we will never know, yet I suspect that the creator of *Richard III* was more concerned with overcoming Christopher Marlowe's Barabas of *The Jew of Malta* than he cared at all about fairness to the actual Richard III. The Richard III of the historians, and of Josephine Tey, is a shadow compared to Shakespeare's great caricature, who out-Marlowes Marlowe's grandest grotesque. It is scarcely fair or even useful to compare Josephine Tey's power of representation to those of William Shakespeare: in such a contest, even Marcel Proust would be certain to lose. Yet the defeat of Tey's best book by the vividness of a Shakespearean villain seems to me a parable of the limitations of the modern mystery as a genre. Its detectives search for a truth that their authors never have the genius to dramatize. If we do not care who killed Roger Ackroyd or whether Richard III actually murdered his nephews, it is because something in us longs perpetually for stronger characterizations than either subliterary writing or history writing can give us. Shakespeare's Richard III, though a myth, will outlast any other.

—H. B.

Margery Allingham
1904–1966

MARGERY LOUISE ALLINGHAM was born in London on May 20, 1904, to Herbert John Allingham, a journalist and editor, and Emily Jane Hughes, a writer. Shortly after her birth her parents moved to a home in Layer Breton, Essex. Allingham began writing at the age of eight, and she continued writing while attending the Perse High School for Girls in Cambridge and the Polytechnic School of Speech Training. She intended to pursue a career in acting and also wrote several plays, one of which, *Water in a Sieve*, was published in 1925; but the critical success of her early novels—her first, *Blackkerchief Dick* (1923), appeared when she was nineteen—impelled her into full-time writing. Since her novels did not provide a sufficient income, Allingham wrote many stories, articles, and reviews for magazines. In 1927 she married the editor and illustrator Philip Youngman Carter, and they settled into a Queen Anne house in Essex, where they remained for most of their lives. In 1929 she introduced her celebrated detective, Albert Campion, in *The Crime at Black Dudley*, and in the succeeding decades he was featured in a score of other mystery novels.

The Campion saga undergoes a variety of mutations during the course of Allingham's career. He begins as a somewhat foolish-seeming, socially inept individual—as different as possible from the cerebral Hercule Poirot of Agatha Christie or the debonair Lord Peter Wimsey of Dorothy L. Sayers—and his manservant, the ex-convict Magersfontein Lugg, is a delightful parody of Wimsey's valet, Bunter. The early Allingham novels mingle detection with the spy or gangster novel (*Mystery Mile*, 1930; *Sweet Danger*, 1933), but later move toward pure detection. In the mid-1930s Allingham also wrote three novels under the pseudonym Maxwell March (*Other Man's Danger*, 1933; *Rogues' Holiday*, 1935; *The Shadow in the House*, 1936).

Sweet Danger introduces Amanda Fitton, then a girl of seventeen. She reappears in several novels, developing a romance with Campion. In *Traitor's Purse* (1941) they are engaged, although Campion has suffered a loss of memory that renders him incapable of understanding the nature of their relationship. Several later novels treat of their married life.

During World War II Allingham temporarily abandoned the detective novel to write two mainstream novels (*The Oaken Heart*, 1941; *Dance of the Years*, 1943), and even after her return to mystery fiction she used Campion with decreasing frequency. Instead, the focus shifts to the policeman Charles Luke, who appears in *More Work for the Undertaker* (1948), *The Tiger in the Smoke* (1952), and other novels. Her last completed novel, *The Mind Readers* (1965), is a mixture of detection and science fiction in its treatment of ESP.

Allingham also wrote a number of short stories (collected in *The Allingham Case-Book*, 1969; *The Allingham Minibus*, 1973; and *The Return of Mr. Campion*, 1989), some of which venture into the macabre, the supernatural, and science fiction. The novel *Cargo of Eagles* was left unfinished at her death on June 30, 1966, and was completed by her husband, who went on to write two subsequent novels about Albert Campion.

❖ *Critical Extracts*

WILL CUPPY   For once this department feels most virtuous and helpful to be recommending a swell thriller of uncommon merit in every direction. Honestly, you can't go wrong with *Death of a Ghost*. It's one of those clever atmospheric things, by turns startling and amusing (though by no means a "funny mystery"), that should please the most fastidious, even if you're practically bedridden with spring fever. Why go elsewhere to be frightened when you can rest assured of a lovely but horrible murder right here—and also of the ministrations of Albert Campion, a Grade A sleuth as good as any now going?

> Will Cuppy, [Review of *Death of a Ghost*], *New York Herald Tribune Books*, 22 April 1923, p. 13

NICHOLAS BLAKE   Though all of the first six novels under review are distinctly above the average of detection-writing, Miss Allingham is awarded without hesitation this month's O.M., or Order of Murder. *Flowers for the Judge* (an attractive but not too relevant title), by its sense of proportion and its all-round excellence, shows up each of its competitors as comparatively unbalanced going, in one direction or another, too far. Miss Allingham has a really unusual talent for creating lovable characters, and—what is more difficult—for the creation of thoroughly convincing unlovable ones: the clerk, Rigget, is a case in point. She takes great pains with her minor characters too: the charwoman, Mrs. Austin, is a devilishly authentic blend of the kind intention and the ghoulish effect. The setting is beautifully done, an old-established publishers, one of whose directors has vanished into thin air within sight of two witnesses while another is found gassed in the firm's strong-room. Not the least of many original things about this book is the way the author makes her heroine, a *chic*, charming, beautiful creature, actually *deteriorate* under the strain of tragedy. How intrepid—and how admirable! Miss Allingham's writing is humorous and supple: I found only one phrase to quarrel with—"most stratas of society"; she can suggest naked drama beneath the dress of sophistication, as witness the cigarette-end incident on p. 19; and she has the rare capacity of making a case-hardened reviewer catch his breath—the trap laid for the detective, Mr. Campion, is brilliantly horrifying. Albert Campion, by the way, can now consider himself elected to my highly exclusive club of Best Fiction-Detectives. The only flaw I found in this admirable book is the motive. Was it really strong enough?

Nicholas Blake, "Going Too Far," *Spectator*, 28 February 1936, p. 364

PHYLLIS McGINLEY   If ⟨Allingham's⟩ *Tiger in the Smoke* is not perhaps the finest flower of all the year's garden, it is definitely a flower and not a weed. Indeed, it is a splendid, gaudy, extravagant bloom, guaranteed to please. For it is the product of a real practitioner, of a writer (if I may drop my horticultural figure) willing to take pains with plot, sufficiently talented to write graceful and perceptive prose, sensitive enough to character to make human beings out of victim, criminal and detective alike.

True, *Tiger in the Smoke* might seem to the purist to own a flaw or two. Although Miss Allingham has invented a new detective, an admirable and fascinating man named Charles Luke—although even Albert Campion figures briefly here as a sop, no doubt, to Allingham readers who expect him—this is not really a detective story at all. Clues do not solve the puzzle. The criminal's identity is not revealed by classic formula, at the close of the book, but long before it. It does not have the precise architectural integrity of the best of Dorothy Sayers (whose *Strong Poison*, for instance, can withstand that ultimate test—rereading).

This is a different genre. It is all suspense, all chase, in the John Buchan tradition. But it is good, very good. From the first wonderful sentence, "It may be only blackmail," to the final clipped paragraph, the story never lags. Fog swirls about a brooding city. A killer of uncommon evil broods in the fog. The forces of right, if a bit naive at times, do triumph over incredible— no, credible—dangers. And everything, if larger than life, is at least parallel to it. What is more, the criminal meets a fate he has deserved, and there is no false or sentimental deploring that fate. A sentimental attitude toward the killer has destroyed as many detective stories recently as bad writing. Here, praise Heaven, there are angels and devils and very little is cited according to Freud.

> Phyllis McGinley, "A Report on Criminals at Large," *New York Times Book Review*, 7 September 1952, p. 26

ANTHONY BOUCHER   It has always been difficult to draw a sharply defined line between the spy novel and science fiction. There is often something science-fictionish about The Plans at stake—which is a direct reflection of reality; there is often something science-fictionish about the secrets for which real-life agents contend. Fictional and (one assumes) factual spies were much concerned with spaceflight even before the first sputnik. Today every major power is rumored to be conducting hush-hush experiments on E.S.P. (extra-sensory perception, or "telepathy") as a serious method of, among other possibilities, military communication; and Margery Allingham's *The Mind Readers*, though it seems to cross the border into pure science fiction, may be more realistic than the reader believes.

The story deals with the extraordinary breakthrough finally achieved by an English research group, and the consequences of this unquestionable proof of the workability of E.S.P. There are agents and double-agents and a murderer, and fortunately Albert Campion is at hand to straighten every-thing out—but all of this conventional thriller-apparatus, though compe-tently handled, tends to get in the way of what telepathy feels like and how it affects people. This is the novel's best feature. It seems fresh and strongly convincing—even after the hundreds of s.f. stories which have covered the same ground.

> Anthony Boucher, [Review of *The Mind Readers*], *New York Times Book Review*, 18 July 1965, p. 28

LeROY PANEK   With *Police at the Funeral,* ⟨. . .⟩ Allingham moved into the very different world of the detective story, one which has marked differences from that of the thriller. None of her new, detective novels deal with monolithic international conspiracies, but shift to the domestic murder as the central concern—almost as if she had read the "fair play" rules about the absurdity of writing a mystery story about such mythical monsters as Master Crooks and Secret Societies. Therefore much of the exotic, wild action disappears, and there are no kidnappings or extended chases in the detective books. Instead of using the whole of England as the ground for the action, the new novels concentrate on specific locales. *Police at the Funeral, Death of a Ghost,* and *Dancers in Mourning* are pretty much confined in terms of place with an attempt to focus on that mainstay of detective writers, the mansion. The atmosphere, sick and oppressive instead of scary, comes from the house and from an examination of the household's relationships and personalities, rather than from the suggestion of ancient and supernatural horror which colors the thrillers. Perhaps most significantly, Allingham disbands the hero-leader and his group of assistants, leaving the detective noticeably isolated in a world in which fast action, quick wits, and the other virtues of the thriller hero are of no use.

In addition to structuring these novels around one major crime which occurs early on and scrapping many of the accoutrements of the thriller, Allingham uses detective story sources—*Police at the Funeral* is certainly based on Conan Doyle's "The Problem of Thor Bridge"—and she incorporates into her books, especially those in the late thirties, the mechanics of the fair play detective story. She does not do this with much enthusiasm or originality, but she does it nonetheless. Chiefly, Allingham uses the "had he but known" formula to call the reader's attention to specific facts, personalities, or relationships, thus producing the signal for the reader to cudgel his brains—if he is so inclined. The first book in which this technique prominently appears is *The Case of the Late Pig,* in which there are seven instances of it throughout the story. This one is fairly typical:

> I stood looking down at the glass in my hand, twirling the ice round and round in the amber fluid, and it was then that I had the whole case under my nose.
>   Unfortunately, I only saw half of it.

There are also prominent, if less pointed, uses of the same technique in *Dancers in Mourning* and *Fashion in Shrouds*. In *The Mysterious Mr. Campion* Allingham recalls being inducted into the Detective Writers' Club and swearing before Dorothy Sayers that "I would never cheat"; and in the detective novels she never does, and she provides the required signposts for the curious reader.

LeRoy Panek, "Margery Allingham," *Watteau's Shepherds: The Detective Novel in Britain 1914–1940* (Bowling Green, OH: Bowling Green University Popular Press, 1979), pp. 136–37

PATRICIA CRAIG and MARY CADOGAN   On the face of it, Amanda Fitton is the detective's wife who seems best fitted to enter into the spirit of the game herself; but in fact she plays very little active part after the first novel in which she appears, *Sweet Danger* (1933). Albert Campion, Margery Allingham's sleuth, who looks foolish but isn't, comes across Amanda while she is acting as miller of Pontisbright. She is seventeen at the time, red-haired, comely and emotionally uncomplicated. She is a competent electrician and mechanic—she goes on to design an aeroplane— engagingly candid and self-possessed, plucky and loyal in the usual way of a young person who is anxious to involve herself in the knockabout enter- prise: 'I should like to point out that I would make a very good aide-de- camp.' Campion replies, 'Or lieut. . . . I often think that's what the poet meant when he said Orpheus and his lieut.'

Humorous understatement is the tone that Margery Allingham adopts to characterize the attachment between Campion and Amanda, but it's carried so far that it turns into comic reticence. 'Look here,' Amanda states when she's lying in bed recovering from a bullet wound acquired in the course of her activities as Campion's second-in-command, 'I shan't be ready for about six years yet. But then—well, I'd like to put you on the top of my list.' As a caricature of the English spirit this ranks with the fictional schoolgirl Jemima Carstairs's 'Oh, chin up, chin up! Chest out, old thing!'; but Campion's rejoinder takes us a stage further in the procedure of expressing affection without overdoing it: 'What's going to change you in six years, you rum little grig?' he wonders. It is a moment of tenderness. ⟨. . .⟩

Campion, the pale, astute young man in horn-rimmed glasses, is given a few things to say on the subject of women which have no particular value:

> Most women . . . muddled through to truth in the most dangerous and irritating fashion. All the same they were not quite so clever as they thought they were, which was as it should be, of course, but odd considering their remarkable penetration in most other practical matters.
>
> It was astonishing how the simple, direct reactions of the ordinary male eluded them . . .

It is astonishing how the simple, direct facts about individual characteristics, the dangers of generalization and complexity in social behaviour elude the popular novelist. However, Margery Allingham writes with gusto and inventiveness and these qualities help to mitigate the more banal assumptions in her novels; it is not until the 1950s that her style becomes impossibly mannered and strained.

Patricia Craig and Mary Cadogan, *The Lady Investigates: Women Detectives and Spies in Fiction* (London: Victor Gollancz, 1981), pp. 203–4, 206–7

TALBOTT W. HUEY   As an anti-hero, Campion stood for values which were seen or felt by his creator as transcending the social organization of a particular era: a keen sense of justice, a responsibility for those in distress, a gentlemanly sense that competence must be accompanied by modesty, etc. This insistence that values which are in part so obviously associated with a certain class and era (Edwardian upper-middle and upper class Britain) have also a transcendental character and are absolute is, appropriately, itself a part of the historical character of the Anglo-American upper-middle class, but cannot be dismissed for that reason. It may be said, for example, that the police have a class character in that they defend the property of the rich against possible depredation by the "criminal classes," but also in discovering and punishing the perpetrator of a heinous, antihuman crime they can be said to be serving the cause of some sort of "purer" or less class-based justice. Campion, while no doubt a gentleman of the old school in a sense, as a seeker for truth and justice can and does define justice in as broad and meaningful a sense as he (and the average reader) can understand, and thus may find employment, so to speak, in 1965 as readily as in 1935. Despite some real trepidation about the postwar world, Allingham in retaining her Great Detective was betting that his function of reassuring the reader that justice will be served would strike a timeless response. And she seems to have been right, at least to the extent that Campion is a successful, appealing, legitimate character, which I certainly think he is. And Campion makes it clear that he is not only the defender of the comfortable classes and their need for social stability but also Nemesis, restoring the moral coherence of the world after evil has been done. Margery Allingham described her moral feelings explicitly in *The Oaken Heart*, a paean to old-fashioned British pluck in the face of the Nazi threat of 1939–40. She described this threat as "the new German experiment" in the "attempt to gain the world by laboriously and meticulously backing the downward drive in the universal equilibrium—at one time the most gigantic and most naively mistaken project since Lucifer got himself kicked out of heaven." And later,

> Nazi doctrine has no aim save slavery and methods which are lies and violence and broken promises, and yet, most terrible of all, a force which is fanatical and spiritual. . . .
> This was plain elementary Wrong. This was the worship of the other god.

Phrased simplistically as it is in religious and sentimental terms, this passage sounds a bit like Colonel Blimp. But it also sincerely and impressively states a faith in abstract good which shines through the fictional works of that time and after, and renders Campion to that extent a man for all seasons.

Talbott W. Huey, "Mr. Campion and the Survival of the Great Detective," *Clues* 3, No. 1 (Spring–Summer 1982): 101

REX W. GASKILL   *Fashion in Shrouds* gives us Rex, the fashion designer, " 'not quite a lady,' " as Tante Martha describes him. Rex has fits of petulance, little coy exuberances and coy wiggles and giggles. Still, before he says "Beddy-byes" in his last appearance in the book, he has informed Campion that he has served as a Tommy in France during World War I, and consequently Campion has identified him as "a natty, demure little soul, only effeminate insomuch as sex shocked him for its ugliness and interested him because it shocked him." We are never quite sure what this means, but it seems to be intended as a compliment.

Finally among those characters of any prominence we have Ricky Silva in *Coroner's Pidgin*, part of Lord Carados's menage who "existed solely to do the flowers as far as anyone knew." Ricky is plump, babyish and gentle with full, childish lips. He cries easily and one is certain that if we could hear him speak it would be with a lisp. He is also a private in the British army during World War II. Of this fact he suggests:

> "I'm having hell, as I tell you, absolute hell." It dawned on Mr.
> Campion that he was probably speaking the truth. The life of a
> man like Ricky Silva as a conscript private in the British Army
> did not bear consideration.

Ricky plays a very minor role in the action of the book and survives the war as far as we know.

The last references in the post-war novels are brief and incidental to the main action. In *Tiger in the Smoke* we have the character of Bill, one of Tiddy Doll's gang, who is effeminate and for whom fear is an excitant. In *The Mind Readers* we have an unnamed minor spy who is variously referred to as "such a dear old lady," "my old queer from the tea shop" and part of "a real old queens' quadrille." Finally in *Cargo of Eagles* we have our first taste of leather. Moo Moo the Dog Faced Boy is the leader of the motorcycle gang and we are assured that he "likes boys mostly."

None of the pictures Allingham presents are likely to cause rejoicing in contemporary gay and lesbian organizations. They are interesting largely because they exist at all at a time and in a genre which usually ignored the issue. They seem less dated, however, when we examine a passage in a P. D. James mystery, *Unnatural Causes*. Ms. James admits to being a fan of Allingham. She is undeniably a modern writer and a good one. Her gay character, Digby Seton, later a second murder victim, sounds familiar:

> He was afraid, too, that I might set up house with a queer. He
> didn't want his money shared with a pansy boyfriend. Poor Old

> Maurice! I don't think he'd recognize a queen if he met one. He
> just had the idea that London, and the West End clubs in
> particular, are full of them.

Allingham creates gay characters which are consistent with the stereotypes that existed in her time. In so doing she demonstrates her facility
with stock types, but even here there is a wealth of detail and she succeeds
in making some of the most completely developed, such as Benny Konrad
and Beaut Siegfried, come alive. She is good enough that they begin to
seem more than a convention while at the same time never violating it.
Their creation provides additional variety. Allingham is never willing simply
to settle for one or two types of people. It is a virtue of her work that all
sorts and conditions of humanity can be found within its pages.

Rex W. Gaskill, "Margery Allingham," *And Then There Were Nine . . . .: More Women
of Mystery*, ed. Jane S. Bakerman (Bowling Green, OH: Bowling Green State University Popular Press, 1985), pp. 52–53

B. A. PIKE   Albert Campion makes his first appearance at the Black
Dudley dinner-table, one murky evening, by candlelight, an uninvited guest
at what rapidly whips up into an eventful weekend party. Described in
general terms by a fellow-guest as "a lunatic . . . just a silly ass" (a catchphrase
that links him with Bertie Wooster and even facets of Lord Peter Wimsey),
the initial account of his appearance bears out this impression. He is "fresh-
faced . . . with two-colored hair," "foolish, pale-blue eyes behind tortoise-
shell-rimmed spectacles," a "slightly receding chin," and a "mouth . . .
unnecessarily full of teeth," through which he speaks in an "absurd falsetto
drawl." Although Miss Allingham does not in later novels insist on the
receding chin, or the protruding teeth and falsetto voice, Campion's features
do not in essentials change over the years; rather, they are modified as she
takes him increasingly seriously.

In the same way, although his persona is decidedly comic at first, there
is yet implicit in the absurdity something of the seriousness of his later self.
Such a question as "Who would dream of the cunning criminal brain that
lurks beneath my inoffensive exterior?" is, in fact, a flippant foreshadowing
of Campion's essential attitude, that of the guileless-looking nonentity whom
it is almost obligatory to underestimate. (In the first book, it is Chris
Kennedy, the beefy young rugger blue, who makes the mistake: " 'You stand

by,' said Kennedy, with something suspiciously like a sneer on his face . . .
'And by the way, I think you're the man to stay with the girls.' There was
no mistaking his inference.") When Miss Allingham tells us that "Mr.
Campion's personality was a difficult one to take seriously," she is establishing
an image of him that persists at least as far as *Flowers for the Judge* in 1936
(where Miss Curley takes some minutes to realize that he is different from
the many "consciously funny young men, most of them ill-mannered nin-
compoops" of her acquaintance, and that his particular "flow of nonsense"
cloaks "more than poverty of intelligence").

Campion's eccentricities save him, in this first book, at least, from the
danger of conventionality. There is, after all, nothing exceptional about his
heroics at Black Dudley; the courage, the resilience, the resource, constitute
the stock-in-trade of the most standard model of fictional adventurer. The
special interest of Campion is that we do not at first know how to take
him—that he proves, for instance, to have an "agility and strength altogether
surprising in one of such a languid appearance": and it is this capacity for
"surprising" that makes him, from the first, an intriguing figure with very
real possibilities for development.

In this introductory adventure, Campion is very much a man of mystery,
quite apart from the uncertainty engendered by his dual personality as
harmless clown and man of action. George Abbershaw, the book's amateur
detective, is at first unable to "place" him, although convinced that they
have met before; and when he does call to mind the circumstances of their
previous encounter, which are never specified, he identifies him, not as
Albert Campion, but as "Mornington Dodd" (the first of several noms-de-
guerre that enliven the earlier novels). Here, too, is the first reference to
Campion's real identity, that of the younger son of a noble house: " 'Campion
. . . is your name, I suppose?' 'Well—er—no,' said the irrepressible young
man. 'But . . . my own is rather aristocratic and I never use it in my business.' "

So alarmed is Abbershaw by his earlier knowledge of Campion, and his
reflections on the irregular nature of his profession, that he suspects him
for a time of the Black Dudley murder; but his conduct is increasingly
reassuring, and his apologia sufficiently disarming to remove any serious
doubts, for the reader at any rate: "I live, like all intelligent people, by my
wits, and although I've often done things that mother wouldn't like, I have
remembered her parting words and have never been vulgar . . . I do almost
anything within reason . . . but nothing sordid or vulgar—quite definitely

nothing vulgar." Elsewhere, we have his additional assurance that most of his commissions "are more secret than shady."

B. A. Pike, *Campion's Career: A Study of the Novels of Margery Allingham* (Bowling Green, OH: Bowling Green State University Popular Press, 1987), pp. 7–8

RICHARD MARTIN   On a number of occasions Margery Alling-ham attempted to formulate her own view of her aims and her achievement. She was, in her own phrase, "an instinctive writer," in the sense that much of what she wrote did not emerge from a clearly thought out thematic plan either of the book in question, or, more generally, of life in any intellectually philosophical sense: "I am by nature an intuitive writer whose intellect trots along behind, tidying, censuring and saying 'Oh my!' It has taken me a very long time to comprehend this and to allow for it." In this statement, Allingham is clearly referring to the painstaking discipline of her writing and at the same time accounting for the continuous maturing process of her work. Yet even the intuitive writer must begin somewhere; why then with the detective story? She herself saw the beginnings rooted in the enjoyment she and her husband shared in reading "lighthearted adventure stories" (Edgar Wallace and P. G. Wodehouse) in the mid-twenties. This enjoyment coupled with the natural urge to write was encouraged by the demand for what she referred to as "a literate and intelligent literature of escape." Allingham defined the much maligned term "literature of escape" as an instrument of solace, "an escape from an intolerable hour." Above all she noted that "any kind of book can provide the necessary vehicle." She drew no careful lines of demarcation between genre and genre, subgenre and subgenre, popular and serious, but rather laid a clear emphasis on a shared humane functionality, which she claimed for her work as for any other literary product. In fact, Allingham saw the modern mystery story within the framework of the application of this theory of escape literature to the crises and upheavals in Western society that began in the mid-thirties.

She said of her own books that they were novels "of the life of the time" in which a sudden death in mysterious circumstances often served to "make characters reveal themselves." Within such an undertaking mystery writing becomes "a kind of reflection of society's conscience," writing which com-bines the telling of home truths with the business of entertainment. Not only is the modern mystery novel part and parcel of the universal literature of escape, but the crime writer is seen to be historically in the tradition of the entertainer with a social function, commenting, often ironically, on faults in the fabric of society.

> Richard Martin, *Ink in Her Blood: The Life and Crime Fiction of Margery Allingham* (Ann Arbor, MI: UMI Research Press, 1988), pp. 17–18

JULIA THOROGOOD   By the turn of the ⟨1950s⟩, Margery had become somewhat disillusioned with the role of the police in society and impatient with their centrality in detective fiction. 'It's a very sour world where the romantic heroes masquerade as police in uniform.' From 1958 Margery showed a new willingness to talk directly about her craft, not merely through asides as she had done in her reviews. She felt ready to pass on her 'trade secrets' and possibly by doing so to help her own work through a period of transition. 'I am by nature an intuitive writer whose intellect trots along behind, tidying, censuring and saying "Oh My!" It has taken me a very long time to comprehend this and to allow for it,' she wrote in 1965.

The debate surrounding the partial abolition of capital punishment (by the Homicide Act of 1957) demanded that detective novelists reassess their craft. The appalling consequences of mistaken deduction in a society where murder is swiftly punishable by death had given edge to the genre since E. C. Bentley's *Trent's Last Case* (published in 1912). Writers had abandoned the essentially Edwardian world of jewel-thieves, coiners and sinister international conspirators, the world in which Margery had started her career, in order to focus with virtual unanimity on the crime of murder. 'It must be murder,' she had explained to their friend Paul Holt for *The Daily Herald*, 'because that is the only crime you get hanged for. Increase the number of crimes for which there is capital punishment and we'd all move away from murder tomorrow.' ⟨. . .⟩

By 1958 there were not more but fewer crimes punishable by death and Margery's attitude to the fictional device of murder had become very much more sophisticated than the explanation she had offered to Paul Holt. In a talk entitled 'Crime for Our Delight', she spoke of the old 'puzzle-novel' growing on into the 'novel of suspense'. It was the 'death of an aspect' which had interested her. 'The killing we harp on is not just an ordinary killing [it is] the new and main literary idea of this century. We seem to be catching up with the Greeks at last. Enormous amount of our stories have this second meaning or main meaning: the way one keeps on murdering one aspect of a person to give birth to another. We kill one relationship and another takes its place. We lose one of ourselves and find another.' This she claimed was true 'of all stories, love, adventure, travel but now we are starting to see it like this and do it deliberately'. In the future 'I see more and more serious writers taking up this two-dimensional kind of story as they begin to see not only the elementary problem but the curious symbolical way in which it can be used.' The old 'chess-problem type of story', she added dismissively, would be 'better served by the cross-word puzzle'.

Julia Thorogood, *Margery Allingham: A Biography* (London: William Heinemann, 1991), pp. 322–24

◈ *Bibliography*

Blackkerchief Dick: A Tale of Mersea Island. 1923.

Water in a Sieve: A Fantasy in One Act. 1925.

The White Cottage Mystery. 1928.

The Crime at Black Dudley. 1929.

Mystery Mile. 1930.

Look to the Lady ⟨*The Gyrth Chalice Mystery*⟩. 1931.

Police at the Funeral. 1931.

Sweet Danger ⟨*Kingdom of Death*⟩. 1933.

Other Man's Danger ⟨*The Man of Dangerous Secrets*⟩. 1933.

Death of a Ghost. 1934.

Rogues' Holiday. 1935.

Flowers for the Judge. 1936.

The Shadow in the House. 1936.

Dancers in Mourning. 1937.

The Case of the Late Pig. 1937.

Mr. Campion, Criminologist. 1937.

The Fashion in Shrouds. 1938.

Mr. Campion and Others. 1939, 1950.

Black Plumes. 1940.

Traitor's Purse. 1941.

The Oaken Heart. 1941.

Dance of the Years ⟨*The Galantrys*⟩. 1943.

Coroner's Pidgin ⟨*Pearls Before Swine*⟩. 1945.

Wanted: Someone Innocent and Other Stories. 1946.

The Case Book of Mr. Campion. Ed. Ellery Queen. 1947.

More Work for the Undertaker. 1948.

Deadly Duo ⟨*Take Two at Bedtime*⟩. 1949.

The Tiger in the Smoke. 1952.

No Love Lost. 1954.

The Beckoning Lady. 1955.

Hide My Eyes ⟨*Tether's End*⟩. 1958.

Crime and Mr. Campion ⟨*Death of a Ghost, Flowers for the Judge, Dancers in Mourning*⟩. 1959.

Three Cases for Mr. Campion ⟨*The Fashion in Shrouds, Traitor's Purse, The Gyrth Chalice Mystery*⟩. 1961.

The China Governess. 1962.

The Mysterious Mr. Campion ⟨*The Case of the Late Pig, Dancers in Mourning, The Tiger in the Smoke*⟩. 1963.

The Mind Readers. 1965.

Mr. Campion's Lady ⟨*Sweet Danger, The Fashion in Shrouds, Traitor's Purse,* "Word in Season: Story for Christmas"⟩. 1965.

Mr. Campion's Clowns ⟨*Mystery Mile, Coroner's Pidgin, More Work for the Undertaker*⟩. 1967.

Cargo of Eagles (with Youngman Carter). 1968.

The Allingham Case-Book. 1969.

The Allingham Minibus. 1973.

The Margery Allingham Omnibus ⟨*The Crime at Black Dudley, Mystery Mile, Look to the Lady*⟩. 1982.

The Return of Mr. Campion: Uncollected Stories. Ed. J. E. Morpurgo. 1989.

☒ ☒ ☒

Nicholas Blake
1904–1972

NICHOLAS BLAKE is the pseudonym of Cecil Day-Lewis, who was born on April 27, 1904, in Ballintupper, Ireland. His father, Frank Cecil Day-Lewis, was a curate in the Church of Ireland, and his mother, Kathleen Blake Squires, was a collateral descendant of Oliver Goldsmith. She died in 1908, shortly after the Reverend Day-Lewis had moved his family to Ealing, West London, and become a vicar in the Church of England.

Day-Lewis attended Wilkie's School and Sherborne School before entering Wadham College, Oxford, in 1923. It was there that he became associated with what was loosely called the "Auden Group," consisting of W. H. Auden, Stephen Spender, and Louis MacNeice. Day-Lewis coedited *Oxford Poetry 1927* (1927) with Auden. At this time he dropped the hyphen in his last name.

After receiving an M.A. from Oxford in 1927, Day Lewis taught at a number of schools in England and Scotland. In 1928 he married Mary King; they had two children. He produced three major volumes of poetry in rapid succession—*Transitional Poem* (1929), *From Feathers to Iron* (1931), and *The Magnetic Mountain* (1933)—and also wrote a volume of criticism, *A Hope for Poetry* (1934). Day Lewis was a member of the Communist party from 1935 to 1938, during which time he produced the treatise *Revolution in Writing* (1935) and edited the anthology *The Mind in Chains: Socialism and the Cultural Revolution* (1937).

In 1935, under the name Nicholas Blake, Day Lewis published *A Question of Proof,* the first of twenty volumes of mystery fiction, most featuring the detective Nigel Strangeways. The success of these novels allowed him to abandon schoolteaching and devote himself to full-time writing. Day Lewis regarded the detective story as a popular substitute for religion, whereby evil is overcome and guilt is purged. His novels feature many autobiographical details, and it is thought that Nigel Strangeways is loosely based upon W. H. Auden. In *Thou Shell of Death* (1936) Day Lewis introduced the character Georgia Cavendish, an explorer whom Strangeways eventually marries. She is, however, killed off in a subsequent novel. In these early novels Day Lewis alternates between the standard detective story and the thriller.

Day Lewis's detective writing was interrupted during World War II, when he served for five years as an editor in the Ministry of Information. In *Minute for Murder* (1947) Nigel Strangeways's career resumes, and in the course of the next several novels he becomes involved with a sculptor, Clare Massinger, who lives with him but does not marry him. Day Lewis also wrote four mystery novels not involving Strangeways: *A Tangled Web* (1956), *A Penknife in My Heart* (1958), *The Deadly Joker* (1963), and *The Private Wound* (1968), which proved to be his last work of detective fiction.

In 1951 Day Lewis was appointed professor of poetry at Oxford. In that same year he divorced his first wife and married Jill Balcon, with whom he had a son, the actor Daniel Day Lewis. In 1954 he became a director of the publishing firm Chatto & Windus. He continued to produce both poetry and prose and translated Virgil's *Georgics* (1940), *Aeneid* (1952), and *Eclogues* (1963). An autobiography, *The Buried Day,* was published in 1960. Day Lewis was the Norton Professor of Poetry at Harvard in 1964–65, delivering lectures that were published as *The Lyric Impulse* (1965). In 1968 he succeeded John Masefield as poet laureate of England, remaining in that position until his death on May 26, 1972. Jill Balcon edited his *Complete Poems* in 1992.

Critical Extracts

UNSIGNED   There is likely to be some speculation about the authorship of this book ⟨*A Question of Proof*⟩, which is said to be the work of one of our most prominent younger poets. It is certainly a very competent and readable first essay in what may be called "highbrow" detective fiction. The dialogue is sprinkled, as one would expect, with a number of literary quotations, but apart from this—for the style is perfectly simple and straightforward—there is nothing to show that the book is the work of a modern poet, although there is a certain significance in the fact that the plot is laid in a preparatory school. As a school story the book is more than competent. It is obvious that the author knows what he is talking about and has given much thought to the relations between boys and masters and to the puzzling psychology of classroom and common-room. Dialogue and description are alike admirable. The detective interest of his tale, though highly ingenious, is less satisfactory. An unpopular boy is found strangled in a "hay-castle" before the school sports. The difficulty, of course, is to suggest a plausible motive for such a crime. Unpopularity, with the staff and the boys, is not a very convincing one; nor, indeed, is it likely that his uncle, the headmaster, who stood to gain financially by his death, would go so far as murder; and the same can be said of the two masters, one of whom was the lover of the headmaster's wife, the other of a housemaid. The only possible motive will probably occur to the intelligent reader before the crime is solved by Nigel Strangeways, the amateur detective. The use of an amateur, who is under no obligation to take either the police or the reader into his confidence, is a happy device for spinning out the story and confusing the issue, but it will not appeal to the connoisseur of scientific detection.

Unsigned, [Review of A *Question of Proof*], *Times Literary Supplement*, 14 March 1935, p. 162

RUPERT HART-DAVIS   We are presented ⟨in *Thou Shell of Death*⟩ with a pre-arranged house-party composed of a famous airman (a mystery man whose life has been threatened), a fishy financier, an Oxford don, a female explorer complete with parrot and bloodhound (a slight lapse here from Aristotle, who says "It is not appropriate in a female character to be manly or clever"), the owner of a road-house, a private detective (he has grown out of his craving for tea), and a "professional peach." With such *dramatis personae*, it is hardly surprising to encounter sudden death and reversal of fortune at every turn. It would be invidious to disclose here any further details of the Plot, but let it be said that Mr. Blake maintains suspense and cumulates excitement with great technical skill. Nor is he one of those writers "who, after a Good Complication, fail in the *Dénouement*." His explanation, in which an Elizabethan dramatist takes part, is as ingenious as could be wished.

Mr. Nicholas Blake, who derives in equal parts from his great progenitors, William and Sexton, must be read by everyone interested in the development of the detective story. In his first book he showed outrageous promise; with his second he steps firmly into the front rank of contemporary detective novelists.

Rupert Hart-Davis, "The Poetics of Detection," *Spectator*, 13 March 1936, p. 484

JOHN STRACHEY   ⟨. . .⟩ Nicholas Blake, who is "in private life" Mr. Day Lewis, has produced in his last detective story, *The Beast Must Die*, an admirable novel. Its author, whether as Day Lewis, or as Nicholas Blake, could not write badly if he tried, but at the risk of saying something very irritating, I am not at all sure that he does not write even better when he is, presumably, pot-boiling as Nicholas Blake, than when he is "giving himself to literature" as Day Lewis.

John Strachey, "The Golden Age of English Detection," *Saturday Review of Literature*, 7 January 1939, p. 13

HOWARD HAYCRAFT   ⟨Blake's⟩ first detective novel, *A Question of Proof* (1935), had, like Michael Innes' maiden effort, a scholastic background. But Nicholas Blake is less insistently "erudite" than Innes, as he is likely to be less pretentious in his writing than Margery Allingham sometimes allows herself to become. Nevertheless his Nigel Strangeways belongs to the same school of studied casualness and insouciance as Albert Campion and John Appleby, and Blake is as insistent as his colleagues on character as the chief determinant of his solutions. His detection, too, is always meticulous and soundly reasoned, if not always predominant.

In fact, in *The Beast Must Die* (1938), undoubtedly his magnum opus to the present date, he largely subordinated the detectival element to a gripping internal study of murder that deserves to stand with the best of Francis Iles. If the rationale of this truly epochal novel is perhaps too complex to be entirely convincing, the fault will be readily forgiven, for the best of the chapters achieve a level of sheer mental suspense that has seldom been surpassed. In *The Smiler with a Knife* (1939), a departure of quite different nature, he turned his back completely on conventional detection to write an unabashed intrigue-adventure yarn in the tradition of John Buchan's Hannay series, converting Strangeways' wife, Georgia, into what Miriam Allen deFord calls "a sort of female Superman." (The allusion is to the American comic-strip character, *not* Shaw's or Nietzsche's.) His other works are more orthodox, in external pattern at least.

Until the Hitler War, Day Lewis and his family lived in a cottage on the Devonshire coast. He enjoys walking, sailing, and shooting (hence he has been called "the poet with a gun"). Tall, with a shock of dark hair and a deeply lined face, he looked to one interviewer like "a young farmer or aeroplane mechanic—strong, almost tough"; but his voice retains an Irish softness. He says that he enjoys writing detective stories, which he considers a harmless release of an innate spring of cruelty present in every one.

This unusual interpretation is typical of "Nicholas Blake's" refreshingly original approach to the genre. He belongs definitely to the Character group of detective novelists, but he senses more than most of his fellows the dangers of being too "highbrow" in an essentially entertainment form. In contrast to the melodramatic intellectualism of some of his colleagues, his books are honest *though* intellectual melodramas. He is one of the rare writers who manage to bring high literacy and thrills together under one cover, without pretense on the one hand or condescension on the other. By any criterion, he is a major figure and force in the modern detective story.

> Howard Haycraft, *Murder for Pleasure: The Life and Times of the Detective Story* (New York: D. Appleton-Century Co., 1941), pp. 190–92

RALPH PARTRIDGE   *Minute for Murder* is the eighth of Nicholas Blake's novels but the first to show his full capacity in this *genre*. For once his remarkable talents have been directed to the implications of his plot, and not merely to imposing on the credulity of his readers. His detective, Nigel Strangeways, ceases to pose as a leisurely superman and deigns to be an ordinary human being, busily employed to all appearance in the Ministry of Information, where the murder takes place. Why should anyone want to drop cyanide into the coffee of the dazzling blonde secretary, who looks "like a damned great carnivorous orchid"? Seven persons had the opportunity; so who had the motive? This time you need not be afraid your intelligence will be underrated. On the contrary it will be put to a severe test. Nicholas Blake faces the fact that motives for murder actually must vary with the characters of murderers; but he accepts his obligations to the reader like a man. All the characters of the potential murderers are presented in a brilliant sequence; he keeps nothing up his sleeve; every card lies face up on the table. Yet what a problem! *Minute for Murder*, if it doesn't purge your soul of guilt, ought to purge Nicholas Blake's for all the faults of its predecessors. May he always write his detection in future with the same courage and receive our universal praise!

> Ralph Partridge, "Intelligent Murder," *New Statesman and Nation*, 26 July 1947, p. 74

NICHOLAS BLAKE   The two commonest remarks made to a detective novelist by his readers are 'I don't know how you can think up such things', and 'I suppose you always begin at the end'. The answer to the first comment is 'Nor do I': the psychologists would no doubt tell us that detective novels are sublimations of an abnormal degree of suppressed violence in their authors—and I, for one, am prepared to let it go at that. Certainly all the detective novelists I know, myself included, are meek inoffensive creatures outwardly, with an almost exaggerated respect for the Law. More positive qualifications for writing this kind of fiction are an ingenious mind, a love of fantasy, a working knowledge of forensic medicine, police procedure and the Law, and a curiosity about the behaviour of human beings under violent stress. ⟨. . .⟩

It is difficult, of course, to isolate the germ of a given detective novel. One of my own books, which developed into a Buchanesque Fifth-Column thriller, originated in my receiving a notice from the Devon Surveyor of Highways instructing me to 'forthwith cut, prune and trim your hedges adjoining the County Roads . . . and also to pare the sides of such hedges close to the bank, and the growth on the top of such hedges at least perpendicular from the Comb . . . in such manner that the said Roads shall not be prejudiced by the shade thereof, and that the Sun and Wind may not be excluded therefrom to the damage thereof'.

Another book of mine began when I saw a child narrowly escape being run down by a road-hog. I started to imagine myself in the mind of a father whose only child had been killed this way: the police are unable to trace the culprit; so the father sets out to find him and take revenge. Revenge, incidentally, uncommon though it is today as a motive for real-life murders, still provides the best motives for detective stories because of the deep atavistic response (the blood-feud) which it exploits, and the strain of fantasy it thus produces. ⟨. . .⟩

My own sleuth started life as an eccentric: but later, as I grew more and more interested in developing the characters and thus distinguishing the possible motives of my suspects, Nigel Strangeways has become progressively more abstract. My aim now is to make him like a piece of blotting-paper, colourless and absorbent: a fantasy figure all eyes and ears, memory and brain-work, with no personality; a foil to the naturalistically-treated suspects. ⟨. . .⟩

In *The Beast Must Die*, the father who is determined to find his child's killer keeps a secret diary, which is a most incriminating document, describing his search and passion for revenge. Extracts from it are given to the reader. Presently the father finds the road-hog he is after, and makes an abortive attempt to kill him, recorded in the diary. Here, when writing the book, I got stuck, until an idea occurred to me which gave the story a twist I had never foreseen. The prospective victim is made to discover the diary: the father, unknown to the victim, discovers that he has discovered it. So he continues to write up the diary, but in such a way now as to give the impression that he has abandoned his intention to murder, frightened out of it by the failure of his first attempt. This twist had the triple effect of (a) putting the victim, who is still 'secretly' reading the 'secret' diary, off his guard, (b) throwing dust in the reader's eye, (c) weakening police suspicion against the father when the murder is finally committed and the diary comes to light.

> Nicholas Blake, "School of Red Herrings," *Diversion: Twenty-two Authors on the Lively Arts*, ed. John Sutro (London: Max Parrish, 1950), pp. 58, 60–65

ANTHONY BOUCHER   From most of the news stories about the appointment of Cecil Day Lewis as Poet Laureate of Great Britain, you would gather that he is one of those lyric dons who dash off an occasional detective story in their lighter moments. In fact the poet is, as "Nicholas Blake," a hard-working professional in crime, who has written a novel almost annually since 1935, and is also one of England's two or three leading reviewers of crime fiction. Blake's stature among mystery novelists is at least as high as that of Day Lewis among poets; he has excelled both in the straight detective puzzle and in the broader study of crime and character, as well as in happy blends of the two methods. And it seems particularly fitting that he should celebrate his laurels by publishing his best novel in a dozen years, *The Private Wound*.

The narrator, an Anglo-Irish novelist visiting County Clare in the disturbed year of 1939, says that his story "began as an idyll, continued into low comedy, and ended in tragedy." It is an intensely penetrating study of sexual passion (and, incidentally, a model of how to write sexy without writing dirty). It is also a powerful story of murder and its aftermath, strengthened by a subplot of Irish politics, and constantly illuminated by the author's lightning flashes of insight into the peculiar relation between the Irish and the English (he himself is both) and the even more incredible relation between man and woman, which few male novelists have understood so well.

Anthony Boucher, [Review of *The Private Wound*], *New York Times Book Review*, 7 April 1968, p. 20

JACQUES BARZUN and WENDELL H. TAYLOR   Ever since Dorothy Sayers made such excellent use of a business agency as the scene of crime in *Murder Must Advertise* (1933), the office murder has become a recognized and popular setting. The large cast of characters, mostly self-willed and at loggerheads, offers rich opportunities for satire and a puzzling tangle of motives. In *Minute for Murder* the author keeps the tensions in the wartime Ministry of Morale quite high but under control. One of the staff, Nigel Strangeways, doing his bit as a writer, is faced with a tougher problem than copy editing when, after an office party, he must find out who put the cyanide in the beautiful secretary's coffee cup—and, of course, why.

Instead of spinning out his tale with the customary interrogation of witnesses, the author gives us actions followed by discussions in which Strangeways and Superintendent Blount sift the meager evidence. It appears that two other crimes—one major and one minor—have taken place on the premises, but neither helps to incriminate or clear any of the seven suspects. Still, the layers of suspicion peel away, leaving detectives and readers with a very small company of "possibles." At that point the skill with which the author prepares his conclusive, dramatic, protracted confrontation scene shows the poet's hand, especially in that control of words by which art conceals art. The critic can only echo Blount's verdict: "a classical case of Nemesis."

Jacques Barzun and Wendell H. Taylor, "Preface," *Minute for Murder* by Nicholas Blake (New York: Garland, 1976), pp. v–vi

HELAINE ROSS   ⟨Harriet⟩ Vane and ⟨Agatha⟩ Troy are what I will call, in the context of this paper, successful characters. Sayers and Marsh create them in a certain image and maintain the integrity of that image through the series of detective novels in which the characters' husbands star. Occasional novels in both series are even dominated by these female characters. By this definition, however, Georgia Cavendish Strangeways and Lady Amanda Fitton Campion, in the novels of Nicholas Blake and Margery Allingham, respectively, are failed characters. Cavendish and Fitton differ from the beginning, and they evolve along widely divergent lines, but both are killed by their creators (the former literally, the latter figuratively). Neither is given the right or room to "live" independently.

Georgia Cavendish is very close to the prototypical female character of these novels, and in one repsect, that of bringing intuition to bear on problems, she has evolved further than either Vane or Troy. But Cavendish dies after appearing in only a few novels; we discover in *Minute for Murder* that she was killed while driving an ambulance during World War II. The cause of Cavendish's demise seems to be at least partly inherent in her character as Blake created it, and partly inherent in problems in the development of her character, but there also seem to be reasons that lie outside the novels, in the characters of the times. ⟨. . .⟩

Even with the limitations Blake imposes on her, Cavendish is given intuition, which Strangeways himself lacks. In *Minute for Murder*, Strangeways sums up the "working relationship" which they had achieved:

> Georgia had helped him in so many of his cases, bringing her
> keen intuitive power to bear upon the facts and hints he
> collected. To become involved in a case again would be to remind
> himself at every step of it how much he had lost.

What the reader must ask is why he had to lose it. It is difficult to believe that Cavendish was a boring character to write about, but she may have been a frustrating one. The reason for her creation may lie in Blake's artistic interest in women. Though he is the only male author considered here, he is at least as interested in the depth of his female characters as the female novelists are. The victim of *Minute for Murder*, for example, is a *femme fatale* who at first seems to be a one-dimensional character, an uncomplicated type who shows up in many detective novels. Blake, however, goes beyond the stereotype to create, after her death, a rich portrait of a woman who was not what she seemed to be: "Oh yes, she looked poised and invulnerable and successful, didn't she? And beneath it there was a panic and chaos." Strangeways is forced to solve this murder without the help of Cavendish's intuition.

Though female intuition is useful to the male detectives, there is a problem with introducing it into a detective novel. One assumption of the formula of these Golden Age novels is that the detective must follow a logical process of deduction so that the reader, engaged along with the detective in solving the puzzle, will have the same opportunity to arrive at the correct solution as the detective does. Dorothy Sayers states in *The Omnibus of Crime* that "the reader must be given every clue—but he must not be told, surely, all the detective's deductions, lest he should see the solution too far ahead." A long intuitive jump that is creative rather than deductive may aid the detective but subvert the detecting reader. To rely heavily on intuition might violate the principle of "fair play" with the reader that Sayers describes. Such a reliance also might force detective novelists to create a new formula, though it is not clear how the formula could *not* menace the bounds and the *raison d'être* of the detective novel.

Cavendish's death could be traced, at least in part, to this threat to the formula of the novel, but she simply may not have had wide appeal. By introducing her, Blake may have hoped to create a team around which he could build succeeding novels (Cavendish does dominate one of the novels in which she appears, *Smiler with the Knife*), but Cavendish's profession clashes with the norm of marriage. Cavendish is described as a strong woman; this strength is so great that when Blake attempts to fit her into a less active role, it is like forcing the proverbial square peg into the equally proverbial round hole. In order to maintain her in character, Cavendish cannot be made to putter around in Strangeways's wake; on the other hand, if she dominates the scene, Blake is in danger of losing Strangeways. Cavendish's dominance places Strangeways in the position of the worrying husband, which robs him of a certain amount of freedom. Blake does not seem to be able to create an equality in their relationship, so he kills Cavendish.

Helaine Ross, "A Woman's Intuition: Wives and Lovers in British Golden Age Detective Novels," *Clues* 2, No. 1 (Spring–Summer 1981): 20–21

EARL F. BARGAINNIER   A specific way in which Blake differs from other British detective novelists of his generation or earlier is the large number of children and teenagers who appear in his work. How many children play even minor roles in the works of the other eleven writers in this volume or in the works of Sayers, Christie or Marsh? In nine novels, young people are conspicuously present, though some are more important than others. The schoolboys who provide the background of A *Question of Proof* and show Blake's understanding of boyish fantasies; the information-supplying rural Dorset boys of *There's Trouble Brewing*, and the delightful John and Priscilla Restorick, the precocious children of *The Corpse in the Snowman*, who trade slang and quips with each other, using such expressions as "spotted pard" and "infant cheeild," may not be absolutely necessary, but they would be missed. The same is true of such teenagers as Sally Thistlewaite, the comic love interest of *Malice in Wonderland* or the emotionally troubled twins Peter and Faith Trubody of *The Widow's Cruise*. On the other hand, children are murder victims in *The Sad Variety* and *The Widow's Cruise*, and in *The Beast Must Die*, a child hit-and-run victim is the motivation for all that happens. In the same novel, another child greatly complicates the plot for both murderer and detective. Finally, in two of the thrillers children are central to the action. In *The Whisper in the Gloom* Bert Hale, aged twelve, and his friends, Copper and Foxy, become involved in an assassination attempt on a visiting Soviet minister. Bert is a scientific "brain" and Foxy is streetwise; together they are the equal of the Hardy boys. Though they undergo considerable danger, they thoroughly enjoy the excitement of their adventures: witnessing a murder, being kidnapped, hiding in secret rooms and riding in helicopters. Adult peril becomes boyish fun in this rather improbable, but comic, novel. (Walt Disney modernized and Americanized it as *The Kids Who Knew Too Much*.) Lucy Wragsby of *The Sad Variety* is another child of twelve; she is kidnapped by communists to obtain a formula from her scientist father. She is incredibly calm during her ordeal, and her intelligence enables her to get a message to the outside. At the same time, she is so appealing that her tough female captor, a woman whose "mental world was one of abstractions, slogans, diagrams, statistics," succumbs to her charm and attempts to prevent her death. As unlikely as the ability of these children to survive their perils may seem, they are still children in their emotions, fears, superstitions and infectious innocent acceptance of their adventures. They are examples of that negative capability so admired by their creator.

Earl F. Bargainnier, "Nicholas Blake," *Twelve Englishmen of Mystery*, ed. Earl F. Bargainnier (Bowling Green, OH: Bowling Green State University Popular Press, 1984), pp. 156–57.

◈ *Bibliography*

Books by Nicholas Blake:
A Question of Proof. 1935.
Thou Shell of Death. 1936.
There's Trouble Brewing. 1937.
The Beast Must Die. 1938.
The Smiler with the Knife. 1938.
Malice in Wonderland ⟨*The Summer Camp Mystery*⟩. 1940.
The Case of the Abominable Snowman ⟨*The Corpse in the Snowman*⟩. 1941.
Minute for Murder. 1947.
Head of a Traveller. 1949.
The Dreadful Hollow. 1953.
The Whisper in the Gloom. 1954.
A Tangled Web. 1956.
End of Chapter. 1957.
A Penknife in My Heart. 1958.
The Widow's Cruise. 1959.
The Worm of Death. 1961.
The Deadly Joker. 1963.
The Sad Variety. 1964.
The Morning After Death. 1966.
The Private Wound. 1968.

Books by C. Day Lewis:
Beechen Vigil and Other Poems. 1925.
Oxford Poetry 1927 (editor; with W. H. Auden). 1927.
Country Comets. 1928.
Transitional Poem. 1929.
From Feathers to Iron. 1931.
The Magnetic Mountain. 1933.
Dick Willoughby. 1933.
A Hope for Poetry. 1934.
Collected Poems 1929–1933; A Hope for Poetry. 1935.
Revolution in Writing. 1935.
A Time to Dance and Other Poems. 1935.
Noah and the Waters. 1936.
Imagination and Thinking (with L. Susan Stebbing). 1936.

The Friendly Tree. 1936.

We're Not Going to Do Nothing (A Reply to Mr. Aldous Huxley's Pamphlet
      What Are You Going to Do about It?). 1936.

A Time to Dance, Noah and the Waters, and Other Poems; with an Essay,
      Revolution in Writing. 1936.

Starting Point. 1937.

A Writer in Arms by Ralph Fox (editor; with John Lehmann and T. A.
      Jackson). 1937.

The Echoing Green: An Anthology of Verse (editor). 1937. 3 vols.

The Mind in Chains: Socialism and the Cultural Revolution (editor). 1937.

Overtures to Death and Other Poems. 1938.

Anatomy of Oxford: An Anthology (editor; with Charles Fenby). 1938.

Child of Misfortune. 1939.

Poems in Wartime. 1940.

The Georgics of Virgil (translator). 1940.

Selected Poems. 1940.

A New Anthology of Modern Verse 1920–1940 (editor; with L. A. G. Strong).
      1941.

Word over All. 1943.

⟨*Poems.*⟩ 1943.

Poetry for You: A Book for Boys and Girls on the Enjoyment of Poetry. 1944.

Short Is the Time: Poems 1936–1943. 1945.

Orion 1 (editor; with others). 1945.

Orion 2 (editor; with others). 1945.

Orion 3 (editor; with others). 1946.

The Graveyard by the Sea by Paul Valéry (translator). 1946.

The Poetic Image. 1947.

Enjoying Poetry: A Reader's Guide. 1947.

The Colloquial Element in English Poetry. 1947.

Poems 1943–1947. 1948.

The Otterbury Incident. 1948.

Collected Poems 1929–1936. 1948.

Selected Poems. 1951, 1957, 1969, 1974.

The Poet's Task. 1951.

The Lyrical Poetry of Thomas Hardy. 1951.

The Grand Manner. 1952.

The Aeneid of Virgil (translator). 1952.

An Italian Visit. 1953.

Collected Poems. 1954.

Notable Images of Virtue: Emily Brontë, George Meredith, W. B. Yeats. 1954.

The Golden Treasury of the Best Songs and Lyrical Poems in the English Language
      by Francis Turner Palgrave (editor). 1954.

Christmas Eve. 1954.

The Chatto Book of Modern Poetry 1915–1955 (editor; with John Lehmann).
      1956.

The Poet. 1956.

The Newborn: D. M. B., 29th April 1957. 1957.

The Poet's Way of Knowledge. 1957.

New Poems 1957 (editor; with Kathleen Nott and Thomas Blackburn). 1957.

Pegasus and Other Poems. 1957.

The Buried Day. 1960.

A Book of English Lyrics ⟨*English Lyric Poems 1500–1900*⟩ (editor). 1961.

The Gate and Other Poems. 1962.

The Collected Poems of Wilfred Owen (editor). 1963.

The Eclogues of Virgil (translator). 1963.

Requiem for the Living. 1964.

On Not Saying Everything. 1964.

The Lyric Impulse. 1965.

A Marriage Song for Albert and Barbara. 1965.

The Room and Other Poems. 1965.

Thomas Hardy (with R. A. Scott-James). 1965.

C. Day Lewis: Selections from His Poetry. Ed. Patric Dickinson. 1967.

Selected Poems. 1967.

The Abbey That Refused to Die. 1967.

A Need for Poetry? 1968.

Saint Anthony's Shirt. 1968.

The Midnight Skaters: Poems for Young Readers by Edmund Blunden (editor).
      1968.

The Poems of Robert Browning (editor). 1969.

For the Investiture of the Prince of Wales. 1969.

The Whispering Roots. 1970.

On Translating Poetry: A Lecture. 1970.

Going My Way? 1970.

Tenure. c. 1970.

A Christmas Way. c. 1970.

The Tomtit in the Rain: Traditional Hungarian Rhymes by Erzsi Gazdas (translator; with Mátyás Sárközi). 1971.

A Choice of Keats' Verse (editor). 1971.

Keep Faith with Nature. 1972.

Crabbe (editor). 1973.

A Lasting Joy: An Anthology (editor). 1973.

Poems 1925–1972. Ed. Ian Parsons. 1977.

Posthumous Poems. 1979.

Complete Poems. Ed. Jill Balcon. 1992.

◈ ◈ ◈

Fredric Brown
1906–1972

FREDRIC WILLIAM BROWN was born in Cincinnati, Ohio, on October 29, 1906, to S. Karl Lewis Brown, a newspaperman, and Emma Amelia Graham. Little is known of his early personal life except that he was small and frail, plagued with allergies that would leave him sickly for most of his life.

Brown's mother died in 1920, and his father the following year, leaving him to the care of a family friend and the financial support of an uncle until 1922, when he graduated from high school. He held a series of office jobs between 1922 and 1927, then enrolled briefly at Hanover College in Indiana and later the University of Cincinnati. In the early 1920s he began corresponding with Helen Ruth Brown, possibly a distant cousin, and married her in 1929.

In 1930 the Browns moved to Milwaukee, where Brown held a succession of jobs, including stenographer, insurance salesman, and detective, to support his wife and two sons. During these years Brown joined the Milwaukee Press Club, where he befriended mystery writer William Campbell Gault. Brown had nurtured an interest in writing since high school, self-publishing a volume of his poetry in the early 1930s, and encouragement from fellow club members inspired him to try writing for trade and professional magazines.

In 1937 Brown began proofreading for the *Milwaukee Journal* and several pulp fiction magazines. Convinced that he could write better than the authors whose work he proofread, Brown began writing fiction and sold his first story to *Detective Story* in 1938. Although the bulk of his work would appear in the mystery and detective magazines, Brown also showed a talent for writing fantasy and science fiction and ultimately forged a link between the two fields. His writing became distinguished for its cockeyed view of a world whose absurdities alternated between the comical and the malevolent. Characters in his stories often had quirky backgrounds, but Brown invariably rendered them as everymen faced with the task of extricating themselves from unusual predicaments.

Brown's fiction output for the pulps increased tremendously in the early 1940s. At the instigation of his agent, Harry Altshuler, he began writing his first novel, *The Fabulous Clipjoint*, in 1944. A gritty view of life in contemporary Chicago, it was rejected by twelve publishers before seeing print in 1947. Critical acclaim for the novel earned Brown a lengthy book contract and led to the development of his series characters, idealistic detective Ed Brown and his experienced uncle Am, a retired circus performer. The book won the Mystery Writers of America's Edgar Allan Poe Award for best novel.

Rejected for military service for health reasons, Brown spent most of the 1940s writing prolifically. His marriage and family life foundered, and he divorced Helen in 1947. Brown married Elizabeth Charlier in 1948 and spent the next decade living a peripatetic life, moving between New York, the Midwest, and the Southwest, trying to make a living as a full-time writer and find an environment suitable for his fragile health.

Brown was a regular presence in the hardcover and paperback markets with unconventional novels that included *The Screaming Mimi* (1949), *Night of the Jabberwock* (1950), *Madball* (1953), and *The Lenient Beast* (1956), and earned the admiration of Mickey Spillane and other colleagues; but his output began dwindling, owing to his precarious health and increasing dependence on alcohol. Partly in response to his debilitation, Brown learned to master the short-short story form in the 1950s.

Brown tried briefly to make a living writing screenplays in Hollywood in the early 1960s but quickly returned to Tucson, Arizona, where he had moved in 1954. Fredric Brown died on March 11, 1972. Although most of his thirty mystery novels are out of print today, interest in his writing in France and the United States led to the reprinting of all his short mystery and detective fiction between 1984 and 1991.

◈ *Critical Extracts*

FREDRIC BROWN   Recently, one of the media of fiction, the comic strip, has brought forth a concept that is genuinely new. Its newness is revolutionary in the truest sense of that term: Superman, by his complete invulnerability, upsets the twin icons of adventure fiction, Menace and Suspense. The guy can't lose.

Pick up the Empire State Building and drop it on Superman's head and it doesn't even muss his hair but it cracks the Empire State Building. Sit Superman on a ton of nitroglycerin and set if off and it doesn't even affect his supersensitive eardrums, which can hear a conversation in a closed building across the street. Let a mob of gangsters fire tommy guns at him and he can sit there with his mouth open and eat the bullets for lunch.

What can you do with a guy like that? Obviously, nothing.

The readers of Superman know that he can't be hurt, that he's never in danger. Other heroes *don't* lose, although they always seem on the verge of losing. Superman *can't*. He's invulnerable.

Yet those kids who follow their hero avidly each night as soon as the paper comes, vicariously identifying themselves with Superman each time he pulls a new feat of strength out of his inexhaustible store, are the pulp and slick readers of tomorrow. What change in taste will result from their diet of invulnerability?

This: The pendulum has, with Superman, reached the end of its swing. It's starting back. Heroes are going to be less tough, progressively more ordinary and more vulnerable. Any tough mug who can lick his weight in wild cats is going to be mild stuff to a graduate of the Superman school.

He can't go on. Superman is the ultimate of invulnerability, strength and toughness. He has spoiled all taste for semi-supermen.

So there comes a tendency toward the story about the perfectly ordinary guy, who isn't a paragon of strength or courage, who, through no fault of his own, gets into a mess of trouble with criminals who are stronger than he, but who through the courage of desperation, manages to pull a fast one and come out on top.

I quote my agent: "Editors feel the tough, Dashiell Hammett type of detective is absolutely dead."

It is my opinion that Superman killed him. R.I.P.

I'll stick to my personal experience. I've found that the stories which have sold most readily to detective markets have been stories in which my protagonist has been an ordinary, everyday you and me type guy. He may be a bit of a coward, until circumstances force him to draw on hidden courage. He doesn't start looking for trouble: he tries to mind his own business until fate drops him spank in the middle of a mess of trouble out of which he has to fight his way unaided.

A shiftless, unambitious veterinarian gets caught in a jam when crooks who have kidnapped a valuable movie dog board him at the vet's kennels. A fat and uncourageous county relief visitor accidentally solves a bank robbery and is captured by the robbers before he can call a copper. A scared apprentice on night watch in an undertaking establishment has unexpected visitors in need of a corpse. A baseball pitcher—

But you get the idea. Having experienced the ultimate in self-identification with a superman who can do anything, the Superman-reader-graduate's reaction is to go to the opposite extreme. An almost Superman will bore him to tears. But he can and does thoroughly enjoy reading about something extraordinary happening to someone as ordinary as he himself is.

And this, I believe, will be the ultimate result of the impact of Superman on the heroes of detective and adventure fiction. The ultra-strong, ultra-clever detective passes into limbo, eclipsed by one stronger than himself.

And the protagonist of the pulp story and the slick adventure story of the future will be increasingly uncolossal. He'll be the chap who puts gas in your car at the filling station, the man who delivers your mail twice every day, the guy who takes your tickets when you enter the movie.

He won't be intrepid, at least until and unless circumstances make him so. He won't have super-sensitive hearing, or be able to disguise himself as your grandmother so well your grandfather couldn't tell the difference. He won't be able to shoot the spots off a playing card half a mile away nor will he be able to jiu jitsu four pugs with one arm tied behind his back.

But he'll be a likable, sympathetic character. A chap that you'd like to meet and know. And, with the help of the author, he'll come out on top in the end, no matter how black things look just before the dawn. That's one requirement of popular fiction that even a Superman isn't husky enough to change.

Fredric Brown, "After Superman, What?" [letter], *Author and Journalist* 25, No. 10 (October 1940): 2

WILL CUPPY   This first full-length opus ⟨*The Fabulous Clipjoint*⟩ by a writer of detective shorts tells of young Ed Hunter's search for the murderers of his father, a linotype operator fatally slugged up an alley. The lad is assisted by his Uncle Ambrose, a wise old carnival fellow quite at home in Chicago's humbler saloons. Problems: Why did Mom, Ed's stepmother, sleep in her clothes that night? Drunk again? What about Claire, the beautiful gun moll? Will Ed go on with his printing job or join the carnival? He's only eighteen, too young to get married and just old enough to jot down his whodunit ideas as narrator of this naive and sometimes pleasing little item.

Just to show how opinions differ, the story is officially said to be "in the tough and rugged tradition of James M. Cain and Raymond Chandler," while we found no likeness whatever to the work of those slick professionals. Seems to us the author has something of his own.

> Will Cuppy, [Review of *The Fabulous Clipjoint*], *New York Herald Tribune Books*, 6 April 1947, p. 19

ISAAC ANDERSON   Script writer Bill Tracy has a wonderful idea for a new radio serial ⟨in *Murder Can Be Fun*⟩. He has been writing soap opera so long that he is completely fed up with it, and he thinks it would be more fun to do a serial about crime and detection. Before he has talked to anyone about the new idea, a man is murdered in precisely the manner described in the script on which Bill was working the previous evening. Bill hopes that it is a coincidence, but when another of his ideas becomes a reality he is seriously worried. The certainty that he is suspected by the police makes it impossible to concentrate upon his work or to do much of anything else except to drink. Finally, the city editor for whom he has formerly worked as a reporter needles him into investigating the case on his own, and the story comes to a speedy and dramatic conclusion. Unless our memory is at fault, this is by far the best thing that Frederick ⟨sic⟩ Brown has done up to this time. It bids fair to be the most ingeniously plotted detective story of the year.

> Isaac Anderson, [Review of *Murder Can Be Fun*], *New York Times Book Review*, 7 November 1948, p. 40

ELIZABETH BULLOCK   Mr. Brown's preceding books have brought him quite an enthusiastic following, and his current one ⟨*The Screaming Mimi*⟩ is not going to let anyone down. It is as fast, smooth, and well-plotted as the others—and it centers around a ripper. Mr. Brown manages to convey a goodly amount of the visceral terror an actual ripper would induce in the reader.

Bill Sweeney of *The Chicago Blade* is in no way anxious to tangle with the ripper, but he is very anxious to tangle with the criminal's latest prey, a blonde dancer by the name of Yolanda Lang. Although his wary, alert hunt takes several days, it only took this glued-to-the-book reader one trance-like sitting.

> Elizabeth Bullock, [Review of *The Screaming Mimi*], *New York Times Book Review*, 27 November 1949, p. 42

UNSIGNED   Take a beautiful blond strip teaser, menaced by a ripper who has already done for three other blondes; a reporter, straight out of *The Front Page*, who wants to know her better; a dog, half wolf, who assists in her act and very efficiently guards her offstage; her agent and manager, who has been a practicing psychiatrist; and a statuette (the screaming Mimi of the title) that turns out to be the key to the whole thing, and you have almost too rich a mixture. Tough, funny, and plausible in a dreadful kind of way.

> Unsigned, [Review of *The Screaming Mimi*], *New Yorker*, 17 December 1949, p. 31

MILTON CRANE   Mr. Brown, whose *Fabulous Clipjoint* and other detective novels are distinguished by imagination, good humor, and unpretentiousness, has now produced a work in which only the first of these qualities can be discerned. *Here Comes a Candle* is the story of Joe Bailey, a pitiful young hanger-on in the numbers racket in Milwaukee, who has been haunted since childhood by that grisly nursery rhyme which concludes:

> Here comes a candle to light you to bed,
> And here comes a chopper to chop off your head.

Why the unhappy Joe is so bedeviled is a long story, and Mr. Brown doesn't make it any shorter in the telling. Little Joe, at the age of three and one-half, had a traumatic experience involving his father, a candle, and a chopper. Two and one-half years later, he led the police to the movie house which the elder Bailey and some associates were about to hold up, and thus encompassed his father's death. (Oedipus-motif on the trombones.)

The candle-chopper story is, of course, an infallible indication of what is to come. At the age of nineteen Joe falls for a nice girl, takes part in some hold-ups, and finally follows his nice girl to Racine where he dies with her in a psychopathic nightmare, in which the candle and chopper make a lurid final appearance.

All this violence is rather below Mr. Brown's usual level of achievement. To make matters worse, he has chosen to enliven his tale of terror with some singularly unfortunate deviations from straight narrative. A half-dozen interludes are presented in a half-dozen different forms—pretentious stylistic vaudeville that makes the book a distressing bore.

Milton Crane, [Review of *Here Comes a Candle*], *Saturday Review*, 9 September 1950, p. 36

JAMES SANDOE   Darius Conn ⟨in *His Name Was Death*⟩ was a meek job printer, honest and harassed until he strangled his wife in passion and discovered an alibi as chancy as it was convenient. Thereafter (and Mr. Brown's proviso is as old-fashioned as a finger worked in needlepoint pointing down the primrose path) he engages in counterfeiting, and when another chance threatens to discover him takes on a succession of hasty murders without compunction.

Mr. Brown is an ingenious craftsman and likes to pin himself within special disciplines. The consequence has a double interest, first for the mad juggling of its narrative about the murderer and the chances which beset him, lucky and unlucky, then for the ingenuities which appear within Mr. Brown's arbitrary pattern. He does appear to feel that a salting of sex is de rigueur and he adds it somberly as if he had been reading Reports on Life Adjustment. For the rest it's very able nonsense which at the last catches you like the mousetrap you set too unwarily.

James Sandoe, [Review of *His Name Was Death*], *New York Herald Tribune Books*, 6 June 1954, p. 12

LENORE GLEN OFFORD   There is something unusually pleasing about Fredric Brown's new mystery, *One for the Road*, perhaps because it partakes somewhat of the easy-going realistic quality of his recent novel

The Office. Set in a small Arizona town, with a reporter on the *Mayville Weekly Sun* as narrator, it gives a genuine feeling of its characters' day-to-day existence, and the mystery fits right in with it. A heavy-drinking lady is found stabbed in her motel room, and our Bob Spitzer gets to write up his first murder case, with the further chance that if he succeeds it may release him from his low-paid slavery to the *Sun*'s proprietor. There's plenty of excitement along with a sound plot handled with unobtrusive neatness.

> Lenore Glen Offord, "The Gory Road," *San Francisco Chronicle*, 24 August 1958, *This World* section, p. 30

ANTHONY BOUCHER   It has been observed that plagiarism from more than one source is research. Similarly, I suppose, a theme that has been used by more than one novelist may be considered in the public domain, and open to anyone clever enough to invent new variations.

When Patricia Highsmith wrote *Strangers on a Train* (1950), the theme of swapping murders, so that A kills B's enemy and B kills A's, was a new and startling one. When Nicholas Blake published *A Penknife in My Heart* (1958), he felt obliged to explain with some embarrassment that he had never seen the Highsmith novel or the Hitchcock film adapted from it until his own manuscript had been completed. Now, with no embarrassed explanations, Fredric Brown treats the same theme in *The Murderers*, and so freshly and skillfully that I doubt if even Miss Highsmith could complain.

Brown's setting is the fringe-world of Hollywood—the failures, the possible future successes, the beat hangers-on—sharply observed and far more alive than the usual tinted glamour portrait of the film capital. His principal killer is an egocentric young actor, trapped by love and debt and ambition; and his astutely devised plot of retribution is quite different from Highsmith's or Blake's, and in some ways more satisfactory than either.

> Anthony Boucher, [Review of *The Murderers*], *New York Times Book Review*, 17 September 1961, p. 50

NEWTON BAIRD   Brown's masterpiece of psychological detection, as well as his best novel, is *The Deep End* (1952), a study of schizophrenia, and a novel that has been neglected. Terror and psychosis are found in a single traumatic episode in childhood. Detection eventually exposes a broader psychological condition, and reveals a psychosis that affects the entire metaphysical existence of the novel. It is close to the kind of psychological condition described by David Abrahamsen in *The Murdering Mind*:

> When a person resorts to violence, it is, in the last analysis, to *achieve power*. By obtaining power, he enhances his self-esteem, which fundamentally is rooted in sexual identity. In the murderer, this sense of true identity is inadequate or lacking. . . .

It should be stated that Abrahamsen goes on to talk about the *whole* identity in the criminal, not the sexual alone. As *The Deep End* dramatizes in the case of Obie, an adolescent, self-esteem is degraded by the reaction to a traumatic guilt experience. The mind fails to sort out the emotions and moral existence goes topsy-turvy. The esteem that is sought rationally in constructive acts becomes instead sought irrationally in destructive acts. Sam Evans, the hero, eventually discovers how this happened to Obie Westphal. First Sam studies the crimes themselves, searches for motive, and finally the meaning behind the motive. The key to motive is self-esteem, and the key to the meaning behind the motive is identity. Sam searches for the lost value of the young mystery figure in the novel.

The Deep End doubles the trauma plot of *The Fabulous Clipjoint*, more clearly and succinctly than *The Screaming Mimi*. In *The Fabulous Clipjoint* the young boy, Ed Hunter, experiences a traumatic shock (the death of a loved one), and turns detective to overcome the shock by uncovering the truth behind the trauma. In *The Deep End*, Sam Evans, a reporter, experiences a traumatic shock (a disintegrating marriage, plus a psychologically disturbing association with violent death), and he turns detective to uncover the truth behind the obsession caused by the shock. Here is how the *Clipjoint* plot doubles in *Deep End*: In *The Deep End* the killings actually originate in a traumatic shock experienced by the young killer (an apparently accidental death he may or may not have caused). The reporter-detective perceives the tangibles and intangibles behind the boy's criminal acts, thus uncovering the psychological cause in the boy's case. Because of his own state of trauma, of guilt and neuroticism, the detective identifies with the boy's state of mind. As he is unearthing the causes of the boy's criminality, he is revealing the cause of his own obsession. The reader, as a result, is better able to understand the crime, its solution, and the criminal mind, because the reader sees the criminal's psychology reflected in the more "normal" mind of the detective. This fictional method is *objectivity in plotting*. The more distant from the crime the detective can become without losing *close* touch with the essentials of the crime, the more objective he can become. The reader is given an opportunity to share in this objective experience, bringing his or her own knowledge to bear upon the case.

Though this is a complex plot construction, Brown makes it clear, simple, and entertaining. Obie Westphal's self-esteem is damaged and traumatized by his parents' (particularly, his father's) reaction to his sister's death when the two children are five and four years old. Sam's self-esteem suffers from his marital instability, followed by his neurotic reaction to a violent death he is sent to report on at an amusement park. The connecting link between detective and young criminal is the loss of self-esteem and self-identity. Obie tries to reestablish his identity and esteem by destructive acts that are fixation rituals of the original traumatic death, much like Yolanda's ritual killing in *Mimi*. Sam seeks to reestablish confidence in himself by controlling the irrational obsession that has acquired mastery of his life and prevents him from feeling normal. The criminal goal is power; the detective goal is happiness. Each seeks to control the evil in his existence, death. That is the meaning of the title and the theme of the story. The "deep end" is death, which can be overcome by order and happiness.

Newton Baird, "Paradox and Plot: The Fiction of Frederic ⟨sic⟩ Brown, Part III," Armchair Detective 10, No. 2 (April 1977): 151–52

BILL PRONZINI   Fredric Brown's vision of the world—indeed, of the entire universe—is paradoxical and slightly cockeyed. Things, in his eye, are not always what they seem; elements of the bizarre spice the commonplace, and conversely, elements of the commonplace leaven the bizarre. Madness and sanity are intertwined, so that it is often difficult to tell which is which. The same is true of malevolence and benignity, of tragedy and comedy, of rationality and irrationality.

The characters that populate Brown's crime and science fiction reflect this paradoxical view. Many are misfits of one sort or another—madmen, dipsomaniacs, retarded individuals (socially as well as mentally), oddball writers and artists, sideshow performers, people with physical handicaps, people with phobias. Some live in fantasy worlds, as did Brown himself with his fiction, because the real world is often too painful to endure. Some have classical educations, and are able to quote from a wide variety of literary sources; yet their intelligence does not always stand them in good stead, and their knowledge—enhanced by their imaginations—ofttimes places them in greater jeopardy, and perhaps brings them greater tragedy, than if they were simpler, less aware individuals.

Brown seems to have felt that the forces, cosmic or otherwise, which control our lives are at best mischievous and at worst malign; that man has little to say about his own destiny, and that free will is a fallacy. The joke is on us, he seems to be saying on numerous occasions (never better than in his fantasy novelette "Come and Go Mad," published in *Weird Tales* in 1949, an exercise in madness and metaphysics that remains, despite its flaws, one of his most powerful pieces of fiction). And it is a joke that all too frequently turns nasty.

Perhaps the underlying source of Brown's vision is his "ardent atheism." In a brief essay entitled "It's Only Everything," first published in a fan magazine in 1965, he wrote that he was "unable to understand . . . people, my contemporaries and predecessors, who give or gave lip-service to the special divinity of Christ and the worship of God and who do or did spend less than their full time and effort and thought in carrying his gospel to the ends of the Earth—and to the rest of the universe, whenever we get there." Yet he admired St. Francis of Assisi and Jesus of Nazareth "and whirling dervishes and anybody else who goeth whole hog with the courage of his convictions. I may not like him, but I understand him. I cannot and never will understand, and hereby spit in the eye of, any passive believer in a revealed religion who gives less than his whole life and thought to what, if it be true, is a matter of such personal and cosmic import that nothing else is worth a tinker's damn."

Fredric Brown had the courage of *his* convictions. And that courage and those convictions are in each and every one of his works of fiction.

Bill Pronzini, "Introduction: Dreamer in Paradox," *Carnival of Crime: The Best Mystery Stories of Fredric Brown*, ed. Francis M. Nevins, Jr., and Martin H. Greenberg (Carbondale: Southern Illinois University Press, 1985), pp. vii–viii

---

GEOFFREY O'BRIEN   The sincere hero serves as a divining rod to detect unreality. The same notion crops up in Fredric Brown's *The Fabulous Clipjoint*—the clipjoint being Chicago, and the hero a suitably naïve lad investigating his father's murder. At first glance this 1948 novel, Brown's first, seems to have its feet reasonably near the ground; but for Fredric Brown no mystery plot was ever more than a pretext for tangential fantasy and speculation. As a science-fiction writer, he pioneered the concept of the "parallel universe," and his crime novels—with their references to chess and Lewis Carroll, their flair for con games and carnival trickery, their unexpected metaphysical flights—make a Wonderland out of back alleys and dimly lit taverns. ⟨. . .⟩

Clipjoint's pivotal scene has nothing to do with crime or clues. The hero's mentor, Uncle Am, an old carny hand of infinite resources, takes him over to the window for a lecture on reality: "That looks like something down there, doesn't it? Solid stuff, each chunk of it separate from the next one and air in between them. It isn't. . . . It's a big mess of almost nothing, that's all. . . . Look, there's a guy walking down Clark Street. Well, he isn't anything either. He's just a part of the dance of the atoms." The laws of hard-boiled fiction are only another layer of illusion; when the hero gets ready to go into action, he consciously models himself on George Raft as Ned Beaumont in *The Glass Key* and psychs himself up by listening to Benny Goodman records.

Geoffrey O'Brien, "After the Crime," Village Voice, 24 February 1987, p. 41

JACK SEABROOK   Brown's ⟨. . .⟩ short mystery, "Don't Look Behind You," is justifiably one of his most famous. It was published in the May 1947 issue of *Ellery Queen's Mystery Magazine* and is a landmark of narrative experimentation. The story begins with a direct address to the reader: "Just sit back and relax, now. Try to enjoy this; it's going to be the last story you ever read, or nearly the last." The speaker is Justin Dean, a printer, but the reader doesn't know it yet, since he tells the first part of the story in the third person, as if it's about someone else. Dean is a meek employee of the Atlas Printing & Engraving Company in Springfield, Ohio, who is approached by Harley Prentice to print counterfeit five and ten dollar bills. Dean moves to New York, where the plan works for a while, until Harley calls from Albany and tells him to dump the plates and burn the remaining bills.

Harley is murdered, and Dean is interrogated by the police and, though they "didn't use clubs or rubber hoses," their harassment causes him apparently to go insane. He is put in a hospital, where he stays until he convinces his doctors that he should be released. Unfortunately, Dean now believes that Harley is alive, and allows himself to be tricked by friends of Harley's, who drive him as far south as the Carolinas and torture him to make him reveal the location of the plates. Finally, they abandon him deep in a swamp. He awakes completely insane and converses with a vision of Harley, who leads him safely out of the swamp. He kills a farm woman, then a man, and goes on the road, killing anyone who stands in his way and taking instructions from "Harley." His goal: to find and kill the men who tortured him. But in the meantime, for fun, he tells the reader about a bet he made with Harley that he could tell a man he was going to kill him with a knife, tell him why and when, and succeed. The intended victim is the reader—this story has been specially bound in this copy of the book to alert the reader, and it ends on this chilling note: "Go on, just a few seconds or minutes, thinking this is just another story. Don't look behind you. Don't believe this—*until you feel the knife.*"

"Don't Look Behind You" is one of Brown's most brilliant stories. Its narrative style is highly unusual and complex, fitting neatly into the world of crime and psychopathy that infuses the tale. The narrator threatens the reader from the start, and tells us about Justin Dean, making sure we understand how dangerous he is before revealing that he is actually Dean himself. This direct address to the reader has appeared in Brown's stories before, but this is the first time the reader is directly involved in the narrative. The idea that Dean is a printer and has specially prepared the reader's edition of the book is unnerving; Brown (through his narrator) is so insistent about it that the reader is compelled to wonder—if even for a moment—whether it might be true. ⟨. . .⟩

"Don't Look Behind You" finds Brown at the top of his form, and it is a perfect short story because it would not succeed in any other form, such as the novel. It has often been mentioned fondly by writers in their discussions of Brown, and is a favorite for reprinting.

Jack Seabrook, *Martians and Misplaced Clues: The Life and Work of Fredric Brown* (Bowling Green, OH: Bowling Green State University Popular Press, 1993), pp. 90–91

▩ Bibliography

The Fabulous Clipjoint. 1947.

The Dead Ringer. 1948.

Murder Can Be Fun. 1948.

What Mad Universe. 1949.

The Bloody Moonlight ⟨*Murder in Moonlight*⟩. 1949.

The Screaming Mimi. 1949.

Compliments of a Fiend. 1950.

Here Comes a Candle. 1950.

Night of the Jabberwock. 1950.

The Case of the Dancing Sandwiches. 1951.

Space on My Hands. 1951.

Death Has Many Doors. 1951.

The Far Cry. 1951.

The Deep End. 1952.

We All Killed Grandma. 1952.

Madball. 1953.

Science-Fiction Carnival: Fun in Science-Fiction (editor; with Mack Reynolds).
        1953.

Mostly Murder. 1953.

The Lights in the Sky Are Stars ⟨*Project Jupiter*⟩. 1953.

His Name Was Death. 1954.

Angels and Spaceships. 1954.

The Wench Is Dead. 1955.

Martians, Go Home. 1955.

The Lenient Beast. 1956.

Rogue in Space. 1957.

One for the Road. 1958.

Honeymoon in Hell. 1958.

The Office. 1958.

Knock Three-One-Two. 1959.

The Late Lamented. 1959.

The Murderers. 1961.

The Mind Thing. 1961.

Nightmares and Geezenstacks: 47 Stories. 1961.

The Five-Day Nightmare. 1962.

Mrs. Murphy's Underpants. 1963.

The Shaggy Dog and Other Murders. 1963.

Daymares. 1968.

Mitkey Astromouse. 1971.

Paradox Lost and Twelve Other Great Science Fiction Stories. 1973.

The Best of Fredric Brown. Ed. Robert Bloch. 1977.

4 Novels ⟨Night of the Jabberwock, The Screaming Mimi, Knock Three-One-Two, The Fabulous Clipjoint⟩. 1983.

Fredric Brown in the Detective Pulps. 1984–91. 19 vols.

Carnival of Crime: The Best Mystery Stories of Fredric Brown. Ed. Francis M. Nevins, Jr., and Martin H. Greenberg. 1985.

And the Gods Laughed: A Collection of Science Fiction and Fantasy. 1987.

❖ ❖ ❖

John Dickson Carr
1906–1977

JOHN DICKSON CARR was born on November 30, 1906 (although 1905 is frequently but erroneously cited), in Uniontown, Pennsylvania. He spent the years 1913–16 in Washington, D.C., when his father, Wood Nicholas Carr, was elected to the U.S. House of Representatives. Returning to Uniontown, Carr became involved in journalism, writing articles on court proceedings and murder cases at the age of eleven and later writing a column on boxing for the local newspaper. He attended the Hill School from 1921 to 1925.

Carr entered Haverford College in 1925. The next year he began writing stories and poems for the *Haverfordian*, the school literary magazine, which he later edited. He graduated from Haverford in 1928 and spent the 1928–29 school year at the Sorbonne in Paris, but most of his time was spent writing a short novel, *Grand Guignol*, serialized in the *Haverfordian* in 1929; he later expanded the work into *It Walks by Night* (1930). This novel introduced the first of Carr's detectives, Henri Bencolin, who was featured in several early novels.

In 1930 Carr moved to New York but traveled widely in England and Europe. He married Clarice Cleaves, an Englishwoman with whom he would have three children, in 1932 and settled in England the next year. Carr became so Anglicized that many readers assumed him to be a British author.

In 1933 Carr published *Hag's Nook* (1933), the first of twenty-three novels featuring the immense private detective Dr. Gideon Fell. The next year he published *The Plague Court Murders*, the first of twenty-two novels involving Sir Henry Merrivale. Throughout the 1930s and 1940s Carr alternated writing novels about Dr. Fell and "H. M."; the latter appeared under the pseudonym Carter Dickson. These novels established Carr as one of the most distinctive writers of mystery fiction's "Golden Age": rigorously adhering to the doctrine of "fair play," they contained bewilderingly complex plots, bizarre methods of murder, an atmosphere of both comedy and the supernatural, and a brisk, vigorous, and at times hyperbolic style. Most of

Carr's works are locked-room mysteries, and he is recognized as the unsurpassed master in this subgenre. Among the best of his novels of this period are *The Mad Hatter Mystery* (1933), *The Three Coffins* (1935), in which Dr. Fell gives a "locked-room lecture," *The Arabian Nights Murder* (1936), *The Peacock Feather Murders* (1937), and *The Reader Is Warned* (1939). *The Burning Court* (1937) is a tour de force in its evolution from an orthodox detective story to a supernatural novel about witchcraft.

In the late 1930s Carr began work for the BBC, and he wrote many plays for British and American radio during World War II. Some of these have been printed in *The Dead Sleep Lightly* (1983), but many remain unpublished. After the war Carr spent years in researching and writing an authorized biography of Sir Arthur Conan Doyle, which was well received upon its appearance in 1949; it won the Edgar Allan Poe Award from the Mystery Writers of America.

In 1948 Carr, disliking the Labour government in England, returned to the United States, purchasing a house in Mamaroneck, New York. When the Labour party was ousted in 1953, Carr returned to England. In 1965 he settled in Greenville, South Carolina, remaining there until his death. In his last two decades Carr wrote innovative "historical mysteries," fusing the detective story and the historical novel. The first such work, *Devil Kinsmere*, had been published in 1934 under the pseudonym Roger Fairbairn (it was later rewritten as *Most Secret*, 1964), while *The Murder of Sir Edmund Godfrey* (1936) is an attempted solution of an actual murder in the seventeenth century. *The Bride of Newgate* (1950) was the first of thirteen historical mysteries that Carr wrote in the last two decades of his life. In 1962 he received the Grand Master Award from the Mystery Writers of America.

Carr, a heavy smoker, developed increasing health problems in his later years that cut down his productivity. He wrote a monthly book review column for *Ellery Queen's Mystery Magazine* from 1969 to 1976, but after *The Hungry Goblin* (1972) he published no more novels. John Dickson Carr died of lung cancer on February 27, 1977. An authorized biography by Douglas G. Greene appeared in 1994.

✦ *Critical Extracts*

DOROTHY L. SAYERS   "Is Mr. Carr Edgar Wallace's successor?"
inquires Mr. Carr's publisher, wistfully. The answer is, "Don't ask silly
questions." From the very first paragraph of *The Mad Hatter Mystery* it is
abundantly clear that Mr. Carr has nothing in common with Edgar Wallace:

> It began, like most of Dr. Fell's mysteries, in a bar. It dealt
> with the reason why a man was found dead on the steps of
> Traitors' Gate, at the Tower of London, with the odd headgear of
> this man in the golf suit. That was the worst part of it. The whole
> case threatened for a time to become a nightmare of hats.

If that is like anybody, it is like G. K. Chesterton. ⟨. . .⟩

Chestertonian also are the touches of extravagance in character and plot,
and the sensitiveness to symbolism, to historical association, to the shapes
and colours of material things, to the crazy terror of the incongruous. Mr.
Carr can lead us away from the small, artificial, brightly-lit stage of the
ordinary detective plot into the menace of outer darkness. He can create
atmosphere with an adjective, make a picture from a wet iron railing, a
dusty table, a gas-lamp blurred by the fog. He can alarm with an illusion
or delight with a rollicking absurdity. He can invent a passage from a lost
work of Edgar Allan Poe which sounds like the real thing. In short, he can
write—not merely in the negative sense of observing the rules of syntax,
but in the sense that every sentence gives a thrill of positive pleasure. This
is the most attractive mystery I have read in a long time.

> Dorothy L. Sayers, [Review of *The Mad Hatter Mystery*], *Sunday Times* (London), 24
> March 1933, p. 7

JOHN DICKSON CARR   "I will now lecture," said Dr. Fell, inexo-
rably, "on the general mechanics and development of the situation which
is known in detective fiction as the 'hermetically sealed chamber.' Harrumph.
All those opposing can skip this chapter. ⟨. . .⟩

"Now, it seems reasonable to point out that the word improbable is the
very last which should ever be used to curse detective fiction in any case.
A great part of our liking for detective fiction is *based* on a liking for
improbability. When A is murdered, and B and C are under strong suspicion,

it is improbable that the innocent-looking D can be guilty. But he is. If G has a perfect alibi, sworn to at every point by every other letter in the alphabet, it is improbable that G can have committed the crime. But he has. When the detective picks up a fleck of coal dust at the seashore, it is improbable that such an insignificant thing can have any importance. But it will. In short, you come to a point where the word improbable grows meaningless as a jeer. There can be no such thing as any probability until the end of the story. And then, if you wish the murder to be fastened on an unlikely person (as some of us old fogies do), you can hardly complain because he acted from motives less likely or necessarily less apparent than those of the person first suspected.

"When the cry of 'This-sort-of-thing-wouldn't-happen!' goes up, when you complain about half-faced fiends and hooded phantoms and blond hypnotic sirens, you are merely saying, 'I don't like this sort of story.' That's fair enough. If you do not like it, you are howlingly right to say so. But when you twist this matter of taste into a rule for judging the merit or even the probability of the story, you are merely saying, 'This series of events couldn't happen, because I shouldn't enjoy it if it did.' ⟨. . .⟩

"You see, the effect ⟨of the locked-room murder⟩ is so magical that we somehow expect the cause to be magical also. When we see that it isn't wizardry, we call it tomfoolery. Which is hardly fair play. The last thing we should complain about with regard to the murderer is his erratic conduct. The whole test is, *can* the thing be done? If so, the question of whether it *would* be done does not enter into it. A man escapes from a locked room— well? Since apparently he has violated the laws of nature for our entertainment, then heaven knows he is entitled to violate the laws of Probable Behaviour! If a man offers to stand on his head, we can hardly make the stipulation that he must keep his feet on the ground while he does it. Bear that in mind, gents, when you judge. Call the result uninteresting, if you like, or anything else that is a matter of personal taste. But be very careful about making the nonsensical statement that it is improbable or far-fetched."

John Dickson Carr, "The Locked-Room Lecture," *The Three Coffins* (New York: Harper & Brothers, 1935), pp. 220–24

NICHOLAS BLAKE   One of those intellectual parlour-games recently in vogue consisted in the proposing of a number of wildly dissimilar phenomena and relating them through a plausible narrative. Let us take, for example, a museum; on its wall a gentleman is found sitting clad in a top-hat and false whiskers; somebody has thrown a lump of coal at one of the inner walls; within also are discovered an attendant tap-dancing at midnight round a mummy-case, two more pairs of false whiskers, and a corpse clutching a cookery-book in its hand. Such, believe it or not, is the situation with which Mr. Carr opens his new book ⟨The Arabian Nights Murder⟩. Mr. Carr could not be unreadable if he tried. But this time I feel he has gone too far. Dr. Illingworth and Sir Herbert Armstrong are figures of too much fun: you will certainly split your sides over them; but the book rather cracks up in the process. The Unicorn Murders is equally readable, and equally damaged by excess. Here the excess is not of comic exuberance but of factual complication. The opening situation presents a man killed in a Marseilles street by something that has left a wound disagreeably suggestive of a unicorn's horn, and a young woman solemnly greeting a friend in a Paris café with the first two lines of "The Lion and the Unicorn." That is good. Better still is the position where a number of people are flood-bound in a castle on the Loire, knowing that the notorious murderer, Flamande, and his famous adversary, Gasquet, are present in disguise, but not knowing the identity of either the criminal or the detective. At this point, however, the story begins to be overloaded with coincidence and further confusion of identities. For those who suspect that J. Dickson Carr and Carter Dickson are one and the same writer, more circumstantial evidence is now forthcoming: (1) the growing family likeness between Dr. Fell and Sir Henry Merrivale; (2) the paradoxical opening gambits of the Arabian Nights Murder and the Unicorn Murders; (3) the fact that in both these books the unusual phrase "you overgrown gnome" appears. By the way, Sir Henry, "quocumque aspicio, nihil est pontus et aer" is not correctly quoted.

Nicholas Blake, "Going Too Far," Spectator, 28 February 1936, p. 364

ALFRED KAZIN   The story of Sir Edmund Godfrey has concerned every historian who has written in general of the later Stuarts, and in particular of the "Popish Plot." It remains a thriller of the first order, full of temptations to the master mind in us all, and stuffed with 250 years worth of dark mystery. On the principle that the apparatus should be worthy of the intent, Mr. Carr has brought a meticulous learning to his task, a good eye, and all the tricks of the trade. Everything in his book is true, save the conclusion, and that, he insists (rather convincingly), is probable. Where such big wigs as Macaulay and David Hume have not been afraid to play detective, Mr. Carr has not been afraid either; the result is that one can read his book with all the high seriousness in the world, but add the keen sense of pleasure we all derive from the amiable solution of another's murder.

Alfred Kazin, [Review of *The Murder of Sir Edmund Godfrey*], *New York Herald Tribune Books*, 22 November 1936, p. 8

E. R. PUNSHON   As a general rule fiction must tend from its very nature to emphasise in life the exception and the abnormal. Oedipus was not continually faced with plague in the city, Lear had had his moments of repose. In the detective novel this emphasis on the abnormal is especially marked, since the crime with which it necessarily deals must remain apart from ordinary experience. How daring, then, is that writer who to the strangeness and the rarity of murder adds the sheer incredibility of the supernatural!

This feat, this welding into one coherent whole of the terror of deliberate murder, of the horror of traffic with the unseen, Mr. Dickson Carr attempts in his new book, *The Burning Court*. To an ingenious and convincing story of the death of an old eccentric—indeed, of two old eccentrics—and of the subsequent investigation he adds as bizarre a study in the macabre and the supernatural as any lover of the occult could desire. Bodies disappear from securely built up vaults, women walk through walls, the dead come to offer greeting to the living, a harmless young man is shown a photograph of his wife guillotined seventy years before, in succession the characters take on the appearance of reincarnations of the actors in the terrible Brinvilliers poisoning drama of the seventeenth century, till in the end both they and we alike are so mazed it is hard for us to tell into what fog of doubt and dread and wonder we have strayed. Then to all his tale of terror Mr. Carr provides the simplest and most convincing of explanations, only in the last few pages to overwhelm the reader once again in a black horror of witchcraft and devil-worship. The book may not be to the taste of all, but as an adventure in diablerie it is a remarkable and outstanding achievement.

E. R. Punshon, "Murder and the Supernatural," *Manchester Guardian*, 9 April 1937, p. 6

ROBERT LEWIS TAYLOR   In the early days of Carr's English travail, his recreational life consisted of frequent trips to Dartmoor, where he got in the mood by staring at the prison and walking in solitude over the mottled barrens. As Holmes had once camped out on the moor near the great Grimpen Mire, Carr sat with a box lunch in the vestigial dwelling places of Neolithic man. Then, infused with a sufficient dosage of the horrors, he would make haste for home and set to work before his humor brightened. Mrs. Carr, who, socially, regarded Neolithic man as a closed book, preferred to spend her time with his present-day descendants, and she usually visited her family. Not long after Miss Sayers' laudatory piece in the *Sunday Times*, the Carrs moved to London, and Carr, his star in the ascendant, took his place in the literary life of the British capital. He was elected to the Savage and Garrick clubs, and, at last, was made a member of the ultimate in mystery writers' groups, the small and snobbish Detection Club in London. Chesterton then reigned as president, handing down decisions on how books were to be written, how the plots unfolded, how the characters drawn, how the standards uplifted in general. Carr put on his best suit for his presentation to his hero, but Chesterton died shortly before the meeting. In all his appearances at the club thereafter, Carr has tried to behave in a manner that he believes Chesterton would have approved. ⟨. . .⟩

Carr feels that ⟨the⟩ high-minded standards ⟨of the Detection Club⟩ have elevated the whole field of English detective fiction. With the shade of Chesterton over his shoulder, he toils with dreadful anxiety to make his work both literary and explicable. First, in the preparation of a new book, he draws up what he calls a "clue outline," marking points in the narrative at which he plans to plant the signposts to the guilt of whichever fiend he is building. Then, with elaborate pains, he makes working sketches of the characters, sometimes promoting minor players to star roles, and the reverse, as he goes, depending on how they respond to the call to creation. He jots down snatches of dialogue as he visualizes the characters and hears their speech in his mind. Plotting is easy for Carr—he habitually sees the entire network of human relations as a slough of intrigue—and the blocking out of the separate scenes is perhaps his favorite chore. He hates the actual writing, however, and does it in anguish, emerging from each long session hollow-eyed and spent. As one of his detective-writer friends has remarked, "This is a hell of a tough rap for a man who has to write four books a year to stay happy."

Robert Lewis Taylor, "Two Authors in an Attic—II," *New Yorker*, 15 September 1951, pp. 39–40

ANTHONY BOUCHER   John Dickson Carr did not actually invent the detective-story-in-a-period-setting, but the current popularity of this form, which so attractively combines the appeals of the whodunit and the historical novel, certainly dates back only a dozen years to Carr's *The Bride of Newgate*; and equally certainly no one is consistently so successful in this hyphenated genre as Carr, who combines genuine understanding of and relish for the past with a comparable understanding and relish in matters of detectival trickery.

The latest Carr historical, *The Demoniacs*, is set in London in 1757, just before the demolition of the dwellings that encumbered Old London Bridge. In one of these ancient ramshackle houses a woman dies of fright (or by an invisible method of murder?); and thief-taker Jeffrey Wynne, one of blind Justice Fielding's forerunners of the modern detective, is up to his ears in a deadly puzzle which includes duels, diamonds, bigamy, bastardy, waxworks and love, with the Rev. Laurence Sterne wandering happily through the pages as comic relief. As always, Carr's settings and dialogue are the next best thing to time travel; and his plotting is a model of its kind.

> Anthony Boucher, [Review of *The Demoniacs*], *New York Times Book Review*, 28 October 1962, p. 55

O. L. BAILEY   John Dickson Carr, master of the arcane, adds to his repertoire the "Victorian Detective Novel" with *The Hungry Goblin*. Once again, Carr, justly famous for his locked-room mysteries, gives us one that is seemingly insoluble—except upon hindsight when, of course, the solution becomes almost obvious.

Set in London a century ago, Carr ornaments the tale with an erudite and entertaining excursion through the life-styles, conceits, and concerns of the time. The story involves a switch in roles of two beautiful women possessing identical physical, social, and intellectual characteristics. Wilkie Collins, whose *The Moonstone* was the first detective novel written in English, is introduced as an actual character in the book, and a key volunteer in aiding the police to solve a thorny case of attempted murder. (Mystery buffs will appreciate the fact that Collins's novel, *The Woman in White*, was built on a similar plot.) The atmosphere is rich, the authenticity convincing, and Carr's stylistic and storytelling skills are quite up to snuff.

O. L. Bailey, [Review of *The Hungry Goblin*], *Saturday Review*, 26 August 1972, p. 62

LeROY PANEK   ⟨. . .⟩ one of the most attractive things about the locked room mystery for Carr was its connection with magic. Fundamentally, it is impossible for someone to be murdered when he is alone in a locked room. Period. It can only be done through some sort of trick or illusion. Magicians, of course, do all sorts of escapes and disappearing acts in which they make their assistants disappear from locked cabinets—this reached epic proportions in the twenties with Raymond's making an elephant disappear— and they themselves escape from straitjackets, locked trunks, and even milk cans. Every trick seems impossible until one reads the secret of the illusion. And the secrets parallel those of the locked room mystery: the magician uses twin assistants, the locks are fakes, etc. Carr does the same thing that the magician does in making the impossible happen through an illusion and by misdirecting our attention by narrative technique, and then, presto, he explains how he did it. As H.M. says in *The Plague Court Murders*, "The fundamental trouble with the locked room situation is that it generally ain't reasonable. I don't mean that it can't be worked, any more than you'd deny one of Houdini's escapes."

Although in *The Three Coffins* Dr. Fell comes close to despair over the evil in human beings, Carr never pretends that his detective stories are about the real world or about real people. His feeling toward the readers who look for reality in the detective story is portrayed in Dr. Illingworth, the Scottish clergyman and Arabic scholar in *The Arabian Nights Murder*. Dr. Illingworth finds a thriller, *The Dagger of Doom*, on the train and after reading it becomes convinced that it is a manual of police work, and thereafter interprets all of the zany events in the novel in the light of adventures of the villainous Dr. Chianti in *The Dagger of Doom* and *The Return of Dr. Chianti*. This becomes wildly absurd. Carr does not pretend that his books are slices of life but frankly identifies them as detective stories full of detective story conventions. Thus in the last chapter of *The Eight of Swords* we get these comments:

>After all, this is only a detective story.
> . . .

> You don't know what you're talking about. And besides, get
> back to the subject. This is the last chapter, and we want to get it
> over with.

And at the end of *To Wake the Dead* Dr. Fell is asked how he would describe
events like those in the novel. He replies: "I call it a detective story." It is
a wild, improbable, fictional entertainment.

LeRoy Panek, "John Dickson Carr," *Watteau's Shepherds: The Detective Novel in Britain
1914–1940* (Bowling Green, OH: Bowling Green University Popular Press, 1979),
pp. 182–83

DOUGLAS G. GREENE　　⟨*It Walks by Night*⟩ begins with an eerie
atmosphere by references to "night monsters . . . with blood-bedabbled
claws." In Carr's hands even an ordinary act like opening a door can be
filled with terror and suspense: "When I turned the knob of that door it
opened with an oiled lock, and the hinges were oiled and soundless, so that
the movement of the door had the odd dreamlike quality of an opening
gulf. . . . I saw, too, faint gleams from a perforated lamp, threading slow
smoke against the weird moving rustle of the dark." Unlike Van Dine, Carr
believed that readers would be involved in the story if it includes romantic
interest. The narrator, Jeff Marle, an American living in Paris, becomes
involved with Sharon Grey—though she is much more anemic than women
in later Carr stories. Bencolin's kindliness in the short stories is downplayed
in *It Walks by Night,* and his sardonic manner and Satanic appearance are
emphasized. His black hair is "parted in the middle and twirled up like
horns." His eyes, earlier described as kindly, are now "dark, veiled." His
smile is "inscrutable"; his face is cruel; and he has a sadistic desire to make
his prey suffer. Even in the "Grand Guignol" version of the novel, Bencolin
admits that "I am fond of sticking pins in my fellow-mortals to see how
they will react." In the later Bencolin novels, his tendency to be theatrical
is exaggerated to the extent that he varies his costume depending on how
close he is to pouncing on the criminal: "When he walks in evening clothes,
with the familiar cloak, top-hat, and silver-headed stick, when his smile is
a trifle more suave and there is a very slight bulge under his left arm—
messieurs, that means trouble. . . ."

It Walks by Night contains Carr's hallmark, an impossible crime, and it
has the typical Carrian plot development. The murder, beheading in a room

all of whose exits are under observation, is one of the bloodiest in detective fiction. Carr's plots were strongly influenced by Chesterton's Father Brown stories, in which physical clues play minor roles and the crime is solved by discovering the pattern which the events form. Carr improved on Chesterton in one way: although the pattern is normally revealed about three quarters of the way into a Carr novel, the criminal is not unmasked until the final scene. Most Carr novels thus have two denouements, allowing him to explain his intricate plots gradually rather than in one undigestible lump at the very end. *It Walks by Night* might easily be used as a textbook of sound plot construction in a detective novel.

> Douglas G. Greene, "Introduction—John Dickson Carr: The Man Who Created Miracles," *The Door to Doom and Other Detections*, ed. Douglas G. Greene (New York: Harper & Row, 1980), pp. 15–16

S. T. JOSHI   ⟨Carr's⟩ foremost strength is narrative drive. This quality he possessed perhaps even in excess of any of his idols—Conan Doyle, Chesterton, even Stevenson and Twain. No writer can keep one reading more than John Dickson Carr. Even if some of his narrative devices are merely tricks—the trick of ending each chapter or section on a startling revelation; the trick of having characters make dramatic entrances like actors in a melodrama—they all work to produce a consuming interest in the puzzle and its attendant circumstances that is not satisfied until the final resolution and explanation. Save in his late works, Carr never wastes a word; his language is always tight and compact, his style almost exhilarating in its forward energy and unceasing flow. ⟨. . .⟩

The most noticeable feature of Carr's detective novels is their combination of intricate plot, supernatural chills, and boisterous humour. *The Eight of Swords* (1934) encapsulates this hybridism when it is remarked: "The whole thing was at once baffling, ludicrous, and terrible." Again, although much of the humour is slapstick and some of the shudders are artificial (as in *Castle Skull*), this picturesque union is on the whole quite effective. The Bencolin novels produce the most harmonious joining of these disparate qualities, as the humour tends to be markedly sardonic and hence appropriate to the grotesque horror of the background and central incidents. In other works humour and horror alternate, sometimes in a blindingly quick fashion. The clowning of Sir Henry Merrivale usually subsides after the actual murder, and occasionally novels that begin with the frothy hilarity of a Wodehouse end with the grimness of Bierce. On still other occasions Carr can create an atmosphere of sustained sombreness, lightened by almost no humour, that ironically is not nearly as far from that of his hated Russian novelists as he would like to believe. *Poison in Jest* (1932) is the earliest and perhaps the best example.

What all this means is that Carr is a master of tone, mood, and atmosphere. In saying this we approach the true greatness and the true distinguishing feature of his work. To be sure, he concocted more elaborate puzzles than anyone in detective fiction; he created three of the most engaging detectives in the field; he wrote one magnificent supernatural novel and his unique historical mysteries; but the fact is that Carr is not a mere logician devising plots like a literary computer wizard. Carr did not ⟨. . .⟩ consider detective stories—or at least his type of detective stories—as belonging to the realm of realism, but rather to the realm of fantasy. The truth is, therefore, that Carr is a great fantaisiste. He could have written some of the finest supernatural fiction of the century if he had been so inclined. In spite of the obvious care he takes in the exact dovetailing of a complicated plot, he is interested not so much in this as in creating a series of images that shock, baffle, and horrify. It is for this end, and this end only, that Carr sets in motion all the narrative and structural skills he has at his disposal: the stage must be carefully set for that arresting tableau which, fleeting as it may be, is the real heart of the work. A man found decapitated as if bending down to the guillotine; a dead woman lying in a waxen satyr's arms; a gun that seems to leap from a wall, hang in midair, and shoot its victim—these are the scenes we remember long after the contrived puzzle is forgotten, and it is they that make John Dickson Carr the supreme colourist in detective fiction.

S. T. Joshi, *John Dickson Carr: A Critical Study* (Bowling Green, OH: Bowling Green State University Popular Press, 1990), pp. 140–41

▨ *Bibliography*

It Walks by Night. 1930.
The Lost Gallows. 1931.
Castle Skull. 1931.
The Corpse in the Waxworks ⟨*The Waxworks Murder*⟩. 1932.

Poison in Jest. 1932.

Hag's Nook. 1933.

The Mad Hatter Mystery. 1933.

The Bowstring Murders. 1933.

The Eight of Swords. 1934.

The Plague Court Murders. 1934.

The Blind Barber. 1934.

The White Priory Murders. 1934.

Devil Kinsmere. 1934, 1964 (as *Most Secret*).

Death-Watch. 1935.

The Red Widow Murders. 1935.

The Three Coffins ⟨*The Hollow Man*⟩. 1935.

The Unicorn Murders. 1935.

The Arabian Nights Murder. 1936.

The Murder of Sir Edmund Godfrey. 1936.

The Punch and Judy Murders ⟨*The Magic-Lantern Murders*⟩. 1936.

The Burning Court. 1937.

The Peacock Feather Murders ⟨*The Ten Teacups*⟩. 1937.

The Four False Weapons. 1937.

The Third Bullet. 1937.

To Wake the Dead. 1937.

The Judas Window ⟨*The Crossbow Murder*⟩. 1938.

Death in Five Boxes. 1938.

The Crooked Hinge. 1938.

Fatal Descent (with John Rhode). 1939.

The Problem of the Green Capsule ⟨*The Black Spectacles*⟩. 1939.

The Reader Is Warned. 1939.

The Problem of the Wire Cage. 1939.

And So to Murder. 1940.

The Man Who Could Not Shudder. 1940.

Nine—and Death Makes Ten ⟨*Murder in the Submarine Zone*⟩. 1940.

The Department of Queer Complaints. 1940.

The Case of the Constant Suicides. 1941.

Seeing Is Believing. 1941.

Death Turns the Tables ⟨*The Seat of the Scornful*⟩. 1941.

The Gilded Man. 1942.

The Emperor's Snuff-Box. 1942.

She Died a Lady. 1943.

He Wouldn't Kill Patience. 1944.

Till Death Do Us Part. 1944.

The Curse of the Bronze Lamp. 〈Lord of the Sorcerers〉. 1945.

He Who Whispers. 1946.

My Late Wives. 1946.

The Sleeping Sphinx. 1947.

Dr. Fell, Detective, and Other Stories. Ed. Ellery Queen. 1947.

The Skeleton in the Clock. 1948.

The Life of Sir Arthur Conan Doyle. 1949.

Below Suspicion. 1949.

A Graveyard to Let. 1949.

The Bride of Newgate. 1950.

Night at the Mocking Widow. 1950.

The Devil in Velvet. 1951.

Behind the Crimson Blind. 1952.

The Nine Wrong Answers. 1952.

The Cavalier's Cup. 1953.

The Exploits of Sherlock Holmes (with Adrian Conan Doyle). 1954.

The Third Bullet and Other Stories. 1954.

Captain Cut-Throat. 1955.

Fear Is the Same. 1956.

Patrick Butler for the Defence. 1956.

Fire, Burn! 1957.

A John Dickson Carr Trio 〈The Three Coffins, The Crooked Hinge, The Case of the Constant Suicides〉. 1957.

Great Stories by Sir Arthur Conan Doyle (editor). 1958.

The Dead Man's Knock. 1958.

Scandal at High Chimneys. 1959.

A Dr. Fell Omnibus 〈The Mad Hatter Mystery, Death-Watch, The Black Spectacles, The Seat of the Scornful〉. 1959.

Three Detective Novels 〈The Arabian Nights Murder, The Burning Court, The Problem of the Wire Cage〉. 1959.

In Spite of Thunder. 1960.

The Witch of the Low-Tide. 1961.

The Demoniacs. 1962.

The Men Who Explained Miracles. 1963.

The House at Satan's Elbow. 1965.

Panic in Box C. 1966.

Dark of the Moon. 1967.

Papa Là-bas. 1968.

The Ghosts' High Noon. 1969.

Deadly Hall. 1971.

The Hungry Goblin. 1972.

The Door to Doom and Other Detections. Ed. Douglas G. Greene. 1980.

The Dead Sleep Lightly. Ed. Douglas G. Greene. 1983.

Four Complete Dr. Fell Mysteries ⟨*To Wake the Dead, The Blind Barber, The Crooked Hinge, The Case of the Constant Suicides*⟩. 1988.

Fell and Foul Play. Ed. Douglas G. Greene. 1991.

Merrivale, March, and Murder. Ed. Douglas G. Greene. 1991.

Speak of the Devil. 1994.

Edmund Crispin
1921–1978

EDMUND CRISPIN is the pseudonym of Robert Bruce Montgomery, who was born on October 2, 1921, in Chesham Bois, Buckinghamshire, England. He attended the Merchant Taylor's School at Moor Park, Middlesex, and later studied modern languages at St. John's College, Oxford, where he received his B.A. in 1943. There he belonged to various musical organizations, serving as president of the University Music Club and organist and choirmaster to St. John's College. From 1943 to 1945 he was a schoolmaster at The Schools, Shrewsbury.

While at Oxford, Montgomery was urged by his friend John Maxwell to read the detective novels of John Dickson Carr. Montgomery read Carr's *The Crooked Hinge* (1938) and was so taken with it that he wrote his own detective novel, *The Case of the Gilded Fly* (1944), under the pseudonym Edmund Crispin. Over the next several years he produced a number of books featuring his sleuth, Gervase Fen, an erudite Oxford don who writes detective stories; these include the novels *Holy Disorders* (1945), *The Moving Toyshop* (1946), *Swan Song* (1947), *Love Lies Bleeding* (1948), *Buried for Pleasure* (1948), *Frequent Hearses* (1950), and *The Long Divorce* (1951), and the short story collection *Beware of the Trains* (1953). During the same period he also composed a great deal of choral music, notably *An Oxford Requiem* (1950).

Crispin's detective work falls into the general pattern of the "fair-play" detective story of John Dickson Carr and others, although enlivened by considerable humor and wit. He is often paired with Michael Innes in his mingling of scholarly erudition with detection. In spite of the hectic action sequences found in several of his novels, Crispin's later mysteries take a greater interest in character development than the solution of the crime.

After the early 1950s Crispin stopped writing mystery fiction but remained active as an editor and composer. Between 1955 and 1974 he edited many anthologies of mystery, horror, and science fiction stories, including seven volumes of *Best SF* (1955–70), two volumes of *Best Detective Stories* (1959–

64), and two volumes of *Best Tales of Terror* (1962–65). In 1959 he wrote the score for the film *Carry On Nurse*. In 1967 he became the crime fiction reviewer for the *Sunday Times* (London).

Crispin married in 1975. After more than twenty years during which he wrote no fiction, he produced another Gervase Fen novel, *The Glimpses of the Moon* (1977). He was planning to write more detective novels as well as crime novels and tales under his own name, but he had apparently written little of this work before he died on September 15, 1978. A posthumous collection of short stories, *Fen Country*, most of which were originally published in the early 1950s, appeared in 1979.

◈ *Critical Extracts*

JOHN HAMPSON   *The Case of the Gilded Fly* is, we are told by the publisher on the jacket, "a detective story by a new writer who calls himself Edmund Crispin." The scene is war-time Oxford, and since the novel also concerns the activities of a repertory company, one may as well follow the author's lead and introduce his characters in the order of their appearance. First the sleuth, Gervase Fen, also a professor of English. Then there is Sheila McGaw, producer at the theatre. A playwright, Robert Warner, his mistress and leading lady, Rachel West, follow. Two more actresses, Yseut and Helen Haskell, half-sisters, come next. Sir Richard Freeman, chief constable, whose hobby of English literature adds to his weight. Then there is Donald Fellowes, a college organist, infatuated with the red-headed Yseut, who happens to be a woman of means, a poor actress, a nasty piece of work and a discard of the playwright's into the bargain. Nicholas Barclay, a spoiled scholar, and Jean Whitelegge, who is in love with Donald, bring us to the Watsonian journalist Nigel Blake, and the walkers-on. All the named characters make the journey from Paddington to Oxford before October 12th, 1940. The final sentence of the opening chapter tells the reader what will happen before October 18th: by the day, out of the eleven characters listed, three "having fordone themselves, desperately are dead." A good beginning, with promising development; the characters are lively and credible. The murderer's motive seems plausible; his methods rather dubious.

Professor Fen, one hopes, will be heard of again; unlike so many amateurs, he is never a bore.

John Hampson, "Fiction," *Spectator*, 24 March 1944, p. 276

WILL CUPPY   Seems that Richard Cadogan ⟨in *The Moving Toy-shop*⟩, a highbrow poet in need of romantic adventure, went to Oxford on vacation, found the body of Miss Emilia Tardy in a toyshop in the Iffley road, got hit on the head, played literary games in the bar with Gervase Fen, professor of English, and otherwise got enough new ideas for several sonnets, we'd say. But why did the toyshop turn into a grocery run by Alice Winkworth? What's this about the late Miss Snaith's will providing that the estate shall go to charity if Emilia doesn't show up in time? Or was Aaron Rossiter, a Dickensy solicitor, lying about that? Scrap of paper reads "07691," and Fen will give you the answers unless he runs into something with his comic automobile named Lily Christine III, or somebody slaps him down for exclaiming, "Oh, my ears and whiskers!"

This successor to *Holy Disorders* and *Obsequies at Oxford* finds Mr. Crispin in an almost alarmingly antic frame of mind, tossing whimsy around regardless and adding more violent amusement whenever there's a broom handle to trip over. What saves the day is that Fen and Richard are expert deducers between their bouts of badinage. Some of the characters are a pleasure to meet, not to mention such local color as dons, proctors, bullers and bowlers and young Mr. Hoskins, a raw-boned student with an irresistible attraction for the ladies. He does it simply by giving them chocolates. And why does Mr. Crispin fling his erudite allusions hither and yon in a way that should cause Michael Innes to chew his nails? Because it's that kind of a whodunit.

Will Cuppy, [Review of *The Moving Toyshop*], *New York Herald Tribune Weekly Book Review*, 8 December 1946, p. 42

JOHN GARRETT   "You have erred perhaps in attempting to put colour and life into each of your statements, instead of confining yourself to the task of placing upon record that severe reasoning from cause to effect which is really the only notable feature about the thing. Crime is common. Logic is rare." The words are Sherlock Holmes's; their victim is naturally

Watson. They serve as a reminder of days when detective fiction aimed to please a more discriminating public, when its practitioners aimed at design and distinction, and when a chasm did not yawn between the few good and the many bad. Most of the present batch lack quality, and appear to have been dashed off without care for craftsmanship, but with an eye perhaps upon film rights.

An exception is Edmund Crispin's *Love Lies Bleeding*, which shows some pleasant wit, great talent for bringing interesting characters vividly to life, a good plot with an exciting climax, and a nicely observed picture of school-life. The headmaster is credible, the school population authentic, and the senile homicidal bloodhound, Mr. Merrythought, a masterpiece of canine creation. But the Oxford don turned detective eludes him, and his detestable so-called modern miss positively creaks. His danger is over-writing, which is the enemy of "colour and life." Why talk of "olfactory delights" instead of "agreeable smells"? Can a doctor speak "vampirically" and a hand be waved "acerbly"? Does it assist a story for a man to "embark on a prolegome-non of discreetly consolatory phrases," or for special formalities to be "hur-riedly consummated"? If Mr. Crispin will court verbal astringency, he can join the small class of reputable authors of detective fiction, who, like the Ancient Mariner, can tell a story which we "cannot choose but hear."

John Garrett, " 'Expense of Spirit . . .," *Spectator*, 16 July 1948, p. 88

FRANCES J. WALLACE   An English detective-story writer with an interest in Elizabethan literature and a flair for composing music is Bruce Montgomery, who under the pseudonym "Edmund Crispin" has produced a number of sophisticated tales involving one Gervase Fen, Oxford don whose sleuthing is seasoned with erudition. The author admits, "as a detective novelist I have a rather specialized audience, chiefly highbrow." ⟨. . .⟩

The author, who is a bachelor, lives at Rockhill House, Brixham, in Devonshire. He has brown eyes, auburn hair, stands a scant six feet, and weighs about 160 pounds. Before the war, Bruce Montgomery—as he prefers to be called—traveled "a fair amount" in Europe, chiefly in France and Germany. He has revealed that his friends consider him to be "lazy, tolerant, politically apathetic, extravagant over food, drink, books, and cigarettes, good-humored, garrulous, and very occasionally witty, much attracted by the other sex, terrified of children, a cat-lover, and a person temperamentally requiring a good deal of solitude."

Among his recreations he lists swimming, the cinema, conversation, and reading. Favorite authors are: detective novelist, John Dickson Carr; "straight" modern novelist, Evelyn Waugh; American writers, Thurber, Mencken, Aiken; and classical authors, Shakespeare, Wordsworth, Smollett, and Thackeray. Montgomery is a Conservative in politics; he is a member of the Church of England.

> Frances J. Wallace, "Edmund Crispin," *Wilson Library Bulletin* 23, No. 10 (June 1949): 750

RALPH PARTRIDGE   Edmund Crispin has been basking in public praise lately; and his fame must have reached the film industry, judging from the internal evidence in *Frequent Hearses*, where the scene of events is a film studio on the outskirts of London. Gloria Scott, a young and apparently successful film actress, drowns herself off Waterloo Bridge. Her death is the signal for a spate of homicide, which Professor Fen and Inspector Humbleby between them are quite unable to prevent: indeed Fen himself almost lands up among the corpses. Edmund Crispin handles the plot with his customary adroitness, but there is something missing from the stock pantomime properties. For one thing, where are the usual comic accessories? No homing pig? No mock heroic bloodhound? Even Fen's car seems to go when it's asked, and no longer backfires uproariously; while Fen himself has dwindled in boisterous exuberance. The only frills that persist (and with those we could easily dispense) are the literary quotations. Fen may be Eng. Lit. Professor at Oxford, but is that any reason why a casual young lady should quote steadily from her repertoire while chasing a murderer in a maze? Altogether *Frequent Hearses* runs on more formal lines than any previous Crispin. The detection is quite straightforward, with a valid motive and the decisive clue well camouflaged.

> Ralph Partridge, "Recent Murders," *New Statesman and Nation*, 4 March 1950, p. 254

ANTHONY BOUCHER   The solution to Edmund Crispin's *The Long Divorce* is far from water-tight and clings too closely to the anything-for-a-surprise, rabbit-out-of-the-hat school; but at least it does no violence to the excellent novel which has been established up to that point. Gervase Fen, rusticating under the attractive pseudonym of "Mr. Datchery," encounters a pretty problem in poison pen letters, an unusually well-characterized group of suspects, local police who are, amazingly, not cut out of cardboard, and a splendid half-witted cat who can see Martian invaders. The civilized wit and charm are all one has come to expect of Crispin; the people are a little stronger, the deduction a little weaker than in previous books.

Anthony Boucher, [Review of *The Long Divorce*], *New York Times Book Review*, 9 September 1951, p. 31

A. E. MURCH   A younger author belonging to this same donnish school of detective story-writers ⟨as Michael Innes⟩ is 'Edmund Crispin' (Robert Bruce Montgomery), also an Oxford man and an educationalist, as devoted as Michael Innes to the polysyllabic adjective, the abstruse noun, and whimsical proper names. His amateur investigator, Dr Gervase Fen, is himself an Oxford don who writes detective stories, when not distracted from his literary labours by mysterious crimes affecting his personal friends, the headmaster of a public school, for instance, in *Love Lies Bleeding* (1948), where the plot turns on the discovery of the original manuscript of a 'lost' Shakespeare play. To offset his somewhat 'precious' literary style, 'Edmund Crispin' has a vein of original humour, a talent for vivid description, unusual settings and intriguing titles—*Frequent Hearses*, *The Moving Toyshop*, *Beware of the Trains*—and is one of the most promising English writers of the *genre* to come to the fore in recent years.

A. E. Murch, *The Development of the Detective Novel* (1958; rpt. Port Washington, NY: Kennikat Press, 1968), pp. 239–40

JAMES SANDOE   Not since Dorothy L. Sayers deserted detection for pious playwriting and her brilliant translation of Dante have we had so conspicuous a loss to another form of artistic expression as the loss of "Edmund Crispin" to Robert Bruce Montgomery's preference for musical composition. Crispin's fantastic floriation was one of the adornments of the Forties and we have waited (in vain) for more than a decade to read another of his bright, ingenious tales about Gervase Fen, the Oxford don with a penchant for unlocking the "locked room." Now Walker and Company, to whom our debt on similar scores is considerable, has published here the one collection (1953) of Crispin's short stories, *Beware of the Trains*, an elegant assembly of hors d'oeuvres, very edible and much too good to be swallowed greedily, gulp upon gulp, as one is tempted to. In welcoming this pretty array and in lieu of a new Crispin might we not ask hopefully for an omnibus (say, *The Case of the Gilded Fly, Love Lies Bleeding* and *The Moving Toyshop*) as solace?

> James Sandoe, [Review of *Beware of the Trains*], *New York Herald Tribune Books*, 10 June 1962, p. 19

ERIK ROUTLEY   In his first book, *The Case of the Gilded Fly* (1944), much of which is very good, he brings us into the chapel organ loft for the climax and then lets us down resoundingly with a totally improbable and grotesque scene based on what he knew best—the names of organ stops. One of the sources of the let-down is the almost complete absence of normal organ stops beginning with 'E'. It's as good an example of the mishandling of special knowledge as you could have in a respectable detective story. *Holy Disorders* (1945), his second novel, is gathered round a west country cathedral and there's a good deal of church music in the surrounding scenery. It was a good point for him to catch out a rascally publican by mentioning the non-existent 'Stanford in E-flat', and indeed none of the musical references goes wrong in this story. But what is far worse, he gives us a textbook example of how not to build up the 'least likely person' solution of a crime. His criminal is altogether too normally attractive until the moment of revelation. The clue of character is totally and unforgiveably hidden.

As he went on he got much better. *Swan Song* (1947) was the best of his 'Oxford' stories—his special knowledge of opera got its chance there. *Love Lies Bleeding* (1948) is perhaps the best of them all: there is some quiet fun in the naming of all the principal characters after church musicians, and in an interview with a thinly disguised impersonation of the Most Important English Musician of that time.

The Long Divorce (1951), his last story, shows perhaps even better what he might have become as a novelist had not other pursuits claimed him. He gives himself a chance to assert a political position in *Buried for Pleasure*

(1948), in which Gervase Fen's crazy intention of getting into Parliament is brought to success after the most offensive speech he could devise for his constituents, and frustrated only by the annulment of his claim on the grounds of irregular operations by his agent. This is reasonably comical: the election anti-speech on the frivolous values which pass for politics in a rustic electorate's mind is a construction worthy of Innes.

It's largely soufflé, beautifully cooked, rarely descending to amateurish sogginess. Crispin has the odd mischievous touch—like Michael Innes (in *The Daffodil Affair*) he mentions his own name once; and in an early chapter of *Frequent Hearses* (1950), which, again from personal experience, is capitally drawn, he mentions the name of another very well known English musician, Geoffrey Bush. That reminds me not to overlook the most important thing to record about Crispin; it is that in a short story, in which he collaborated with this same Geoffrey Bush, he produced the best intellectual leg-pull I have personally met since Agatha Christie's *Roger Ackroyd*. It is called 'Baker Dies', and may be found in some anthologies, having been originally published in the *Evening Standard*. Crispin, more than Michael Innes, excelled in short stories. At least two of his full-length books would have gone better as short stories. But one thing can be said of him: he writes like a master, and he has the edge on Innes when it comes to creating characters.

Erik Routley, *The Puritan Pleasures of the Detective Story* (London: Victor Gollancz, 1972), pp. 163–64

T. J. BINYON   ⟨*The Glimpses of the Moon*⟩ is Edmund Crispin's first full-length work since *The Long Divorce*, which appeared in 1951. Those who have been waiting for this moment for the past twenty-six years may find, after a first hurried reading, their joy slightly clouded by disappointment. For though *The Glimpses of the Moon* offers several dead corpses making night hideous, a criminal or two and some policemen, it is not a detective story in the mould of the author's earlier work, but a comic novel constructed round a crime (or crimes), set in darkest Devon.

As before, Gervase Fen is a central character, but he acts throughout more as observer than detective. And although he is allowed a long monologue after the classical model to sum up events in the final chapter, his exposition seems parodic in intent and performance. The climax of the book—a hilarious chase across the countryside involving cows, horses, motor-cycles, cars and men on foot, which ends under an evil-minded electricity pylon known locally as the Pisser—violates all canons, since it has very little to do with the plot and introduces a number of characters, delineated in detail, who never appear again.

A second reading, however, alleviates the disappointment and makes it clear that *The Glimpses of the Moon* is in fact a logical successor to the earlier novels, with the difference that an exuberant fancy, which had hitherto been held partially in check by the exigencies of the form, has here been allowed to blossom freely.

T. J. Binyon, "Criminal Proceedings," *Times Literary Supplement,* 26 August 1977, p. 1037

ROBIN WINKS   Edmund Crispin and his literary critic turned detective, Gervase Fen, have never been among my favorites, but *The Moving Toyshop* is a clever and delightfully constructed, if totally preposterous, example of the Oxbridge sub-school of crime fiction. The exposition of the problem—a poet, Richard Cadogan, stumbles into a toy shop on the Iffley Road in Oxford, and a body therein, only to have toy shop as well as body disappear before he can bring the police—is especially good, even if the solution, based on the nonsense verse of Edward Lear, is rather too donnish.

Robin Winks, "Robin Winks on Mystery," *New Republic,* 24 September 1977, p. 38

ROBERT BRUCE MONTGOMERY   "Edmund Crispin" was born in April, 1942. His fleshly envelope, however, appeared under the name of Robert Bruce Montgomery on October 2, 1921. It happened thus:

I was with one of those rare creatures, a genuinely bookish actor, in a pub in Oxford. We normally talked books. And we did so on this occasion. How the conversation got round to John Dickson Carr I can't quite remember, but I do remember the tone of mingled reproof, reproach and amusement with which my friend said, "Oh, haven't you read John Dickson Carr?" I was a bit of an intellectual snob in those days, and thought the detective story rather beneath my notice. However, you didn't ignore advice about books from John Maxwell (my friend), and on our way back to my lodgings he called in at his, and he lent me a copy of *The Crooked Hinge*.

I went to bed with it not expecting very much. But at two o'clock in the morning I was still sitting up with my eyes popping out of their sockets at the end of one of the sections—I think the third—with the doctor looking after the nerve-racked maid saying, "You devil up there, what have you done?"

And of course I finished the book that night. It was to be a seminal moment in my career and to alter it entirely, for although subsequently I read and enjoyed other detective-story writers, in particular Michael Innes and Gladys Mitchell, it was Carr primarily who induced me to try my hand at one myself, thus creating Edmund Crispin. The reasons for the pseudonym are very dull and obvious so I shan't bother you with them here. Anyway, I wrote a book called *The Case of the Gilded Fly*—in the U.S.A. called *Obsequies at Oxford*—and was lucky enough in both countries to have it accepted by the first publisher to whom it was sent: Gollancz in Britain and Lippincott in the States. The influences of John and of Michael Innes, not to mention a few other people such as M. R. James, are obvious in it. So, though I was to have been a civil servant, I became first a schoolteacher, while the war lasted, and afterwards took to writing and composing full time. ⟨. . .⟩

⟨. . .⟩ for a long time I lay fallow, living on my fat and writing and composing very little. Then fairly recently I realized that I was beginning to run out of money, and went back to writing Crispin novels, the first of them being *The Glimpses of the Moon*, published over here (May 1977) by Gollancz, and due to be published in the States by Walker. I'm also embarking on a new series under my real name, Bruce Montgomery, for another publisher, and this though it will consist entirely of crime stories will embrace crime stories of every possible kind, from armchair detection through spy fiction and humor to atmospheric horror stories. The name of the first one I shall be publishing under my own name, by the way, is *What Seems to Be the Trouble?* (American publication not yet arranged). It's predominantly comic, and of course, as the title indicates, largely about doctors.

⟨. . .⟩ My favorite detective story writers are of course John Dickson Carr, Michael Innes, Gladys Mitchell, Elizabeth Daly, Rex Stout, Eric Ambler, Margery Allingham, Pamela Branch (very little known), H. C. Bailey, Nicolas Freeling and Agatha Christie. I have no great liking for spy stories or, come to that, for the more so-called "realistic" type of crime story (e.g. Higgins). I believe that crime stories in general and detective stories in particular should be essentially imaginative and artificial in order to make their best effect. Another way of putting it would be to say that I make Jacques Barzun's distinction between the novel and the tale and think that you try to mix the two things at your peril.

Robert Bruce Montgomery, "Edmund Crispin," *Armchair Detective* 12, No. 2 (Spring 1979): 183, 185

WILLIAM A. S. SARJEANT   The first criminal case in which Fen was involved was the murder of a composer, Alan Pasmore, at Amersham, Buckinghamshire, in 1935. Fen was already interested in criminology, and it was after dinner with the Chief Constable of that county that he was shown the dossier of the case and worked out its solution, though the murderer was not apprehended.

The next chronicled case in which he was involved probably took place in 1938, the Oxford adventure of the prowling poet and the corpse in the toyshop. Several other adventures, however, seem to have gone unchronicled. One in which Scotland Yard were impressed, if not with Fen's abilities, at least with the difficulty of excluding him from a case, took place at Caxton's Folly, which we know to have been the home of the plump publisher Erwin Spode; but we have so far learned no details of this affair.

Then came the war and Fen's involvement, at the time of the Battle of Britain (August–September 1940), with spies, witchcraft and murder in the cathedral town of Tolnbridge. In that adventure, he was captured, tied up and left to be gassed in an isolated cottage. Fortunately, Geoffrey Vintner guessed his likely fate and saved him by arranging for the gas supply of the whole district to be turned off. ⟨. . .⟩ There were further perils to survive before that adventure was over and Fen's associates in that case were relieved enough when it was behind them. Yet on October 4th of that year, when returning by rail from "one of those innumerable educational conferences which spring up like mushrooms to decide the future of this institution or that, and whose decisions, if any, are forgotten two days after they are over," Fen was already wondering "whether he would be allowed to investigate another murder, supposing one occurred." His wish was dramatically fulfilled by the murder of an actress in a room in his own college, but ironically his identification of the murderer to the police was to occasion him only regret.

Perhaps even Fen could not find murders to investigate all the time, for the next adventure on record took place almost seven years later, in January 1947, when Wagner's operas were at last emerging from the wartime cloud of anti-German feeling into renewed public acceptability. The two murders, in whose solution Fen's percipience and imagination prove crucial, actually seem to have facilitated that Oxford performance of *Die Meistersinger!*

When a call to speak at a school speech-day took him to Castrevenford, Warwickshire, in the summer of that year, Fen found himself, not only involved with two murders and one near-murder, but also with a hope of recovering a lost Shakespearean manuscript. That hope, alas, fades in the flames of a blazing car, and Fen is left only with an Elizabethan miniature as a souvenir of what might have been his greatest literary achievement. In the meantime, Fen has survived several hazards, including the frightening episode in a darkened wood, when he and an injured girl faced a murderer with a revolver and a torch and were only saved by an elderly bloodhound. ⟨. . .⟩

The last extended chronicle of Crispin treats with two murders and dismemberings in the autumnal Devonshire countryside; but it is much more a portrait of a variety of colourful and entertaining people and their hilarious interaction. Despite the macabre moving around of three severed heads and their repeated rediscovery, it was an adventure in which murder took a back seat and Fen's identification of the culprits seemed almost an irrelevancy. Nevertheless, it was another in the roster of his successes.

And now we must wait in hope that another hand will take up pen and chronicle the hitherto unrecorded adventures of Gervase Fen. Soon may that day come; but we may just doubt whether any other writer will have the elegant style, wry observation, and sheer entertaining wit of "Crispin." In a host of Sherlockian imitators and parodists, there is not yet a second Doyle detectable; and I fear we may have to wait long for another "Crispin."

William A. S. Sarjeant, "Obsequies about Oxford: The Investigations and Eccentricities of Gervase Fen," *Armchair Detective* 14, No. 3 (Summer 1981): 207–9

MARY JEAN DeMARR   Crispin's indebtedness to his great forebears of the Golden Age is perhaps most obvious in his style—especially if style is defined broadly to include tone as well as more limited matters of language. Crispin never took his materials seriously; his plots are ingenious, as carefully worked and as inventive as those of Agatha Christie, but his use of language, literary and allusive as well as witty, is more in the vein of Dorothy L. Sayers, Nicholas Blake and Michael Innes. His sense of discipleship is most dramatically revealed by the names he chose for himself and for one of the central characters in his first novel, *The Case of the Gilded Fly*. The character in Innes' *Hamlet, Revenge!* called Gervase Crispin gave him his pseudonymous surname and his detective's Christian name. In addition, one of the main characters, the one through whose eyes most of the action is seen, is called Nigel Blake, clearly a combination of the names of author Nicholas Blake and his detective Nigel Strangeways. And Inspector Humbleby, of the later novels and many stories, obviously pays homage through his name to Innes' Appleby.

One of the most obvious devices from the Golden Age which Crispin kept, though only for a time, was the use of maps and charts. His earliest three novels all contain them: thus *The Case of the Gilded Fly* has a plan of part of Fen's college at Oxford, *Holy Disorders* contains a chart of part of a cathedral, while *The Moving Toyshop* rejoices in two diagrams—a simple map of part of Oxford and a chart of the murder scene. After these first three novels, however, Crispin dropped this device, perhaps a sign of his increasing confidence and independence of his masters.

Crispin's delight in language is everywhere apparent. Puns and wordplay abound, and the reader must be alert not only to follow clues but also to be sure not to miss much of the humor. Some jokes are extraneous to the plot proper and seem put there largely for the sake of the fun; for example, in *The Glimpses of the Moon*, Fen is engaged in writing a book on some contemporary British novelists and, jaded in that attempt, decides to write a novel of his own. Lonely in self-imposed solitude, he has been talking out some of his ideas to his only living companion, a cat; inspired perhaps by its lack of attention as well as by his own dislike of the novelists he has been studying, he decides his novel will be called *A Manx Ca*. The hasty reader, interested primarily in the extravagant plot of this novel with its many farcical twists and turns, or in the eccentric characters displayed in abundance, might skim past this passage, wondering only at the carelessness of printers and proofreaders who allowed such an obvious typographical error to slip past them. The more thoughtful and literary reader would pause to recall the oddity in conformation of the manx breed of cats and then to become amused over the implied comment that something is missing from much of the most respected of contemporary fiction. But this subtle literary comment is unnecessary, not even clearly relevant to major concerns of Crispin's present novel, and it merely forms an added kind of in-joke for the observant reader to enjoy. Nevertheless, this sort of literary exuberance helps to create the very special kind of appeal that Crispin's novels have for their devoted readers.

> Mary Jean DeMarr, "Edmund Crispin," *Twelve Englishmen of Mystery*, ed. Earl F. Bargainnier (Bowling Green, OH: Bowling Green University Popular Press, 1984), pp. 253–54

⊗ *Bibliography*

The Case of the Gilded Fly ⟨*Obsequies at Oxford*⟩. 1944.

Holy Disorders. 1945.

The Moving Toyshop. 1946.

Swan Song ⟨*Dead and Dumb*⟩. 1947.

Love Lies Bleeding. 1948.

Buried for Pleasure. 1948.

Frequent Hearses ⟨*Sudden Vengeance*⟩. 1950.

The Long Divorce. 1951.

Beware of the Trains: Sixteen Stories. 1953.

Best SF: Science Fiction Stories (editor). 1955–70. 7 vols.

Best Detective Stories (editor). 1959–64. 2 vols.

Best Tales of Terror (editor). 1962–65. 2 vols.

The Stars and Under: A Selection of Science Fiction (editor). 1968.

Best Murder Stories 2 (editor). 1973.

Outwards from Earth: A Selection of Science Fiction (editor). 1974.

The Glimpses of the Moon. 1977.

Fen Country. 1979.

Erle Stanley Gardner
1889–1970

ERLE STANLEY GARDNER was born in Malden, Massachussetts, on July 17, 1889, to Grace Adelma Gardner, whose family tree extended back to the *Mayflower*, and Charles Walter Gardner, a mining engineer. His father's work entailed much traveling, with the result that Erle spent time in Mississippi, Oregon, and the Klondike before graduating from Palo Alto High School in 1909.

Gardner was a diligent student, but his greater interest in boxing led to the termination of his law studies at Valparaiso University in Indiana after less than a year. He continued to read law while apprenticed to an attorney and was admitted to the California bar in 1911. Gardner set up a practice in Oxnard, outside Los Angeles, and soon earned a reputation as a lawyer with unorthodox but highly effective techniques. He married Natalie Talbert in 1912 and had a daughter with her, Natalie Grace, the following year.

Gardner's enthusiasms as a sportsman and experiences as an attorney served him well when he turned to writing fiction in his spare time. Following his first professional sale in 1923, he wrote prolifically for the Western, adventure, and detective pulp magazines, under his own name and a number of pseudonyms. Although a contributor to *Black Mask* during the years that Dashiell Hammett, Raymond Chandler, and other writers were perfecting the hard-boiled style of writing in its pages, Gardner shunned the hard-boiled label and preferred to think of himself as a writer of mystery tales. His adventures of dilettante detective Lester Leith, human fly crimestopper Speed Dash, and numerous other series characters all demonstrate a faith in the principal of self-reliance and the triumph of good over evil.

In less than a week in 1932, Gardner wrote a novel entitled *Reasonable Doubt* featuring lawyer detective Ed Stark. The title was changed to *The Case of the Velvet Claws* and its protagonist's name to Perry Mason when the book was published in 1933. A second Mason novel, *The Case of the Sulky Girl*, which originally had featured another lawyer detective before Gardner changed him at the request of the publisher, appeared later that year. Ultimately, Gardner would write eighty-two adventures of Perry Mason, assistant Paul Drake, secretary Della Street, and district attorney Hamilton Burger, at the rate of two to three novels per year. Although reviewers criticized the books as formulaic and the characters as two-dimensional, Gardner defended them as fast-paced, crowd-pleasing tales of ratiocination that put all the clues necessary to solve the crime in the reader's hands before the denouement in the courtroom. Their enormous popularity allowed Gardner to give up his law practice and write full-time.

The Perry Mason stories made an international celebrity out of Gardner and his habit of working on more than one story at a time with the help of a dictaphone and a pool of secretaries. As a result, his A. A. Fair pseudonym, under which he wrote twenty-nine adventures of the quirky detective team of Donald Lam and the wisecracking, overweight Bertha Cool between 1939 and 1980, was one of the worst-kept secrets in publishing. Gardner also wrote nine adventures of district attorney Douglas Selby between 1937 and 1949.

Although much of Gardner's life after 1933 was devoted to writing the Perry Mason novels and to their adaptation for film and television, he pursued interests as a sportsman and produced books on travel and the American legal system. Following World War II, he helped found the Court of Last Resort, in which a committee of legal experts investigated the convictions of supposedly innocent people. He received the Mystery Writers of America's Edgar Allan Poe Award in 1952 and their Grand Master Award in 1961. Gardner's fame was augmented by the popularity of the long-running 1960s television show *Perry Mason*, starring Raymond Burr.

Although Gardner separated from his first wife in 1935, he supported her until her death in 1968. That same year he married Agnes Jean Bethell, one of his secretaries and the presumed role model for Della Street. When Gardner died of cancer at his California ranch on March 11, 1970, worldwide sales of his fiction totaled more than 300 million copies.

❖ Critical Extracts

WILL CUPPY   Introducing a new writer in whom his publishers have what they might call unbounded faith, they "claim the credit for being the first to prophecy that Erle Stanley Gardner will find a place immediately as one of the most popular authors of detective fiction." We hope so, although we truly believe that Mr. Gardner, whose line is extreme simplicity and forthrightness of the Dashiell Hammett, early Hemingway, late Wallace type, must submit his Muse to certain disciplines if he would scale the heights. This maiden volume ⟨The Case of the Velvet Claws⟩ features Perry Mason, a fighting criminal lawyer, who undertakes to clear up a mass of blackmail involving a writer for Spicy Bits, the owner of the dirty sheet, his wife, a rising politician and other perfectly horrid people, all trying to uncover secrets in the lives of the others and all deficient in passable manners. In fact, Mr. Gardner treats you to an orgy of lowlife, straight talk, unexpected happenings and remorseless sleuthing; and we hope that somebody will kick this department if we are ever heard saying "Well," "damn," "Okay," or "Oh, my God!" We don't want to be a wet blanket, so we'll bet that when Mr. Gardner learns to conserve, tame and point his material, he'll make an agreeable baffler of the hard-boiled school.

    Will Cuppy, [Review of The Case of the Velvet Claws], New York Herald Tribune Books, 5 March 1933, p. 14

ISAAC ANDERSON   The basic pattern of Mr. Gardner's Perry Mason stories is always the same, but the variations that he is able to introduce into that pattern are so ingenious that each story is at least as interesting as any of the previous ones. Always when Mason accepts a retainer he does so without knowing much more about the case than that it looks interesting. Usually, if not always, the murder takes place after his entry into the case, and his client is suspected upon what appears to be irrefutable evidence. Mason's conduct of the case is invariably characterized by legal trickery and practices that appear to be, and sometimes are, more than dubious. And always there is a courtroom scene in which one of Mason's tricks utterly confounds the prosecution and results in a complete solution of the mystery. The prosecution is well aware that Mason is going to try to trick them, but it is never prepared for his trick when it comes. Neither, for that matter, is the reader, even though he has read all the earlier Perry Mason stories.

    Mr. Gardner has a genius for attention-compelling titles, and his stories, definitely including The Case of the Sleepwalker's Niece, fulfill the promises that the titles make. His next book is to be called *The Case of the Stuttering Bishop*, and what a title that is!

Isaac Anderson, [Review of *The Case of the Sleepwalker's Niece*], *New York Times Book Review*, 22 March 1936, p. 17

ERLE STANLEY GARDNER   So far as technique is concerned, the technique of the mystery story varies with various types of mystery.

There is the hard-boiled mystery. The hero is usually a private detective, big, tough, and with an almost unlimited capacity to absorb and dish out punishment. During the course of the story, everything is thrown at him, including the kitchen sink. He takes them all in his stride, and in due time, polishes off the villain with several well placed shots from his six-shooter, grabs the heroine and kisses her on the mouth—hard.

Then there is the intellectual type of story in which the British influence predominates. There is a murder y'know. And, dash it all, something just doesn't fit. Some little clue that's out of place, and the bally clues just *won't* fit into the proper pattern. During the course of this story, there is ample opportunity for the reader to review everything that has happened. The detective usually prepares a chart along about the middle of the book, showing where everyone was at the time of the murder. The detective and some bosom companion sit up late of nights in smoke-filled rooms, discussing the possibility that each of the persons involved may have committed the murder, marshalling the facts against each suspect in turn, and then offsetting them with at least one apparently insurmountable obstacle. ⟨. . .⟩

Then, there's the sophisticated type of mystery in which the police officers are frankly puzzled. The district attorney is utterly bewildered, and "my friend the gifted What'shisname refuses, at first, to be interested because he's working on his treatise concerning the application of glaze in the Ming Dynasty." But at length, he is persuaded to accompany the district attorney to the scene of the crime, where he is terribly bored by it all, being infinitely superior to all of the characters in the book—as well as the reader, by implication. He smiles at the district attorney, makes some enigmatical remark, and returns to his investigation of the Ming vases. Whereupon, it turns out that his enigmatic remark, which was disregarded by the exasperated attorney, is the most significant clue of all, and the district attorney finally gets him back on the case for another half hour and another cryptic remark. ⟨. . .⟩

It is possible to write the stories classified under each type in a variety of ways. There is what has been so lately and cleverly tagged as the "had-I-but-known" style of presentation. There is the first person, naive type of narration in which the heroine is so extremely innocent that the reader wants to yell at her, "Don't go there. Don't meet him in that deserted house," but the heroine pushes blithely on. Not until she gets in the old house, and suddenly realizes that it is a trap, does she fully awaken to the horror of the situation. Then it is too late. There are no lights. The dark silence of rooms cluttered with cobwebs is broken by the ominous sound of someone breathing—

Personally, I like a story that is just a little short of the hard-boiled school. A mystery story that has an element of humor, a puzzling plot, and a style of narration that makes for swift action. You play perfectly fair with the reader. You give him not only the facts that the detective has, but you let him see the approximate significance of those facts; and you throw the story at him with such a bewildering rapidity of pace that he loses his breath about the second chapter and never gets it back until he turns the last page.

That, of course, is the ideal toward which I strive, the goal I seek to attain.

Erle Stanley Gardner (as "A. A. Fair"), "A Method to Mystery," *Writer* 57, No. 8 (August 1944): 233–34

ALVA JOHNSTON   There have been criticisms to the effect that his work shows signs of haste, but this is irrelevant fault-finding. What Erle's public wants from him is not artistic finish, but productivity. The true Gardner fan wants more Gardner, not better Gardner. Their demand is that he brace up and quit babying himself and turn out twelve novels a year instead of six.

Will Cuppy, the Longinus and Quintilian of mystery critics, has complained that Gardner uses the same formula too often. In most detective stories, characters are twisted like Monterey cypresses and probability is fearfully maltreated, because of the iron rules of the mystery. No literary form except the sonnet is governed by such inflexible rules. At the last minute a magical solution must be pulled out of the hat, proving that the reader misunderstood everything and everybody all along. In the Perry Mason stories, Gardner has a formula within a formula. Not only must there be a surprise solution at the end, but that solution must be brought about by Perry's cross-examination of witnesses in a courtroom. It is also practically a statutory requirement that Perry, in his unparalleled services for his clients, should get himself in dire peril of being arrested as an accessory after the fact and of being hauled up before the grievance committee of the Bar Association. The result is that, while Erle invents an endless diversity of detail, a sameness of pattern runs through most of Perry's exploits. But the charge against the average mystery writer is that he resembles mystery writers too much. Erle is accused of resembling only himself.

Alva Johnston, *The Case of Erle Stanley Gardner* (New York: William Morrow, 1946), pp. 14–15

ANTHONY BOUCHER   Back in 1939 there appeared what readers then thought was an extraordinary first novel: *The Bigger They Come*, by A. A. Fair, which introduced Donald Lam, ex-lawyer turned private detective, with the best gimmick of forcing the law to frustrate itself since the Randolph Mason stories of Melville Davisson Post.

It's now common knowledge that "Fair" was a pseudonym for Erle Stanley Gardner—a slight surprise, since the average Fair story, with the same pace and ingenuity, has more characterization and humor than the average Gardner—and today the Fair and Gardner names appear together on the title page of *Beware the Curves*, which chronicles Donald Lam's most outrageously adroit legal maneuver since that unforgettable first book.

Here Donald, stoutly assisted by Bertha Cool, starts as a private detective on a routine tracing job and winds up as a lawyer (if disbarred) masterminding a murder defense through a series of astonishing twists, going so far as deliberately getting his client convicted and ending with a wholly cynical and immoral balancing of the scales of justice. I'm a major admirer of Gardner's Perry Mason; but even I wish Mr. G. would more frequently abandon Mason to give us the ironic vigor that comes only from Lam.

Anthony Boucher, [Review of *Beware the Curves*], *New York Times Book Review*, 9 December 1956, p. 32

KINGSLEY AMIS   There would be a lot to be said for not noticing ⟨Perry Mason⟩ at all, if it were not for the hideous frequency of his appearances in print and on television. I am afraid there can be very few people in our culture who would not know that, although Mason is not in the strict sense a detective, is a mere lawyer employing the Drake Detective Agency to do his legwork for him, he does investigate crimes, ending up ten times out of ten by winning one of those objection-overruled-objection-sustained rituals in concert with the D.A. and the judge. The TV films faithfully reflect the Erle Stanley Gardner novels in their portrayal of the inevitable three-stage progress from seeing-the-client through seeing-the-witnesses to going-to-court, with an expected unexpected revelation at the end. Mason has an impressive claim to being considered the most boring foe of criminality in our time, which is saying something if we make the effort to remember such cobwebbed figures as Inspector French (in the work of Freeman Wills Crofts) or Philo Vance (S. S. Van Dine). The nullity of Mason is nowhere better displayed than in his relations, or lack of any, with his assistant—I cannot bring myself to say girl Friday—Della Street. Della Street, whose name appears in full every time Gardner mentions her, answers the telephone and listens to Mason telling her that the law is not a rat-race unless you run with the rats. Oh, and sometimes she worries because Mason looks so tired. Nothing more; whereas the vital role of the assistant in detective fiction is to encourage and provoke the great man to reveal his hidden inner nature.

Kingsley Amis, "My Favorite Sleuths," *Playboy* 13, No. 12 (December 1966): 344

CHARLES W. MORTON   ⟨*The Case of the*⟩ *Velvet Claws* was turned down by several publishers before it reached acceptance by Thayer Hobson at Morrow. Despite his own ten years of success as a pulp writer before that, Gardner counts Hobson as his discoverer and patron. "Once his respect has been given to his editor or his publisher," says Willis Wing, "Gardner is easily the most loyal of men." ⟨. . .⟩

How much advice Gardner ever needed is debatable.   What he lacked in urban sophistication he made up for with his inventiveness and quickness to learn. Hobson is credited with guiding him into specializing in a character rather than trying to turn out new characters in a new locale in each book, as most of his contemporaries were doing. Hobson felt that faced with a large output of book-length mystery fiction, the booksellers would find it best to go along with an author who stuck to a major character, made no basic change in the situation of the character, and produced novels about him with regularity. While others were erratic in production, as the comparatively short list of Dashiell Hammett books indicates, shifting their setting and experimenting with new characters, Hobson pressed Gardner to standardize his work with Perry Mason, even to the extent of using the same unchanging title formula for each story.

Neither of the principals foresaw the dimensions that Perry Mason would eventually attain. Something over twenty years ago Gardner was trying to explain why he had launched the Bertha Cool–Donald Lam series under the pseudonym A. A. Fair. His thirty or forty titles up to that time had sold around thirty-five million copies, but Gardner was hunting for a change, partly to stimulate his own production and partly as protection against a decline in Perry's following. His feeling at the moment seemed to be that Perry's clock was running down.

"It's like this," he said. "You create a character and some more to go with him. You invent situations for those characters. And you write thirty-five books about those characters and their situations, and you might be said, in a sense, to have skimmed the cream from those characters."

Charles W. Morton, "The World of Erle Stanley Gardner," Atlantic Monthly 219, No. 1 (January 1967): 83

FRANCIS M. NEVINS, JR.   Gardner created Paul Pry for *Dime Detective* magazine around 1930, and during the Depression years steered him through a sizable number of novelet-length capers. Pry is one of several less colorful variants of Simon Templar created by Gardner for the pulps, the most famous of these creations probably being the light-fingered Lester Leith. Like his prototypes, Pry is a professional opportunist, making an excellent living in the midst of nationwide depression by lifting loot from the less nimble witted members of the criminal fraternity. He is assisted in his extractions by a hulking Tonto with the improbable name of Mugs Magoo, who has the inestimable advantages of a photographic memory for faces and an encyclopedic knowledge of the underworld. Mugs had been "camera-eye" man for the metropolitan police force, but lost his right arm in an accident and his job in a political shakeup. He had become an alcoholic bum, scratching for whiskey money by selling pencils on the street, when Pry had come upon him, sobered him up, put him on a strict quota of one quart a day, and made him his partner.

Just as certain aspects of Mugs Magoo suggest him as the source for Leslie Charteris' fabulous Hoppy Uniatz, certain characteristics of Paul Pry might well have influenced Rex Stout's delineation of Nero Wolfe. In particular, Pry's habit of working out his grand stratagems while beating (to render his mind limpid and relaxed) on one of the Oriental drums in his collection foreshadows Wolfe's trait of pushing his lips out and in, out and in, when he is working out the solution to a murder-puzzle. Unfortunately, the reader is seldom told the details of Pry's plans, so that all too often one experiences only a comfortable blur before Pry pulls the rabbit out of the hat.

Francis M. Nevins, Jr., "Notes on Some Uncollected Gardners," *Journal of Popular Culture* 2, No. 3 (Winter 1968): 489

FRANK E. ROBBINS   Bertha ⟨Cool⟩, you will understand, is a strong-minded woman well able to take care of herself. She is also a big woman; for years, after abandoning her diet, she weighed about 275 pounds, and it took an attack of flu and pneumonia in 1941 to reduce her weight by 100 pounds to 160. More recently it has remained at 165 pounds, and is mostly bone and muscle, for since her illness Bertha has taken up fishing, which has given her a fine tan and presumably helps to keep her in condition, although she still likes her sugar and cream and enjoys loafing in her apartment on a lazy Sunday. When she and Donald were in New Orleans in 1942 she ate three pecan waffles for breakfast and scandalized a waiter by putting catsup on her steak.

Aside from her heft, Bertha has flowing white hair which gives her a deceptively motherly, or grandmotherly, appearance, and little glittering gray eyes. She uses bifocals, and likes to wear loose clothes. She has a peculiarly effortless way of walking and even in her fattest days didn't waddle. She is a cigarette smoker—brand not specified, uses a long carved ivory cigarette holder, and wears diamonds on her left hand.

But though Bertha's physical characteristics are striking enough her habits of speech and her mental attitudes are even more so. She is probably the most profane person in the detective business; in fact almost the only profane person in that line of work, as they are described to us by the masters of detective fiction. Even the hard-boiled lads, like the Continental Op or Philip Marlowe, scarcely ever utter as much as a damn, but that is one of the commonest words in Bertha's vocabulary, and she makes free use of others too which you won't hear used even in a political campaign and much less in the bosom of the family. As she puts it, she likes profanity, loose clothing, and loose talk.

Bertha is also a realist, which in her case chiefly means that she has a high regard for money. Her doodling when she interviews a client in the office is apt to concern the amount she thinks the client is good for; her tips hardly ever exceed a dime, and she voices strenuous objection to Donald's including "Regards and best wishes" in a collect telegram. One brief conversation, in which Bertha is the first speaker, goes like this: "You mean she turns down money?" "Exactly." "I don't get it." And she doesn't; if there is money to be had she is hot on its trail, and if there is money in the office it is kept in the locked cash drawer of Bertha's desk and doled out with marked reluctance. She makes a good many investments, some of them safe and bringing good returns, some of them gambles, and she is quick to bet on a horse race when she thinks that Carl Keetley's system of handicapping has presented her with a sure thing.

Frank E. Robbins, "The Firm of Cool and Lam," *The Mystery Writer's Art*, ed. Francis M. Nevins, Jr. (Bowling Green, OH: Bowling Green University Popular Press, 1970), pp. 138–40

MARVIN LACHMAN   There has been endless speculation over the years regarding the Perry Mason–Della Street relationship. Initially, the relationship is merely one of employer and employee with an occasional kiss or embrace by way of congratulations at the successful conclusion of a hard case. At first Della is not entirely convinced that Perry is infallible and in two of the first three recorded cases she expresses doubt about the correctness of his approach. She is never to doubt him again as gradually they become closer and romance rears its beautiful head. In *The Case of the Caretaker's Cat* (1935) the case requires their going up to Santa Barbara on a fake elopement and honeymoon. When Mason first mentions the elopement Della has "a quick gasping intake of breath"; at his suggestion of a honeymoon "her eyes opened wide." However, further developments in the case cause Mason to return to Los Angeles alone and Della says in parting, "You deprived yourself of your honeymoon." Apparently at this point they had still not fully consummated their relationship.

However, there is ample evidence, especially during the late 30's and early 40's, that there was real intimacy between them though Gardner went to considerable pains to disguise this. Thus when Mason and Della go on a sea voyage to the Orient together (*The Case of the Substitute Face*, 1938) he says that they occupied separate cabins. When they are out of town on business he places them in separate rooms of the same hotel suite. However, no one is really deceived. There is too much evidence to the contrary, such as Mason packing a valise of Della's clothes (including underthings) in *The Case of the Substitute Face*, or sitting, matter-of-factly, in his pajamas when he discusses a case with her in *The Case of the Dangerous Dowager* (1937).

Even more significant are the scenes in *The Case of the Crooked Candle* (1944) and *The Case of the Half-Awakened Wife* (1945) where we come upon them lying together all alone. While Gardner does not get more specific than, on each occasion, to have Mason fall asleep with his head in Della's lap, he does admit to Perry planning a little hideaway in the country, just for them, in the later book.

Relatively early in their relationship, Perry may have grown fearful of Della's getting too inclined to change his ways. He tells her in *The Case of the Sleepwalker's Niece* (1936), "Listen, kid . . . take me as I am. Don't try to make me the way I should be because then you might find that I was guilty of that greatest sin of all, being uninteresting." He also convinces her that he would not let any wife of his work. Della, therefore, refuses five separate proposals of marriage from Perry Mason. Once she says to him, "You're not the marrying kind . . . I don't think you need a wife, but I know damn well you need a secretary who's willing to go to jail occasionally to back your play." Della does, in fact, get arrested five times "in the line of duty." She also suborns a witness and conceals evidence to help Perry. On at least four occasions she risks death by physical violence while helping him on cases.

Marvin Lachman, "The Case of the Unbeaten Attorney; or The Secret Life of Perry Mason," *Armchair Detective* 4, No. 3 (April 1971): 149–50

DOROTHY B. HUGHES   The Hammett comparison was some-thing that was to plague Gardner throughout his early years. In 1930 Hammett had published *The Maltese Falcon*, which made history in the detective field, and which, in Gardner's opinion, turned Cap Shaw, the *Black Mask* editor, into such a worshiper of Hammett that he tried to have all his other authors write like him. Gardner felt that he himself was slighted in the magazine because only those authors who *would* imitate Hammett received first class treatment.

Gardner never imitated anybody. He was his own man. When he was accused of imitation, as he was in those early days by book editors, book critics, and slick magazine editors—in other words by all those who had not followed his development in the pulps—it was, in one of his favorite expressions, a red flag to a bull. His angry refutations were not against Hammett but against those who compared him to Hammett. Although the two were not close personal friends, they were good working friends.

> Dorothy B. Hughes, *Erle Stanley Gardner: The Case of the Real Perry Mason* (New York: William Morrow, 1978), p. 101

J. KENNETH VAN DOVER   In quality as in quantity, the D.A. series is the least of Gardner's three principal novel series. The D.A. concept is even more tightly constricted by formulas than that of Perry Mason. A few stereotyped relationships form the predictable core of every Mason novel: Mason–female client, Mason–district attorney, Mason–Della Street. These necessary tensions are infinitely repeatable because they are inherent in the institutional premises: a lawyer must have a client and a secretary; he must confront a district attorney. The conventions which prescribe the essential relationships in the D.A. series are both too many and too accidental. ⟨. . .⟩

Each of the D.A. novels follows a definite pattern. Someone commits a murder. ⟨In *The D.A. Calls It Murder* (1937)⟩ *The Blade* ⟨a newspaper⟩ blames ⟨Doug⟩ Selby ⟨the district attorney⟩ for acting too slowly to apprehend the perpetrator (or, in the several cases where Selby's office initially misidentifies the corpse, for acting too precipitously). *The Blade* outlines its own theory of the crime (imitating the district attorney's counterplot in the Mason series). Selby, Brandon, and Sylvia rush around the countryside interviewing witnesses until they uncover the real culprit. *The Clarion* celebrates Selby's triumph.

As the series continued, Gardner inserted two other recurring conventions. One involves the introduction of Selby's old flame, Inez Stapleton, a dark beauty who has decided to earn his respect by becoming a lawyer herself. Inez offers Selby one predictable legal adversary; Alphonse Baker Carr offers another, more important one. "Old A.B.C." is what Perry Mason would recognize as a most competent jury-bribing pettifogger. Carr is in some ways Gardner's revenge on Mason; he is a Mason with an unlocked id. Mason exercises his exciting lack of scruples on behalf of innocent clients; Carr merely extends his unscrupulousness to include his choice of clients. Though he always comes up just short in his struggle with Selby, Carr's witty self-possession makes an attractive contribution to the series.

Ultimately the action of the D.A. novels is too forced; the motivations too contrived. The symmetries are not subtle: *Blade/Clarion*, police chief/sheriff, Inez/Sylvia, Carr/Selby. There is simply no reason for *The Blade* to keep insisting upon its naive counterplots; and the abundance of misidentified corpses suggests that Gardner was hard-pressed to invent temporary advantages for Selby's opponents. The characters in short are too obviously puppets, and the action is too clearly programmed by external considerations. After completing a volume or two, the reader returns to the series not to wonder at Selby's ingenuity, but at Gardner's. He ceases to identify at all with the actors in the fable.

Nonetheless Gardner's ingenuity is sufficiently wonderful to be enjoyed as such. And the small-town environment he evokes has its pleasant aspects. His portraits of the comfortable Brandon kitchen or, in *The D.A. Calls a Turn* (1943), of the solidarity of the large Freelman family, suggest a nostalgia for domestic values largely missing from his other two more cosmopolitan series.

J. Kenneth Van Dover, "Erle Stanley Gardner," *Murder in the Millions: Erle Stanley Gardner, Mickey Spillane, Ian Fleming* (New York: Frederick Ungar Publishing Co., 1984), pp. 76–78

JAMES BAIRD   A typical Erle Stanley Gardner story features interesting and engaging characters, fast action which is moved along primarily by dialogue, and a plot with more twists and turns than a bowl of Chinese noodles. The reader is given just enough information to keep him or her from being totally lost, and somewhere in the welter of material are placed a few details which, properly interpreted, will clear up the mystery and tie up all the loose ends.

Gardner did not come by this pattern or his writing skills by nature, but only after ten years of study and work at his craft. At first he thought that the way to make characters interesting was to make them bizarre, and his early pulp fiction introduces such unusual characters as Señor Lobo, a romantic revolutionist; Ed Jenkins, the phantom crook; El Paisano, a character who could see in the dark; Black Barr, a western gunfighter; and Speed Dash, a human-fly detective who could climb up the side of buildings to avoid locked doors. Gardner also created the more conventional detective figures Sidney Giff, Sam Moraine, Terry Clane, Sheriff Bill Eldon, and Gramps Wiggins, about each of whom he was to write complete novels later.

Lester Leith is a character from this period who was one of Gardner's favorites and whose stories reveal typically Gardnerian twists. Leith is a detective who specializes in solving baffling cases of theft (particularly of jewels) merely by reading newspaper accounts of the crimes. Leith steals the missing property from the criminals, sells it, and donates the money he gets to charity, keeping a percentage as a commission which he uses to maintain himself in his luxurious life-style (which even includes employing a valet). The fact that the police are never able to pin any crimes on Leith himself is the more remarkable because his valet, Scuttle, is actually a police undercover agent planted in Leith's home specifically to catch the detective in shady deals. In the series devoted to this character, Gardner puts an extra spin on the pulp-fiction device of the crime-fighter with a secret identity. Usually, the character with a secret identity must remain outside the law because he has special powers which would create problems if he were revealed (for example, Superman) or must use special extralegal methods (the Green Hornet). In the Lester Leith series, Scuttle, the valet with the secret identity, is a crime-fighter who remains inside the legal system in order to catch a detective who is so clever that he stays outside the law. A further irony is that Leith, who has amazing intellectual ability, never figures out that he has a spy operating in his own household, a feature which amuses the thoughtful reader.

James Baird, "Erle Stanley Gardner," *Critical Survey of Mystery and Detective Fiction,* ed. Frank N. Magill (Englewood Cliffs, NJ: Salem Press, 1988), Vol. 2, pp. 689–90

▣ *Bibliography*

The Case of the Velvet Claws. 1933.
The Case of the Sulky Girl. 1933.
The Case of the Lucky Legs. 1934.
The Case of the Howling Dog. 1934.
The Case of the Curious Bride. 1934.
The Clew of the Forgotten Murder. 1935.
The Case of the Counterfeit Eye. 1935.
This Is Murder. 1935.
The Case of the Caretaker's Cat. 1935.
The Case of the Sleepwalker's Niece. 1936.
The Case of the Stuttering Bishop. 1936.
The D.A. Calls It Murder. 1937.
The Case of the Dangerous Dowager. 1937.
The Case of the Lame Canary. 1937.
Murder Up My Sleeve. 1937.
The Case of the Substitute Face. 1938.
The Case of the Shoplifter's Shoe. 1938.
The D.A. Holds a Candle. 1938.
The Bigger They Come ⟨Lam to the Slaughter⟩. 1939.
The Case of the Perjured Parrot. 1939.
The Case of the Rolling Bones. 1939.
The D.A. Draws a Circle. 1939.
Turn On the Heat. 1940.
The Case of the Baited Hook. 1940.
The D.A. Goes to Trial. 1940.
Gold Comes in Bricks. 1940.
The Case of the Silent Partner. 1940.
The Case of the Haunted Husband. 1941.
Spill the Jackpot. 1941.
The Case of the Turning Tide. 1941.
The Case of the Empty Tin. 1941.
Double or Quits. 1941.
The D.A. Cooks a Goose. 1942.
The Case of the Drowning Duck. 1942.
Owls Don't Blink. 1942.
The Case of the Careless Kitten. 1942.

Bats Fly at Dusk. 1942.
The Case of the Smoking Chimney. 1943.
The Case of the Buried Clock. 1943.
Cats Prowl at Night. 1943.
The Case of the Drowsy Mosquito. 1943.
The D.A. Calls a Turn. 1944.
The Case of the Crooked Candle. 1944.
Give 'Em the Ax ⟨*An Axe to Grind*⟩. 1944.
The Case of the Black-Eyed Blonde. 1944.
The Case of the Golddigger's Purse. 1945.
The Case of the Half-Wakened Wife. 1945.
Over the Hump. 1945.
The D.A. Breaks a Seal. 1946.
Crows Can't Count. 1946.
The Case of the Backward Mule. 1946.
The Case of the Borrowed Brunette. 1946.
Two Clues. 1947.
The Case of the Fan Dancer's Horse. 1947.
Fools Die on Friday. 1947.
The Case of the Lazy Lover. 1947.
The Case of the Lonely Heiress. 1948.
The Land of Shorter Shadows. 1948.
The Case of the Vagabond Virgin. 1948.
The D.A. Takes a Chance. 1948.
Bedrooms Have Windows. 1949.
The Case of the Dubious Bridegroom. 1949.
The Case of the Cautious Coquette. 1949.
The D.A. Breaks an Egg. 1949.
The Case of the Negligent Nymph. 1950.
The Case of the Musical Cow. 1950.
The Case of the One-Eyed Witness. 1950.
The Case of the Fiery Fingers. 1951.
The Case of the Angry Mourner. 1951.
Top of the Heap. 1952.
The Case of the Moth-Eaten Mink. 1952.
The Case of the Grinning Gorilla. 1952.
The Court of Last Resort. 1952.
The Case of the Hesitant Hostess. 1953.

Some Women Won't Wait. 1953.

The Case of the Green-Eyed Sister. 1953.

The Case of the Fugitive Nurse. 1954.

The Case of the Runaway Corpse. 1954.

The Case of the Restless Redhead. 1954.

Neighborhood Frontiers. 1954.

The Case of the Glamorous Ghost. 1955.

The Case of the Sun Bather's Diary. 1955.

The Case of the Nervous Accomplice. 1955.

The Case of the Guilty Client. 1955.

The Case of the Terrified Typist. 1956.

The Case of the Demure Defendant. 1956.

The Case of the Gilded Lily. 1956.

Beware the Curves. 1956.

The Case of the Lucky Loser. 1957.

You Can Die Laughing. 1957.

The Case of the Screaming Woman. 1957.

The Case of the Daring Decoy. 1957.

Some Slips Don't Show. 1957.

The Case of the Long-Legged Models. 1958.

The Case of the Foot-loose Doll. 1958.

The Count of Nine. 1958.

The Case of the Calendar Girl. 1958.

The Case of the Deadly Toy. 1959.

Pass the Gravy. 1959.

The Case of the Boy Who Wrote "The Case of the Missing Clue" with Perry Mason. 1959.

The Case of the Mythical Monkeys. 1959.

The Case of the Singing Skirt. 1959.

The Case of the Waylaid Wolf. 1960.

The Case of the Duplicate Daughter. 1960.

Kept Women Can't Quit. 1960.

The Case of the Shapely Shadow. 1960.

Hunting the Desert Whale. 1960.

The Case of the Spurious Spinster. 1961.

Bachelors Get Lonely. 1961.

The Case of the Bigamous Spouse. 1961.

Shills Can't Cash Chips ⟨Stop at the Red Light⟩. 1961.

Hovering over Baja. 1961.

The Case of the Reluctant Model. 1962.

Try Anything Once. 1962.

The Case of the Blonde Bonanza. 1962.

The Case of the Ice-Cold Hands. 1962.

The Hidden Heart of Baja. 1962.

The Case of the Mischievous Doll. 1963.

Fish or Cut Bait. 1963.

The Case of the Stepdaughter's Secret. 1963.

The Case of the Amorous Aunt. 1963.

The Desert Is Yours. 1963.

The Case of the Daring Divorcée. 1964.

Up for Grabs. 1964.

The Case of the Phantom Fortune. 1964.

The Case of the Horrified Heirs. 1964.

The World of Water. 1964.

The Case of the Troubled Trustee. 1965.

Cut Thin to Win. 1965.

The Case of the Beautiful Beggar. 1965.

Hunting Lost Mines by Helicopter. 1965.

Widows Wear Weeds. 1966.

The Case of the Worried Waitress. 1966.

Traps Need Fresh Bait. 1967.

Off the Beaten Track in Baja. 1967.

The Case of the Queenly Contestant. 1967.

Gypsy Days on the Delta. 1967.

The Case of the Careless Cupid. 1968.

Mexico's Magic Square. 1968.

Drifting Down the Delta. 1969.

The Case of the Fabulous Fake. 1969.

Host with the Big Hat. 1969.

The Case of the Murderer's Bride and Other Stories. Ed. Ellery Queen. 1969.

Cops on Campus and Crime in the Streets. 1970.

All Grass Isn't Green. 1970.

The Case of the Crimson Kiss. 1971.

The Case of the Crying Swallow. 1971.

The Case of the Irate Witness. 1972.

The Case of the Fenced-In Woman. 1972.

The Case of the Postponed Murder. 1973.

The Amazing Adventures of Lester Leith. Ed. Ellery Queen. 1980.

The Human Zero: The Science Fiction Stories of Erle Stanley Gardner. Ed. Martin
    H. Greenberg and Charles G. Waugh. 1981.

Whispering Sands: Stories of Gold Fever and the Western Desert. Ed. Charles G.
    Waugh and Martin H. Greenberg. 1981.

Pay Dirt and Other Whispering Sands Stories. Ed. Charles G. Waugh and Martin
    H. Greenberg. 1983.

The Adventures of Paul Pry. 1989.

Dead Men's Letters. 1990.

The Blonde in Lower Six. 1990.

Honest Money and Other Short Novels. 1991.

Chester Himes
1909–1984

CHESTER BOMAR HIMES was born in Jefferson City, Missouri, on July 29, 1909. His parents, Joseph and Estelle Bomar Himes, were both teachers. The family lived in several cities in the southern and midwestern United States, finally settling in Ohio. Himes graduated from Glenville High School in Cleveland in 1926 and studied for less than a year at Ohio State University before withdrawing, as his schoolwork was suffering because of his frequent carousing, gambling, and associating with pimps and criminals. In December 1928 he was convicted of armed robbery and sentenced to twenty years' hard labor in the Ohio State Penitentiary. He served seven years. During his incarceration Himes wrote many works of fiction, including a story based upon a tragic fire that broke out in the prison and killed 300 men. These tales began appearing in various magazines, including such black weekly newspapers as the *Atlanta World* and the *Baltimore Afro-American*.

Some time after his release in 1936 Himes joined the Ohio Writers' Project and went on to become a feature writer for the *Cleveland Daily News*. He was also involved with the labor movement and the Communist party. He married Jean Johnson in 1937. In 1942 Himes moved to California, where he worked at a variety of odd jobs in shipyards in Los Angeles and San Francisco. When he received a Rosenwald Foundation Fellowship in 1944, he moved to New York City to write. His first published novel, *If He Hollers Let Him Go* (1945), is a grimly realistic tale drawing upon his shipyard experiences. His first five novels were explosive studies of the situation of the black man in a racist society. They feature a considerable amount of autobiography, such as *Cast the First Stone* (1952), a story of prison life. These novels enjoyed only moderate success in America and brought in such a small income that Himes was forced to work at a number of menial jobs to support himself. He separated from his wife in 1951 and later divorced her. When he noticed that he was being hailed in Europe as a powerful voice of social criticism, Himes decided to emigrate. He moved to the island of Majorca in 1954 and spent the rest of his life there and in Paris.

Himes was persuaded by the editor of the publishing house Gallimard to write detective novels for its crime series, La Série Noire. The result was his famous Harlem thrillers, such as *For Love of Imabelle* (1957), *The Real Cool Killers* (1959), and *The Heat's On* (1966). Many of these novels appeared in French translations before being published in English. One of them, *La Reine des pommes* (1958; an expanded version of *For Love of Imabelle*), won the Grand Prix Policier in 1958. Most of these works feature two black police detectives, Grave Digger Jones and Coffin Ed Johnson, and are characterized by fast-paced action and much violence. Himes occasionally returned to the protest vein of his early works, as in the mordant satire *Pinktoes* (1961) and his two volumes of autobiography, *The Quality of Hurt* (1972) and *My Life of Absurdity* (1976).

In the late 1950s and early 1960s Himes was romantically involved with a German woman, Marlene Behrens; sometime later he married an Englishwoman, Lesley Packard, with whom he remained until his death in Moraira, Spain, of Parkinson's disease on November 12, 1984. His *Collected Stories* appeared in 1990. His unfinished novel *Plan B* was published in a French translation in 1983 and in English in 1993.

Critical Extracts

RICHARD WRIGHT   Jerky in pace, *If He Hollers Let Him Go* has been compared with the novels of James M. Cain, but there is more honest passion in 20 pages of Himes than in the whole of Cain. Tough-minded Himes has no illusions: I doubt if he ever had any. He sees too clearly to be fooled by the symbolic guises in which Negro behavior tries to hide, and he traces the transformation by which sex is expressed in equations of race pride, murder in the language of personal redemption, and love in terms of hate.

To read Himes conventionally is to miss the significance of the (to coin a phrase) bio-social level of his writing. Bob Jones is so charged with elementary passion that he ceases to be a personality, and becomes a man reacting only with nerves, blood and motor responses.

Ironically, the several dreams that head each chapter do not really come off. Indeed, Himes's brutal prose is more authentically dreamlike than his consciously contrived dreams. And that is as it should be. In this, his first novel, Himes establishes himself not as what has been quaintly called a New Negro but as a new kind of writing man.

> Richard Wright, "Two Novels of the Crushing of Men, One White, One Black" (1945), cited in Michel Fabre, *Richard Wright: Books and Writers* (Jackson: University Press of Mississippi, 1990), pp. 212–13

ANTHONY BOUCHER   Chester Himes's novels about Harlem police detectives Grave Digger Jones and Coffin Ed Johnson are still not well known in this country, although they are highly successful in France—where Himes now lives, and where the first novel in the series, *For Love of Imabelle* (1957), received the Grand Prix de Littérature Policière. Possibly this may be because racial humor is such a delicate matter in these times. Himes's stories are the wildest of camps—grotesque, macabre, black humor (using "black" in a quite nonracial sense); and because they are about Negroes many readers may feel embarrassed. If a white writer created so many shiftless or vicious denizens of Harlem, he would be accused of using derogatory stereotypes. But since Himes is himself a Negro, it would appear that the enjoyment of these cruel and fantastic nightmares is *au fait* rather than ofay.

If you are unacquainted with this extraordinary series, now is a good time to catch up: the prize-winning first has just been republished as *A Rage in Harlem*, and the sixth (in this country; there have been more in France), which includes a pleasing postlude to that first, is *Cotton Comes to Harlem*, the first time one of these stories has appeared in hard covers. It has some weaknesses (over-explicit sex and occasional plot confusion), but many splendidly strange notions, including the conflict between Back-to-Africa and Back-to-the-South movements and the peculiar plot-function of a bale of cotton. The French, apparently, take all of this parodistic violence as a True Picture of America (*"Mais, mon cher, c'est indisputable! N'a-t-on pas trouvé les même vérités dans Sartre et Brecht?"*); we may have our reservations . . . and still find this carnival of gallows humor somewhat disturbing.

> Anthony Boucher, "Criminals at Large," *New York Times Book Review*, 7 February 1965, p. 43

JOHN A. WILLIAMS   *Williams:* There's a rash of books, I hear (I haven't read them)—detective books—in which there are black detectives, and of course one of these books was made into a movie with Poitier, *In the Heat of the Night.* Do you feel that these people are sort of swiping your ideas?

Himes: No, no. It's a wonder to me why they haven't written about black detectives many years ago. It's a form, you know, and it's a particularly American form. My French editor says, the Americans have a style of writing detective stories that no one has been able to imitate, and that's why he has made his *Série Noire* successful, by using American detective story writers. There's no reason why the black American, who is also an American, like all other Americans, and brought up in this sphere of violence which is the main sphere of American detective stories, there's no reason why he shouldn't write them. It's just plain and simple violence in narrative form, you know. 'Cause no one, no one, writes about violence the way that Americans do.

As a matter of fact, for the simple reason that no one understands violence or experiences violence like the American civilians do. The only other people in the white community who are violent enough for it are the armed forces of all the countries. But of course they don't write about it because if the atrocities were written about the armies of the English and French in Africa, they would make among the most grisly stories in the history of the world. But they're not going to write about them. These things are secret; they'll never state them.

American violence is public life, it's a public way of life, it became a form, a detective story form. So I would think that any number of black writers should go into the detective story form. As a matter of fact, I feel that they could be very competent. Anyway, I would like to see a lot of them do so. They would not be imitating me because when I went into it, into the detective story field, I was just imitating all the other American detective story writers, other than the fact that I introduced various new angles which were my own. But on the whole, I mean the detective story originally in the plain narrative form—straightforward violence—is an American product. So I haven't created anything whatsoever; I just made the faces black, that's all.

Williams: You know, I'm always amazed when I read your books. Here you've been out of the country for twenty years, but I'm always amazed at your memory of things and how accurate you are in details, like the guns that the cops use. In rereading the screenplay last night, there was the business of the drop slot in the car. How do you come by all this knowledge?

Himes: Well, some of it comes from memory; and then I began writing these series because I realized that I was a black American, and there's no way of escaping forty some odd years of experience, so I would put it to use in writing, which I have been doing anyway. I had always thought that the major mistake in Richard Wright's life was to become a world writer on world events. I thought that he should have stuck to the black scene in America because he wouldn't have had to live there—he had the memory, so he was still there, but it was subconsciously, which he discovered when he went back to write *The Long Dream* and the sequel (which was never published, I don't think).

Well, then, I went back—as a matter of fact, it's like a sort of pure homesickness—I went back, I was very happy, I was living there, and it's true. I began creating also all the black scenes of my memory and my actual knowledge. I was very happy writing these detective stories, especially the first one, when I began it. I wrote those stories with more pleasure than I wrote any of the other stories. And then when I got to the end and started my detective shooting at some white people, I was the happiest.

> John A. Williams, "My Man Himes: An Interview with Chester Himes," *Amistad I*,
> ed. John A. Williams and Charles F. Harris (New York: Vintage, 1970), pp. 48–50

STEPHEN F. MILLIKEN   In each of Himes's detective novels there is ⟨. . .⟩ at least one stunningly attractive black woman among the major characters, but the function of these women is possibly even more limited and precise than that of the gunsels and pistoleros, and they vary only minutely from novel to novel. Imabelle was the prototype, and those who followed her resembled her far more closely than Jackson resembled his errant twin, physically and psychologically. Imabelle is "a cushioned-lipped, hot-bodied, banana-skin chick with the speckled brown eyes of a teaser and the high-arched, ball-bearing hips of a natural-born *amante*." Iris, Deke's woman in *Cotton Comes to Harlem*, is "a hard-bodied high-yellow woman with a perfect figure . . . and her jiggling buttocks gave all men amorous ideas." Ginny, of *The Heat's On*, has "the high sharp hips of a cotton chopper . . . the big loaded breasts of a wet nurse," and a "big, wide, cushion-lipped mouth." Leila, Casper Holmes's sultry, sullen, and

conniving wife in *All Shot Up*, blatantly underscores her share of the natural
endowments common to all these Afro-American Aphrodites with a sure
clothes sense and a spectacular wardrobe:

> She was rather short and busty, with a pear-shaped bottom and
> slender legs. She had short wavy hair, a heart-shaped face, and
> long lashed, expressive brown eyes; and her mouth was like a red
> carnation.
>
> She wore gold lamé slacks which fitted so tight that every
> quiver of a muscle showed. Her waist was drawn in by a black
> leather belt, four inches wide, decorated with gilt figures. Her
> breasts stuck out from a turtleneck blue jersey-silk pullover as
> though taking dead aim at any man in front of her.

None of these women are squares; innocence is apparently the exclusive
province of young males in Himes's Harlem, but, with a few exceptions—
most notably Leila Holmes and Sister Heavenly, the aging ex-whore, faith
healer, and drug dealer of *The Heat's On*—they lack the willpower to actively
manipulate events. They are all madly in love with one man, though not
at all indifferent to other attractive males who pass their way. They are
virtuoso sexual athletes, aggressive and demanding ⟨. . .⟩ They have extraordinary physical courage—Iris punches Coffin Ed in the nose after he finishes
choking her, and Imabelle so effectively defends herself against a huge man
who grabs her in the street, slashing him with a knife, that sadistic onlookers
comment on his "leaky veins"—but when they are faced with an overpower-
ing threat they lapse into terror and promise sexual delights in return for
safety. "You'll want me when you've had me," Ginny babbles at the inexora-
ble, terrifying Coffin Ed, determined to wring information out of her at any
cost: "You won't be able to get enough of me. I can make you scream with
joy. I can do it in ways you never dreamed of." The function of these women
in the novels is, quite simply, to be desired and to be frightened. They offer
literary thrills that have obvious and direct affiliations with the realms of
sex and sadism. "I hate to see people tearing at one another like rapacious
animals," Lieutenant Anderson sadly remarks to Grave Digger and Coffin
Ed, after the two detectives have succeeded in frightening Iris into betraying
her man, the despicable Deke. "As long as there are jungles there'll be
rapacious animals," retorts Grave Digger, with calm authority. The world
of detective fiction is, in effect, a stalking ground for primeval predators,

and the picture would hardly be complete without a generous sprinkling of succulent victims.

Stephen F. Milliken, *Chester Himes: A Critical Appraisal* (Columbia: University of Missouri Press, 1976), pp. 249–51

EDWARD MARGOLIES   ⟨. . .⟩ Himes's humor is not confined to description. The crimes his characters commit will at times become a kind of grim joke they play on themselves; there is a macabre quality to their violence that one associates with the Keystone Cops or the more sadistic animated cartoons. To illustrate: A motorcyclist in flight from a pursuing police car has his head neatly severed by several sheets of steel that have slipped off the side of a truck. The headless cyclist drives on for a distance before the vehicle crashes (*All Shot Up*, 1960). A sneak thief who has just managed to scissor carefully through the back of a church lady's skirt in order to snip off the money bag that hangs from her waist (while his partner engages her in "holy" conversation) is shortly thereafter hit from the rear by a truck and sent flying through the air like a bird (*Cotton Comes to Harlem*, 1965). A long wicker basket filled with loaves of bread stands in front of a supermarket. A young man lies down on the mattress of bread and is promptly stabbed to death (*The Crazy Kill*, 1959). A crook who is simultaneously trying to kill a goat and crack open a safe accidentally shoots off a half-pint bottle of nitro-glycerine that blows himself up with the goat, the safe, and the entire house (*The Heat's On*, 1965). A bartender leans over the counter and axes off the arm of an unruly knife-wielding customer (*The Real Cool Killers*, 1960). A gunman, Big Six, shuffles through the streets of Harlem with a hunting knife stuck through his head. A woman with two children on their way to see a horror movie shouts at him. "You ought to be ashamed of yourself frightening little children" (*All Shot Up*). At a huge outdoor street revival, presided over by the grotesquely garbed Sweet Prophet, pandemonium breaks loose when a rumor gets out that one of the converts was poisoned drinking the holy water that had been blessed by the Prophet (*The Big Gold Dream*, 1960). And on a less grim note, a tire thief watches his tire sail away from him down the steep incline of Convent Avenue knocking a couple of policemen off their feet (*All Shot Up*).

Himes's humor is verbal as well as physical. He burlesques some of the old-fashioned moral platitudes of the pulp writers. In *For Love of Imabelle*, for instance, a con man who has been passing himself off as a federal agent "apprehends" Jackson, the simple-minded victim of a gang of thieves that has promised to convert his real money into counterfeit money ten times its value. In order to avoid jail, Jackson bribes his captor with money he steals from his boss. Upon receiving the payoff, the marshall admonishes: "Let this be a lesson to you, Jackson. . . . Crime doesn't pay." Himes's humor reflects the hard cynical wit of the urban poor who know how to cheat and lie to the white world to survive physically, and cheat and lie to themselves to survive psychologically.

Edward Margolies, "Chester Himes's Black Comedy: The Genre Is the Message," *Which Way Did He Go? The Private Eye in Dashiell Hammett, Raymond Chandler, Chester Himes, and Ross Macdonald* (New York: Holmes & Meier, 1982), pp. 66–67

JAMES SALLIS   Though the Harlem novels develop in a fairly clear line from the modern detective novel as established by Hammett (particularly *Red Harvest*) and Chandler, they were never true genre pieces, fulfilling few traditional expectations, and as they continued, they in fact withdrew further from preconceived notions of the detective story. Specific crimes are solved in the early books (albeit rather incidentally), but there is a progressive movement towards concentration on the scene itself, on Harlem as symbol, using the detective story framework as vehicle for character and social portraiture. And as this shift occurs, absurdities, incomprehensible events and grotesqueries proliferate. The books close on greater disorder and confusion than they began with, as James Lundquist observes in his book-length study of Himes: "Order and reason are left farther and farther behind as the crimes Grave Digger and Coffin Ed must solve and the means of solution become ever more outrageous." This is of course nihilism—and a near perfect reversal of Gide's description of the detective story as a form in which "every character is trying to deceive all the others and in which the truth slowly becomes visible through the haze of deception."

Himes did not plan this evolution; it grew quite spontaneously out of the material he was working with in the Harlem novels, and what he himself was. In *My Life of Absurdity* he describes writing these novels:

> I would sit in my room and become hysterical thinking about
> the wild, incredible story I was writing. But it was only for the
> French, I thought, and they would believe anything about
> Americans, black or white, if it was bad enough. And I thought I
> was writing realism. It never occurred to me that I was writing
> absurdity. Realism and absurdity are so similar in the lives of
> Amerian blacks one can not tell the difference.

These trends culminate—there was a five-year delay between the final
two, and it seems unlikely there will be more—in *Blind Man with a Pistol*,
surely the apotheosis of Himes's detective novels. Assigned to find the killer
of a cruising white homesexual, Grave Digger and Coffin Ed roar through
a landscape of crazy preachers, children eating from troughs, the cant of
black revolutionaries, and a gigantic black plaster-of-Paris Jesus hanging
from the ceiling with a sign reading *They lynched me*. (Lundquist has called
the first chapter of this book "one of the strangest in American literature.")
Neither the original nor subsequent murders are solved; the sole connecting
link is an enigmatic man (*or men*) wearing a red fez. The two detectives
are confounded and frustrated at every turn: politically protected suspects,
payoffs and neatly contrived "solutions," diversionary cleanup campaigns
and bureaucracy. Halfway through the novel they are taken off the case,
in fact, and assigned to investigate Harlem's swelling black riots. "You
mean you want us to lay off before we discover something you don't want
discovered?" Grave Digger asks point blank. But he already knows; they all
do, and the rest is little more than ritual dance. This is where Himes' work
breaks off most surely from its forebears. With Hammett, Chandler or Ross
Macdonald, the corruption, however profound, would at last be penetrated;
with Himes, it is so pervasive, its signature so universal, that it cannot be.

James Sallis, "In America's Black Heartland: The Achievement of Chester Himes,"
Western Humanities Review 37, No. 3 (Autumn 1983): 195–96

MICHAEL DENNING   ⟨. . .⟩ beginning with *All Shot Up*, there is
a growing sense that the real criminals have gotten away, that the end of
the chain of incrimination is outside Harlem and that it has been arbitrarily
cut, so as not to lead into the white world. In *All Shot Up* and *Cotton Comes
to Harlem*, this is figured by the appearance of a white Southerner, not fully
explained and yet somehow connected. In *All Shot Up* the Harlem politician
Caspar Holmes shoots the Southerner at the end to prevent him from

talking, leaving Grave Digger and Coffin Ed infuriated, unable to pursue the case further because of Holmes' political power. And in *Cotton Comes to Harlem*, the real criminal, Colonel Calhoun, the organizer of the bizarre Back-to-the-Southland movement, an attempt to recruit cotton pickers in Harlem, manages to escape at the end to the South.

This tendency comes to a conclusion in *Blind Man with a Pistol*. At this point Himes has largely worked through the awkwardnesses of his transitional books. Here the original comic absurdity is joined to his social vision, and the detective genre is twisted to a postmodernist experimentation that makes this a just contemporary of Ishmael Reed. Here nothing is solved. The police department wants them to forget about solving the murders, which are leading out of Harlem to political bosses and the Syndicate; instead, the police want Grave Digger and Coffin Ed to find out who is "behind" the riots. The book becomes a broad social satire, with a memorable sense of the convergence of three marches: the Brotherhood march, the Lynched Black Jesus march, and the Black Power march, a confrontation that Grave Digger and Coffin Ed can't stop in their usual way by drawing pistols and yelling "Don't make graves." Instead they are as confused as anyone, including the reader, as several plots disintegrate into the riot.

The conclusion, a rewriting of ⟨Amiri⟩ Baraka's play *Dutchman*, is a subway encounter between blacks and whites which leads to a blind man firing off a pistol, creating a panic and then a riot. When asked by their bosses whether they have discovered who incited the riot, Jones and Johnson answer, "a blind man with a pistol." Despite the patness of Himes' moral—he says in the preface to the book that "I thought of some of our loudmouthed leaders urging our vulnerable soul brothers on to getting themselves killed, and thought further that all organized violence is like a blind man with a pistol"—what is striking about the image is its allusion to the first of the books, when Coffin Ed is blinded by acid and then fires his pistol at random, and eventually slugs his own partner. As so often in Himes, the grotesque overwhelms both the conventional action and the moral of the genre, leaving us with emblems of absurd and comic violence.

> Michael Denning, "Topographies of Violence: Chester Himes' Harlem Domestic Novels," *Critical Texts* 5, No. 1 (1988): 17

H. BRUCE FRANKLIN   The most seminal influence in the development of the hard-boiled, rough-and-tough school of detective fiction

is of course that former Pinkerton detective, Dashiell Hammett, whose masterpiece *Red Harvest* appeared, appropriately enough, in 1929. Hammett's craft developed, along with many other writers of this school, in the main organ of hard-boiled detective fiction, the pulp magazine *Black Mask*, especially in the early 1930s. During this period a convict in the Ohio State Penitentiary, an aspiring young author named Chester Himes, subscribed to *Black Mask*. So Himes's interest in detective fiction did not suddenly emerge, as he suggests in *My Life of Absurdity*, in 1957. Far more significant, Himes—as former criminal, as a convict, and as a Black man—was in a position to develop the contradictions of this proto-fascist detective fiction to their full logical absurdities.

Himes's Black killer-detectives protect the people of Harlem by enforcing upon them the law and order of white capitalist America, doing this with a brutal and often literally blind violence their white colleagues can no longer employ with impunity, often committing more crimes than they solve. They embody what they represent, the ultimate stage of social disorder masquerading as order. For in their blindness and rage, they are always in the process of discovering that the real criminals are the masters of American society, and that the people Coffin Ed and Grave Digger are attacking are their own brothers and sisters, daughters and sons. And all this is shadowed forth in a story Himes published in 1933, while still a convict, almost a quarter-century before the first of his Harlem detective novels.

This story is "He Knew," published in *Abbott's*, December 2, 1933. It is told, in the third person, from the point of view of a pair of hard-boiled Black detectives, John Jones and Henry Walls, as they follow an assignment on a December night in a waterfront district of "dismal warehouses and squalid tenements." The white precinct captain has explained, " 'I'm putting you two men on this job because it's a Negro neighborhood and I believe that it's Negroes who are pulling these jobs. You fellows are plodders and it's plodders we need.' " Walls has "splotched, yellow, mulish features." Jones is a "tough dick," with a "hard black face." Like Coffin Ed, he has two sons and a teenaged daughter.

The climax comes in a scene with some revealing similarities to the key event in *For Love of Imabelle*, the first of the Harlem detective novels. In *For Love of Imabelle*, Coffin Ed and Grave Digger confront some gangsters in a waterfront warehouse; one of them hurls acid into Coffin Ed's face, temporarily blinding him and permanently turning his face into a hideous mask (he is subsequently known as Frankenstein, and he bears great resemblance to Stephen Crane's "The Monster"); Coffin Ed blindly empties his .38, accidentally hitting a light-switch, thus plunging the room into total darkness; now in double blindness, he begins "clubbing right and left with the butt of his pistol," and accidentally knocks Grave Digger unconscious; more blind mayhem ensues. In "He Knew," Jones and Walls have a shootout in a pitch-black warehouse with a gang of young hoodlums, killing three of them. When the white cops come and light is restored, they all bend over the bodies. One of the white cops wonders what the father of any of these dead young men would feel like. Jones knew—hence the title—because two of them are his own sons.

"He Knew" is the imaginative core of one of the main themes of the Harlem detective series, the infinite forms of violence perpetrated by Blacks on Blacks, forms embodied by the two detectives as much as by the criminals they hunt.

> H. Bruce Franklin, *Prison Literature in America: The Victim as Criminal and Artist* (New York: Oxford University Press, 1989), pp. 223–25

GILBERT H. MULLER   The sense of evil pervading Himes's Harlem universe arises typically from the pursuit of money—that archetypal incarnation of capitalist values. The clear absence of honest capital in Harlem activates the absurd pursuit of money in any form by Hymes's dedicated villains, who would simply imitate their more sedate white counterparts in the pursuit. Clearly the dividing line in this Harlem universe is between the select and corrupt haves and the disenfranchised mass of have-nots. Ideological conflict, expressed in the absurdist action writing Himes perfected, occurs across this line or chasm separating the poor, a sprawling lumpenproletariat, and the amoral criminal rich, who attain their financial advantage or power through a series of ruses, thefts, con-games, and deceptions.

This frantic pursuit of money so central to bourgeois ethics can be traced in many of Himes's detective plots. In *For Love of Imabelle*, several preposterous scams—including the classic raising of money by turning ten-dollar into hundred-dollar bills, and the selling of fraudulent gold stock, as well as the search for a trunk of gold (which turns out to be fool's gold)—animate the action. In *The Heat's On*, pursuit by contesting criminals and various law enforcement agents of a lost heroin shipment worth $3 million results in outrageous, grotesque parody of the spirit of capitalism. Similarly, a bale of cotton containing $87,000 misappropriated from Harlem residents by Reverend Deke O'Malley in a phony back-to-Africa scheme triggers the conflict in *Cotton Comes to Harlem*. In *The Big Gold Dream*, the very title suggests the omnipotence of money—in this case, a maid's substantial numbers winnings and the criminal pursuit of it—that dictates the savage action. In *All Shot Up*, eight lives are extinguished for $50,000 in political payoff money. Within a culture ruled by such materialist pursuits, the ludicrous spirit of capitalism manifests itself in the frenetic, violent, criminal pursuit of money.

If mock capitalist intrigue is the source of the essential conflict between good and evil in Himes's Harlem crime fiction, the author seems more intent on exploring the absurdist implications of this phenomenon than in lodging a protest about it in the spirit of Richard Wright. "I wasn't showing the Negro as an oppressed, downtrodden people," he states in *My Life of Absurdity*, "but simply as an absurdity." Creating almost implausibly grotesque action in an equally absurd world, Himes turned time and again to a rereading of Faulkner—specifically *Sanctuary* and *Light in August*—to sustain the harrowing comedy of his crime fiction. "I could lift scenes straight out of Faulkner and put them down in Harlem and all I had to change was the scene." Faulkner, Himes's "secret mentor," suggests the extent to which Himes was shifting the boundaries of the world of detective fiction, bringing into focus through a range of comic devices a world in which evil and anarchy can scarcely be restrained.

Gilbert H. Muller, Chester Himes (Boston: Twayne, 1989), pp. 86–87

NORA M. ALTER   ⟨Himes's⟩ turn toward increasing violence has ⟨. . .⟩ a more specific reason. It is not Harlem that is changing, but Himes's vision of Harlem. And this evolution cannot be explained by the influence of changes in the detective genre. True, other contributors to the *Série Noire*, such as Chandler and Hammett, featured strong and hard boiled detectives. But Marlowe and Sam Spade, however coarse, solve their problems through intellect and deductive reasoning. I rather believe that, on the level of the plot, the violence of Coffin Ed and Grave Digger Jones is a direct consequence of their difficult role as black detectives maintaining a white law in the black world of Harlem. As Digger explains, "colored hoodlums had no respect for colored cops unless you beat it into them or blew them away" (*Cotton Comes to Harlem*). In contrast to *A Rage in Harlem*, where they still commanded respect, in the last novel of the series, *Blind Man with a Pistol* (1969), Jones and Ed will almost completely lose their authority among the blacks. In fact, they are threatened and attacked by a group of teenagers with a racial agenda: " 'We're the law,' Coffin Ed said. . . . 'Then you're on whitey's side.' " The two detectives justify their violence against blacks—men and women—by a paradoxical double argument: their brutality is necessary to curb crime, but it is also excusable because they belong themselves to the very people they brutalize. They think that it is the only way for them to gain respect because their official title no longer holds any weight and the traditional means of questioning are no longer effective. For them, violence is an "innocent" feature of their profession as detectives in contrast to "the white men on the force who commit the pointless brutality" (*Cotton Comes to Harlem*). Yet, by the end of the series, they fail not only the citizens of Harlem who reject them, but also the white world of the police precincts which also rejects them:

> Now after twelve years as first-grade detectives they hadn't been promoted. Their raises in salaries hadn't kept up with the cost of living . . . when they weren't taking lumps from the thugs, they were taking lumps from the commissioners. (*Blind Man with a Pistol*)

The direct cause of their failure seems to be a double alienation, from both blacks and whites. Which means that they experience a growing double gap in communication or, more generally, a double collapse of their mediating function between the two worlds.

Nora M. Alter, "Chester Himes: Black Guns and Words," *Alternatives*, ed. Warren
Motte and Gerald Prince (Lexington, KY: French Forum, 1993), pp. 15–16

▨ *Bibliography*

If He Hollers Let Him Go. 1945.
Lonely Crusade. 1947.
Cast the First Stone. 1952.
The Third Generation. 1954.

The Primitive. 1955.

For Love of Imabelle. 1957, 1958 (French; as *La Reine des pommes;* tr. Minne
     Danzas), 1965 (as *A Rage in Harlem*).

Il pleut des coups durs. 1958 (French; tr. C. Wourgaft), 1959 (as *The Real Cool
     Killers*).

Couché dans le pain. 1959 (French; tr. J. Hérisson and Henri Robillot), 1959
     (as *The Crazy Kill*).

Dare-dare. 1959 (French; tr. Pierre Verrier), 1966 (as *Run Man, Run*).

Tout pour plaire. 1959 (French; tr. Yves Malartic), 1960 (as *The Big Gold
     Dream*).

Imbroglio negro. 1960 (French; tr. J. Fillion), 1960 (as *All Shot Up*).

Ne nous enervons pas! 1961 (French; tr. J. Fillion), 1966 (as *The Heat's On*).

Pinktoes. 1961.

Une Affaire de viol. 1963 (French; tr. André Mathieu), 1980 (as *A Case of
     Rape*).

Retour en Afrique. 1964 (French; tr. Pierre Sergent), 1965 (as *Cotton Comes
     to Harlem*).

Blind Man with a Pistol ⟨*Hot Day, Hot Night*⟩. 1969.

The Autobiography of Chester Himes, Volume I: The Quality of Hurt. 1972.

Black on Black: Baby Sister and Selected Writings. 1973.

The Autobiography of Chester Himes, Volume II: My Life of Absurdity. 1976.

Miotte. 1977.

Le Manteau de rêve. Tr. Hélène Devaux-Minie. 1982.

Plan B. 1983 (French; tr. Hélène Devaux-Minie), 1993 (ed. Michel Fabre
     and Robert E. Skinner).

Collected Stories. 1990.

Michael Innes
1906–1994

MICHAEL INNES is the pseudonym of John Innes Mackintosh Stewart, who was born on September 30, 1906, in Edinburgh, Scotland, to John and Eliza Jane Stewart. His father taught in Scotland, and the Stewart household was undoubtedly bookish. After attending schools in Scotland, Stewart attended Oriel College, Oxford, receiving a B.A. in 1928. In 1929 Stewart won the Matthew Arnold Memorial Prize, and in 1930 he took his first teaching position at the University of Leeds in Yorkshire, England. He taught at the University of Adelaide in Australia from 1935 to 1945. Stewart then lectured at Queen's University, Belfast, Ireland (1946–48), before finally returning to Oxford, where he was first a Student (i.e., Fellow) of Christ Church College and then (from 1969) a Reader in English Literature. He married Margaret Hardwick, a physician, in 1932; they had three sons and two daughters.

Oxford plays a great part in the fiction of J. I. M. Stewart the Oxford don and Michael Innes the mystery writer. Under his real name, Stewart wrote novels with scholarly themes and eccentric characters, a concern for the role of art in society, and a frequent reliance on witty dialogue. Stewart also wrote a number of highly regarded academic works, including critical biographies of James Joyce (1957), Rudyard Kipling (1966), Joseph Conrad (1968), and Thomas Hardy (1971). In 1963 he published *Eight Modern Writers* in the Oxford History of English Literature series.

As Michael Innes, Stewart was the creator of many detective novels featuring John (later Sir John) Appleby. The detective first appeared in *Death at the President's Lodging* (1936). Appleby is a witty, donnish, and erudite sleuth who is a self-proclaimed conversationalist. Much of the dialogue of the Appleby stories is concerned with rather arcane literary and academic matters, and many of the novels also contain liberal doses of humor and farce.

The early Appleby novels, such as *Hamlet, Revenge!* (1937) and *Lament for a Maker* (1938), were praised for their intricate plots, comic situations, and wit. But some critics have complained that Innes's dialogue is pretentious and irrelevant to the plot. Appleby has also been compared to S. S. Van Dine's Philo Vance, who could not escape the pose of a snobbish dandy. Nonetheless, the Appleby stories have been a popular success.

Several novels of Innes's middle and later period depart from the traditional detective story and become spy stories and thrillers, although always leavened with humor and even buffoonery. Innes detected the influence of fellow Scotsmen John Buchan and Robert Louis Stevenson in these works. Innes also wrote many short stories; some are collected in *Appleby Talking* (1954), *Appleby Talks Again* (1956), and *The Appleby File* (1975), but many remain uncollected.

In 1974 Innes published *The Mysterious Commission*, the first of several novels featuring the painter Charles Honeybath. Innes teamed up his two detectives in *Appleby and Honeybath* (1983).

Michael Innes died on November 12, 1994.

Critical Extracts

NICHOLAS BLAKE   Dons and beaks, there is no doubt about it, make capital murderers. Fiction, crime-fiction in particular, has accustomed us to the highly spiced dishes of malice and uncharitableness served up at High Tables, to the steamy atmosphere of sedition and privy conspiracy pervading Common Rooms. In actual fact, all the blood feloniously spilt in our academies of learning during the last hundred years would probably go into a medium-sized ewer. But that is unimportant. The tradition is the thing; and detection-writers are only following in the irreproachable steps of Lord Tennyson, who—it will be remembered—spoke of "don or devil" in the same breath.

Mr. Innes, postulating a university midway between Oxford and Cambridge—at Bletchley, to be precise—kills off Dr. Umpleby, President of St. Anthony's, and surrounds the corpse with bones. The Fellows of this college are very strong on anthropology: so Inspector Appleby has plenty of suspects to start with. Appleby, by the way, is a graduate of St. Anthony's, and quite one of the most intelligent, charming and cultured detectives on the books. He needs to be, too; for he is pitting his wits against some of the most formidable brains in England, and—as we learn in the sequel—half the Common Room have something to conceal. *Death at the President's Lodging* is the most brilliant first novel I have had the luck to read. It is perhaps too complicated to become a classic in this *genre*. But Mr. Innes commands such a battery of wit, subtlety, learning and psychological penetration that he blows almost all opposition clean out of the water.

Nicholas Blake, "Dons and Beaks," *Spectator*, 30 October 1936, p. 770

E. R. PUNSHON   Obviously, in the higher sense of the word, little current fiction, few of the day's books for that matter, can lay claim to be "literature," but the notion that a detective novel is by its nature inferior is merely a specially silly instance of attaching a label and then using that label to judge by. But since some such idea does seem to exist, the warmest of welcomes is due to Mr. Michael Innes's *Lament for a Maker*, which has at least as good a claim to be "literature," is at least as worthy of the attention of the intelligent reader as any piece of fiction published for many a long day. It is remarkable for strong and clear characterisation and for power of narrative as well as for those distinctive qualities of the detection tale, suspense and mystery logically developed to a reasonable conclusion. The book gives, too, the somewhat rare pleasure of seeing words treated with a fine sensibility, and there is in addition both humour and that agreeable flavour of scholarship given to a book when there is felt to be behind it a background of culture and of knowledge.

The story has its faults: the opening is too long—even too Scottish,— and Mr. Innes depends too much upon coincidence and on such base mechanical tricks as conversations overheard to carry on his tale, so that at times the situations seem to be built up artificially instead of arising, as they should, from the natural flow of narrative. Few readers, however, will forget the portrait of the aged "sutor" or the picture drawn of the old laird, aloof in his solitary castle, as a man driven by the whips of the pursuing fates. In contrast there are the sketches of quiet Scottish village life, with its small, everyday excitements. Comparisons are not only odious, they are useless; but it may at least be said that, as there is one glory of Sayers and another of Crofts, so now there is a glory of Michael Innes.

E. R. Punshon, "Literature and Mystery," *Manchester Guardian*, 1 July 1938, p. 7

WILL CUPPY   Says Superintendent Hudspith to Inspector Appleby at a high spot of this remarkable tale ⟨*The Daffodil Affair*⟩: "We're in a sort of hodgepodge of fantasy and harum-scarum adventure that isn't a proper detective story at all." Be that as it may—and Hudspith is probably too modest—the two New Scotland Yard experts are in a honey of a mystery, one that will grace any list of 1942 leaders, and maybe it's the best of all this author's uniformly first-class work. True, there was a little heckling when Michael Innes went fantastic in *Appleby on Ararat* last year; which only means that beetle-browed chasers of clews and other terribly earnest and literal citizens would do well to avoid Innes altogether, leaving him to the rest of us, whose name must be legion. Whatever the mixture should be called, it contains the aforementioned fantasy, strictly tough-minded, the kind of fun that ran riot in the Ararat yarn, psychic phenomena of a rare order, a climax that ought to please even the lower brows and dozens of quieter thrills for more stuck-up and finicking customers. ⟨. . .⟩

The Daffodil Affair is really too good to read with the radio going, a habit to which we fear many mystery fans are prone. Better turn it off or read something else, for Mr. Innes will provide all the mental exercise you need, what with literary allusions, hunks of science and that sort of thing. The story has murder in plenty, but the main show is the special mood and the people, among whom Daffodil, the equine wonder, is not least. Mr. Innes uses him for one of the most impressive curtain lines in quite some time. We mean this item is Grade A plus.

Will Cuppy, [Review of *The Daffodil Affair*], *New York Herald Tribune Books*, 4 October 1942, p. 25

ANTHONY BOUCHER   Innes, at his most inimitable, writes not fantasy in its specialized sense but fantasias—wondrous concatenations of improbabilities which just *might* happen, related with a singular combination of detached and delicate wit and vigorous Stevensonian story-telling. This one ⟨*Christmas at Candleshoe*⟩ has little mystery and no formal detection; but it offers on the side of wit the detailed creation of three centuries in the history of a minor branch of British aristocracy. It is sparklingly reminiscent of early Huxley or even of the broader humor of Osbert Lancaster. On the side of melodrama there's a criminous siege of an ancient manor defended only by a troop of children captained by a splendid boy who is a lineal descendant at once of Jim Hawkins and of the children who embarked on Richard Hughes' innocent voyage. This is hardly a novel to suit any conventional taste (and heaven knows why it is related largely in the present tense), but readers weary of private eyes and idiot heroines may well find it one of the most captivating items of the year.

Anthony Boucher, [Review of *Christmas at Candleshoe*], *New York Times Book Review*, 1 November 1953, p. 32

A. E. MURCH   John Innes Mackintosh Stewart, born near Edinburgh in 1906, distinguished himself in the world of letters while still at Oxford, and after a period as lecturer at Leeds University accepted an appointment in Australia, as Professor of English at Adelaide University. As "Michael Innes" he has written many novels and short stories of his Scotland Yard detective, Inspector John Appleby (later Sir John), a scholarly sleuth with a "weakness for cultivated reverie" and a habit of overfrequent conversational references to the classics and the lesser-known poets. The first in the series, *Death at the President's Lodging* (1936), with its very complicated plot, is set in a provincial university, described with satirical humour and a wealth of detail. *Hamlet, Revenge!* (1937) brings a detective drama to complicate an amateur Shakespearean performance in an English country house. In his third novel, *Lament for a Maker* (1938), Michael Innes came to full stature in the *genre*, and produced one of the most memorable detective novels of recent years. The title itself is derived from the fifteenth century historical poem, William Dunbar's *Lament for the Makaris*, the setting is Scotland, gloriously portrayed, while the method of presentation and the plot itself are cleverly modernised from Wilkie Collins's *The Moonstone*. The literary quality of this novel has not been reached again in Michael Innes's later work, though his popular detective, erudite as ever, has continued to appear in a long series of slight tales, with his name in the title of each volume, and has regained something of his former stature in *The Long Farewell* (1958), which shows Sir John grappling with a complicated mystery that calls for his own special blend of scholarship and detective skill.

A. E. Murch, *The Development of the Detective Novel* (1958; rpt. New York: Greenwood Press, 1968), pp. 239–40

ALLEN J. HUBIN   For a good many years I have seldom regretted an encounter with Michael Innes's Sir John Appleby. In his previous case (*Death by Water*), it did appear that retirement from Scotland Yard was sitting uncomfortably on Appleby's shoulders, but his adjustment is now happily complete in *Death at the Chase*. This is a fine puzzle, in the revered mold of the formal detective story, well shored with affability and stout characters. Sir John, wandering one day, trespasses onto the property of an aging recluse—who, by his own account, undergoes annual attempts on his life for his failings in the French Resistance. Appleby might have taken the whole thing for advancing senility, had not a large and lethal stone come off the roof and whistled past his ear. From here on, the plot thickens in the best Innes tradition.

> Allen J. Hubin, [Review of *Death at the Chase*], *New York Times Book Review*, 15 March 1970, p. 44

MICHAEL INNES   I think a species of nostalgia was at work ⟨in the creation of Appleby⟩. English life and manners had a compelling fascination for me—and the more so because, as a Scot who had scarcely crossed the border as a boy, my experience of them had been comparatively brief. And at once keen but impressionistic! So as Appleby moves through his early adventures he reflects something of this situation. He is within a society remembered rather than observed—and remembered in terms of literary conventions which are themselves distancing themselves as his creator works. His is an expatriate's world. It is not a real world, controlled by actual and contemporary social pressures, any more than is, say, the world of P. G. Wodehouse.

But the sphere of Appleby's operations is conditioned by other and, as it were, more simply mechanical factors. Why does he move, in the main, through great houses and amid top people: what an Englishman might call the territory of *Who's Who?* It might be maintained that it is just because he likes it that way. ⟨. . .⟩

But this isn't quite the fact of the matter. In serious English fiction, as distinct from a fiction of entertainment, the great house has long been a symbol—or rather a microcosm—of ordered society; of a complex, but on the whole harmonious, community. ⟨. . .⟩

But Appleby, like many of his fellow-sleuths in the genre, roams these great houses for a different and, as I have said, technical reason. The mansion, the country seat, the ducal palace, is really an extension of the sealed room, defining the spatial, the territorial boundaries of a problem. One can, of course, extract a similar effect out of a compact apartment or a semidetached villa. But these are rather cramping places to prowl in. And in detective stories detectives and their quarry alike must prowl. At the same time, they mustn't get lost. And this fairly spacious unity, the Unity of Place in Aristotle's grand recipe for fiction, conduces to an observance of those other unities of time and action which hold a fast-moving story together. And just because Appleby is leisured and talkative, urbane and allusive; just because he moves among all those people with plenty to say themselves; just because of this he wisely seeks out that rather tight *ambiance*.

Michael Innes, "John Appleby," *The Great Detectives*, ed. Otto Penzler (Boston: Little, Brown, 1978), pp. 13–15

LeROY PANEK   When Charles Honeybath gets involved with crooks in *The Mysterious Commission*, the narrator gives us this insight into his motivation:

> He was no longer Honeybath R.A. He was once more Honeybath Minor . . . and his main ambition in life was one day to become a King Scout.

Here, Innes says, is the final displacement of the adventure story. Adventure tales, to gain credibility, need to shunt their readers into a world which is not their own, usual, humdrum one. Thus, they take us to other places and to other epochs. But the most important displacement is moving the hero, and the reader, out of the adult world into the world of childhood. Children, first of all, need to learn things about danger, commitment, and action which adults are supposed to know. Children also supposedly derive enjoyment from risk and danger while adults know that these things are foolish. For these reasons, the adventure story is almost always some sort of growth story. With these things in mind—and remembering Buchan's Gorbals Die-Hards in *Castle Gay*—Innes shifts focus from the adult hero to the child hero. In *The Case of the Journeying Boy*, it is Humphrey who first recognizes the dangers and at the end demonstrates his identity by spelling out his name

in huge letters on an Irish hillside. Groups of young people also play significant roles in *Operation Pax, Appleby Plays Chicken, Christmas at Candleshoe*,
and *An Awkward Lie*. By using them in these books, Innes not only shows
us those who naturally engage in adventure and whose fantasy lives can
benefit from it, he also shows the limits of the spy story or the adventure
yarn as simple escape entertainment. As Appleby notes in *Death by Water*,
"spy stories, unless recklessly romanticized, are necessarily so disagreeable."
Here, Innes's purpose in his detective novels holds for his adventure novels.
They intend to comically entertain us and to add a seasoning of character-
shaping action, as the detective books add problem-solving. They do not
intend to introduce us to real life with its excessive violence and difficult
moral decisions. Just as in the detective books, therefore, his thrillers show
us people remote from us learning about life, and they also punish minor
foibles and small dishonesties, leaving real causes of evil, whether personal
or international, unexamined. By a strange twist, however, Innes realized
the pathos of modern life and its moral dwindling from the resolute action
pictured in the adventure story. In *Eight Modern Writers*, after considering
the moral tradition of Stevenson and Scott, Innes/Stewart remarks that:

> If gentlemen are no longer put to making calculations [when to
> punch a gangster]—except, indeed, in conditions of mass
> slaughter—it is perhaps the gentlemen who are doing the
> escaping, after all.

In his thrillers, however, he is too sophisticated and aware of himself to be
able to provide muscular examples for his gentle readers.

LeRoy Panek, "The Novels of Michael Innes," *Armchair Detective* 16, No. 2 (Spring
1983): 129

JOHN D. NEVILLE   A recurrent theme in Innes' fiction concerns
art, particularly the theft of art. ⟨. . .⟩ *From London Far* deals with large scale
art theft. In *Silence Observed* there is forgery of art, deception, and murder.
Appleby solves the mystery which takes place in a fashionable gallery in
London. In this novel Lady Appleby, herself an artist, becomes involved
in the sleuthing and finds herself in great danger. Just as Sir John solves the
mystery, so does he rescue his wife in the nick of time. Charles Honeybath, a
famous portrait artist, becomes involved in several of the mysteries that

concern art. In *The Mysterious Commission* Honeybath is tempted by the offer of a huge fee to paint the portrait of an unnamed person in an unannounced location. He sets off in a chauffeured limousine. On arriving at an isolated mansion far from London, he realizes that he has been drugged en route. Then Honeybath finds himself involved in a bank robbery. In his absence, his studio has been used to permit burglars to tunnel into the vaults of the bank next door. And for what purpose is the portrait, Honeybath's best work to date, painted? To answer that, the artist must become an amateur detective, and he finds himself caught in a war between two rival ruthless gangs of criminals. Somehow, he is able to solve the mystery with the aid of the police in a credible fashion. Honeybath appears again in *Honeybath's Haven*, in which Edward Lightfoot, Honeybath's contemporary and friend from years before, drowns in a pool at Hanwell Court, an exclusive home for the elderly. One cannot help but sympathize with Charles Honeybath as he contemplates a move into an old folks home and in doing so first meets a plethora of peculiar inmates, and then has his friend Lightfoot die a mysterious death there. Sensing foul play, Honeybath investigates and begins to feel that his proposed haven is instead a sanctuary for criminals. Again, the forgery and theft of art figures prominently in the solution. *Money from Holme* also involves art as the supposedly dead artist Sebastian Holme turns up alive at a memorial exhibition of his work. But is it really Sebastian Holme or an imposter? Once again forgery of art plays a major role in an Innes novel.

John D. Neville, "Michael Innes," *Clues* 5, No. 2 (Fall–Winter 1984): 122–23

GEORGE L. SHEPER   For Michael Innes the Great Good Place is, was, and always will be Oxford University. Margaret Yorke has demonstrated that Oxford has many more detective fiction connections than does Cambridge: more stories are set in Oxford, more detectives are Oxford-connected, and so too are more detective writers. It is even true that more detective writers *live* near Oxford: "It cannot be coincidence that eight writing members of the Crime Writers Association live within fifteen miles of the centre of Oxford and only two live as close to Cambridge." Why should this be? For anyone familiar with both universities, there is no mystery. Cambridge boasts a Chair in Criminology, but Cambridge, "strong on science, deals with criminological facts whereas our subject here is crime in fantasy." Cambridge is wide and tranquil, surrounded by "flat fenland exposed to cobweb-dispersing winds"; the ancient university town has a modern, suburban feel. At Cambridge "the eye is led ever upwards and one is aware, always, of the sky." However, the "heavens are not conspicuous above Oxford, where the climate is prone to fog and the atmosphere induces introspection." Oxford is centrally located, a great industrial center. The gray stones and "dreaming spires" of the university and its colleges are tucked into the bustling city, behind great formidable walls and amid wonderfully winding streets and alleys in a medieval fashion. Everything on the score of mystery tilts toward the dark blue of Oxford rather than the light blue of Cambridge.

Innes knows Oxford inside and out, first from his experiences as an undergraduate and then as a don for twenty-five years. He has written with great familiarity and poignancy about Oxford in the J. I. M. Stewart magnum opus, the Oxford Quintet called A Staircase in Surrey. But he has also introduced an Oxfordian note quite often in the Innes mysteries as well. In them there is no dark satiric vision of university life. In Innes one encounters only a Chestertonian whimsicality. Neither Innes, nor Appleby, nor any of Innes's donnish protagonists ever conveys the sense that he feels the validity of his deepest commitments and values is seriously threatened or called into question. As Krouse and Peters testify in their article on murder in academe: "Innes's vision of academe has remained essentially intact"; his academic novels reveal his "essential reverence for university tradition and innocence. He takes it for granted that his professors' learning is vast, their integrity almost unchallengeable, and their flaws not serious enough to discredit their calling." Innes's approach is always one of good-natured and high-spirited humor.

> George L. Sheper, Michael Innes (New York: Frederick Ungar Publishing Co., 1986), pp. 86–87

J. I. M. STEWART   Michael Innes had continued on the market with detective stories which (like Matthew Arnold in Max Beerbohm's cartoon) were not always wholly serious—being fairly regularly tinged, that is to say, with fantasy and extravagance. But another, and distinct, strain, emerged in some of them. It goes back not to Conan Doyle and G. K. Chesterton, but—I suppose—to two countrymen of my own, Robert Louis

Stevenson and John Buchan. I have been told that *Lament for Maker* smells strongly of *The Master of Ballantrae*, and although my memory of that story (read in 1924) doesn't quite respond to this, I am in no doubt about the validity of the general proposition. And that the detective element has to be rather awkwardly edged into *Lament for a Maker* is evident from the fact that my indefatigable official sleuth, John Appleby, arrives at Castle Erchany, the scene of action, only in the last third of the book. The mystery he investigates is not particularly memorable, but I regard this novel as leaving something in the mind, all the same—which is a quality not owned by the numerous Innes stories at all often.

The next book of any note is, I think, *The Secret Vanguard*, published in 1940 and set in the months immediately before the outbreak of the Second World War. It is essentially a spy thriller—and again Appleby, yet more awkwardly, undertakes the job of making it a detective story as well. There are, of course, many sorts of spy thrillers, and this one belongs to the sub-species that concerns a haunted man. Only my haunted man is a girl, and she is being haunted because she has, all-unawares, become involved in a totally preposterous espionage situation which no professional fabricator of spy stories would now look for in a moment. Secret agents pass information in railway carriages by spouting Swinburne to one another with bogus stanzas thrown in: absurdities like that. Yet the actual hunting of the girl, Sheila Grant, over a Scottish moor, is a different thing: far and away, I judge, the most empathic writing I have anywhere achieved. The chapters entitled 'Hawk' and 'Hare' are to my mind as good as such unassuming things can be. But again they have their derivations. Thus there comes a point at which Sheila is suddenly confronted by 'a curve of steel':

> For the first time she realized fully the significance of a railway
> line over such country as this. Unlike the undulating and heather-
> covered moor, it was something which, granted any sort of
> visibility at all, it would be virtually impossible to cross
> unobserved. And where a straight line might give scope for
> manoeuvre, this half-circle of track was like a pair of open jaws.

I believe the situation here comes straight from Buchan's *Prester John*. But almost immediately there follow the chapters called 'Sheila Travels without a Ticket', *'Johnny Cope'*, and 'Two in a Cage'. Here—and particularly in the appearance of Harry McQueen, the blind fiddler who peddles his 'poems of a Moray loon' up and down the line, and who can find his way through the glens by listening to the echoes from his instrument—I am drawing upon memories of my childhood. Harry's 'cage' is the stronghold, he believes, of that Alexander Stewart, the 'Wolf of Badenoch', who had burned down Elgin Cathedral at the close of the fourteenth century. The juxtaposition of Harry's crazy imaginings and the closely worked minute-by-minute account of Sheila's flight has the felicitousness that does sometimes drop unbidden into a writer's grasp. Here—to vary the figure—it lands me on a perch from which I descend clumsily enough. The closing chapters of *The Secret Vanguard* are a huddle of spy-and-detective stuff much lacking in clarity and credibility.

> J. I. M. Stewart, *Myself and Michael Innes: A Memoir* (New York: W. W. Norton, 1987), pp. 124–25

T. J. BINYON   Innes's detective is John Appleby, who rises from inspector to commissioner of the Metropolitan Police, acquiring a knighthood and a wife—the sculptress Judith Raven—on the way. He first appears in *Death at the President's Lodging* (1936; US title *Seven Suspects*). Though Appleby may toy with fingerprints and timetables, police routine and procedure are never important, and are never treated with conviction. Indeed, the novels have little connection with reality at all; they are intellectual conceits, in which a complex, logical plot is set against an elaborate, often highly artificial background peopled with eccentric characters, whose conversation is witty, amusing, and erudite, but often irrelevant to the matter at hand. In the earlier novels the author sometimes allows his delight in creating improbable, baroque narrative edifices to get out of hand; and he is inclined to solve difficulties of plot by melodramatic event. As detective stories, the more sober later works are probably to be preferred. In method Innes could be compared with Ellery Queen and John Dickson Carr; he is a better writer than both, however; and an important difference is that he is always concerned to entertain. The detective element is unmistakably there, but it is not absolutely paramount, as it is with Queen and Carr. Appleby himself is somewhat characterless on his first appearance; though he acquires a more definite, individual persona in later works, especially when seen with his wife, at first he is more a mind than a physical presence. His looks are mentioned only as an indication of his social class: the dean of St. Anthony's College reflects that Appleby 'was remarkably young, and

... had all the appearance of being—indeed quite plainly *was*—what Mr. Deighton-Clerk still liked to think of under the designation "genteel" '. And again, 'he took another glance at Appleby—the man was indubitably a gentleman.' Appleby exhibits other characteristics of the amateur police-man: he takes pleasure in being wilfully enigmatic, and his speech is stuffed with literary illusions, though he is academically whimsical rather than facetious. ⟨...⟩ Whatever their defects as detective stories, the books are always immensely lively, and are written with great charm and wit.

> T. J. Binyon, *"Murder Will Out": The Detective in Fiction* (New York: Oxford University Press, 1989), pp. 93–95

▣ *Bibliography*

Books by Michael Innes:

Death at the President's Lodging ⟨Seven Suspects⟩. 1936.

Hamlet, Revenge! A Story in Four Parts. 1937.

Lament for a Maker. 1938.

Stop Press ⟨The Spider Strikes⟩. 1939.

The Secret Vanguard. 1940.

There Came Both Mist and Snow ⟨A Comedy of Terrors⟩. 1940.

Appleby on Ararat. 1941.

The Daffodil Affair. 1942.

The Weight of the Evidence. 1943.

Appleby's End. 1945.

From London Far ⟨The Unsuspected Chasm⟩. 1946.

What Happened at Hazelwood? 1946.

A Night of Errors. 1947.

The Journeying Boy ⟨The Case of the Journeying Boy⟩. 1949.

Three Tales of Hamlet (with Rayner Heppenstall). 1950.

Operation Pax ⟨The Paper Thunderbolt⟩. 1951.

A Private View ⟨One-Man Show⟩. 1952.

Christmas at Candleshoe. 1953.

Appleby Talking ⟨Dead Man's Shoes⟩. 1954.

The Man from the Sea. 1955.

Old Hall, New Hall ⟨A Question of Queens⟩. 1956.

Appleby Talks Again. 1956.

Appleby Plays Chicken ⟨*Death on a Quiet Day*⟩. 1956.
The Long Farewell. 1958.
Hare Sitting Up. 1959.
The New Sonia Wayward. 1960.
Silence Observed. 1961.
A Connoisseur's Case ⟨*The Crabtree Affair*⟩. 1962.
Money from Holme. 1964.
Appleby Intervenes: Three Tales from Scotland Yard ⟨*One-Man Show, A Comedy
    of Terrors, The Secret Vanguard*⟩. 1965.
The Bloody Wood. 1966.
A Change of Heir. 1966.
Appleby at Allington ⟨*Death by Water*⟩. 1968.
A Family Affair ⟨*Picture of Guilt*⟩. 1969.
Death at the Chase. 1970.
An Awkward Lie. 1971.
The Open House. 1972.
Appleby's Answer. 1973.
Appleby's Other Story. 1974.
The Mysterious Commission. 1974.
The Appleby File. 1975.
The Gay Phoenix. 1976.
Honeybath's Haven. 1977.
The Ampersand Papers. 1978.
Going It Alone. 1980.
Lord Mullion's Secret. 1981.
Sheiks and Adders. 1982.
Appleby and Honeybath. 1983.
The Michael Innes Omnibus ⟨*Death at the President's Lodging, Hamlet, Revenge!,
    The Daffodil Affair*⟩. 1983.
The Second Michael Innes Omnibus ⟨*The Journeying Boy, Operation Pax, The
    Man from the Sea*⟩. 1983.
Carson's Conspiracy. 1984.
Appleby and the Ospreys. 1986.
The Michael Innes Treasury ⟨*The Case of the Journeying Boy, Hamlet, Revenge!,
    Appleby's End*⟩. 1986.

Books by J. I. M. Stewart:
Montaigne's Essays: John Florio's Translation (editor). 1931.
Educating the Emotions. 1944.

Character and Motive in Shakespeare: Some Recent Appraisals Examined. 1949.

Mark Lambert's Supper. 1954.

The Guardians. 1955.

A Use of Riches. 1957.

James Joyce. 1957, 1960.

The Man Who Wrote Detective Stories and Other Stories. 1959.

The Man Who Won the Pools. 1961.

The Last Tresilians. 1963.

Thomas Love Peacock. 1963.

Eight Modern Writers. 1963.

An Acre of Grass. 1965.

The Aylwins. 1966.

Rudyard Kipling. 1966.

The Moonstone by Wilkie Collins (editor). 1966.

Vanderlyn's Kingdom. 1967.

Joseph Conrad. 1968.

Vanity Fair by William Makepeace Thackeray (editor). 1968.

Cucumber Sandwiches and Other Stories. 1969.

Shakespeare's Lofty Scene. 1971.

Avery's Mission. 1971.

Thomas Hardy: A Critical Biography. 1971.

A Palace of Art. 1972.

Mungo's Dream. 1973.

The Gaudy. 1974.

Young Pattullo. 1975.

A Memorial Service. 1976.

The Madonna of the Astrolabe. 1977.

Full Term. 1978.

Our England Is a Garden and Other Stories. 1979.

Andrew and Tobias. 1980.

The Bridge at Arta and Other Stories. 1981.

A Villa in France. 1982.

My Aunt Christina and Other Stories. 1983.

An Open Prison. 1984.

The Naylors. 1985.

Parlour 4 and Other Stories. 1986.

Myself and Michael Innes: A Memoir. 1987.

Ngaio Marsh
1899–1982

NGAIO MARSH was born on April 23, 1899, in Christchurch, New Zealand. Marsh's given name, pronounced "ny-o," is a Maori word for a flowering tree native to New Zealand. Marsh's parents, Henry Edmund and Rose Elizabeth Seager Marsh, were both amateur actors. Marsh attended St. Margaret's College from 1910 to 1914 and then studied painting at the Canterbury University College School of Art from 1915 to 1920; but she remained enthusiastic for and active in the theatre throughout her life, working variously as an actress, director, and producer.

Marsh lived in England from 1928 to 1933, where she worked as an interior decorator, and it was at this time that she produced the works for which she is best known: mystery novels featuring the gentleman detective Roderick Alleyn (named for the Elizabethan tragedian Edward Alleyn), the first of which, *A Man Lay Dead*, appeared in 1934. This novel, like those of Dorothy L. Sayers and Margery Allingham, upholds many of the conventions of Golden Age detective fiction, but variations and innovations become apparent in subsequent volumes. Alleyn is an aristocrat with high-society ties, a subtle charm, and a frequently used knowledge of literature. In this respect, he falls within the tradition of genteel, bookish detectives of the Golden Age. However, Marsh also enlivens Alleyn with some physical prowess and even entangles him in a romantic relationship with the painter Agatha Troy. Marsh also breaks with the convention of introducing the murder at the beginning of the story, and on some occasions she makes no secret of the identity of the murderer.

Along with her presentation of more rounded characters, Marsh's continuing interest in painting and the theatre become significant influences in the Alleyn stories. In *Enter a Murderer* (1935), Marsh's second Alleyn mystery, the theatre provides the setting, and Marsh's reliance on theatrical language and devices become apparent. In *Vintage Murder* (1937), *Overture to Death* (1939), and others, the influence of the theatre is most clearly detected in the method of murder (a huge falling champagne bottle and a piano that fires bullets).

Marsh's interest in painting is evident in her rich descriptions of scenery and setting, especially in her four mysteries set in New Zealand (*Vintage Murder*, 1937; *Colour Scheme*, 1943; *Died in the Wool*, 1945; *Photo-Finish*, 1980). She also wrote several books on New Zealand.

In 1934 Marsh returned to New Zealand to assist her ailing parents. When World War II broke out, she worked as a Red Cross ambulance driver while continuing to do much theatre work. A concern with espionage seeps into her wartime writing, as in *Colour Scheme* and *Died in the Wool*. For the rest of her life she resided alternately in New Zealand and England.

Despite the enormous popularity of her Alleyn mysteries, most of which became best-sellers, Marsh consistently claimed that the theatre was her primary interest. She was producer for D. D. O'Connor Theatre Management from 1944 to 1952, directing Shakespeare productions and many other plays; in 1946 she became director of the first all–New Zealand Shakespearean company, the Canterbury University College Student Players. She also adapted several of her own novels into plays: *The Nursing Home Murder* (1936), *Surfeit of Lampreys* (1950), *False Scent* (1961), and *Murder Sails at Midnight* (1972; adapted from *Singing in the Shrouds*). She also wrote the lyrics for *A Unicorn for Christmas* (1965), with music by David Farquhar. Although they have been performed, none of these plays has been published. In her autobiography, *Black Beech and Honeydew* (1965), discussion of her detective fiction is notably scarce.

Marsh won many awards and honors, including a D.Litt. from the University of Canterbury and, in 1977, the Grand Master Award from the Mystery Writers of America. In 1966 she became a Dame Commander of the British Empire. Ngaio Marsh died on February 18, 1982. Inspector Alleyn made his last appearance in the posthumously published *Light Thickens* in the same year. Her *Collected Short Fiction*, edited by Douglas G. Greene, was issued in 1989.

◈ *Critical Extracts*

UNSIGNED   Miss Ngaio Marsh has again written a model detective story ⟨*Overture to Death*⟩. An eminent writer of this class of fiction recently criticized Miss Joanna Cannan's first detective story on the ground that she concealed the real character of the murderer and gave inadequate clues to his identity. But these habits are all too common even among more experienced writers of detective stories. Miss Marsh is an exception to the rule and, indeed, in her present novel she tends in the opposite direction and makes clues and motives sufficiently transparent for any intelligent reader to discover the criminal. In this case the novel is so well written that this transparency need not detract from the reader's enjoyment. Nevertheless it is clear that the novelist who writes detective stories is nowadays being confronted with an awkward dilemma; if he conceals the motive and is parsimonious with the clues he is accused of cheating; if he makes plain the motive and is generous with clues he is liable to be blamed for presenting too simple a problem.

Unsigned, "Death at the Piano," *Times Literary Supplement*, 11 March 1939, p. 152

WILL CUPPY   Since Ngaio Marsh is the best mystery writer going, and since *Death and the Dancing Footman* is her best book, it ought to be quite an important event in fandom—assuming that we know what we are talking about, or even partly. Certainly, this department can't remember another baffler that ever struck it with the one hundred per cent impact of this one. Which is only to say, maybe, that it is exactly suited to one reader's taste, and by that we mean exactly. If Miss Marsh is getting tired of all-out praise of this sort, she'll just have to get used to the fact that nobody in her racket begins to touch her for writing grace and that few possess her skill at creating potential corpses and suspects, building a puzzle and other essentials of ground and lofty detectivism. There hasn't been anybody in the least like her since the palmiest days of Dorothy L. Sayers with whom her work may have some sort of affinity which posterity will properly evaluate. These two belong in the same bracket, somehow, as all the rabid Sayers fans probably know by now.

Will Cuppy, [Review of *Death and the Dancing Footman*], *New York Herald Tribune Books*, 14 September 1941, p. 18

DOROTHY CAMERON DISNEY   Ngaio Marsh has already proved that in her ironic and witty hands the mystery novel can be civilized literature. *Colour Scheme* has everything—style and atmosphere, humor which is never forced, a striking and unusual background, and a group of characters, English, Maori and New Zealander, who are fascinating and completely credible. ⟨. . .⟩

No gore is spilled in *Colour Scheme* until nearly two hundred pages have passed. By that time Miss Marsh has taken the reader through a tour of the thermal springs and volcanic regions of New Zealand and immersed one of her chief characters in a bath of boiling mud. This appears to be an old New Zealand custom. ⟨. . .⟩

Colour Scheme is a must for everyone who wants the kind of mystery story that would bore anybody who is fascinated by Terry and the Pirates.

Dorothy Cameron Disney, "Murder in an Exotic Background," *New York Times Book Review*, 11 July 1943, p. 4

EDMUND WILSON   I had often heard people say that Dorothy Sayers wrote well, and I felt that my correspondents had been playing her as their literary ace. But, really, she does not write very well: it is simply that she is more consciously literary than most of the other detective-story writers and that she thus attracts attention in a field which is mostly on a sub-literary level. In any serious department of fiction, her writing would not appear to have any distinction at all. Yet, commonplace in this respect though she is, she gives an impression of brilliant talent if we put her beside Miss Ngaio Marsh, whose *Overture to Death* was also suggested by several correspondents. Mr. De Voto has put himself on record as believing that Miss Marsh, as well as Miss Sayers and Miss Allingham, writes her novels in "excellent prose," and this throws for me a good deal of light on Mr. De Voto's opinions as a critic. I hadn't quite realized before, though I had noted his own rather messy style, to what degree he was insensitive to writing. I do not see how it is possible for anyone with a feeling for words to describe the unappetizing sawdust which Miss Marsh has poured into her pages as "excellent prose" or prose at all except in the sense that distinguishes prose from verse. And here again the book is mostly padding. There is the notion that you could commit a murder by rigging up a gun in a piano in such a way that the victim will shoot himself when he presses down the pedal, but this is embedded in the dialogue and doings of a lot of faked-up

English country people who are even more tedious than those of ⟨Sayers's⟩
The Nine Tailors.

Edmund Wilson, "Who Cares Who Killed Roger Ackroyd?" (1945), *Classics and Commercials: A Literary Chronicle of the Forties* (New York: Farrar, Straus, 1950), pp. 259–60

ANTHONY BOUCHER   The folk mind "writes" in a way almost
impossible for a conscious creator to duplicate, fusing divergent elements,
erasing unnecessary (and even necessary) transitions and explanations, and
shaping a sort of magic not subject to critical analysis. One would swear
that deliberate imitation of the folk manner would lie beyond the skill of
even a highly capable professional writer; yet Ngaio Marsh brings off the
feat beautifully in *Death of a Fool*.

The Mardian Morris Sword Dance and Play of the Five Sons, performed
annually on the first Wednesday after the winter solstice, is as tantalizingly
half-meaningful, as hauntingly evocative as anything you've ever read in
the annals of folklore; and it furnishes a superb background for murder (of
the "impossible" genre, and very neatly resolved). Roderick Alleyn, now a
superintendent, has little to do but stage a somewhat foolish "reconstruction"; but the other characters are unconventional and attractive and the
varying levels of village life admirably depicted. It's a long novel; but the
eery magic of Sword Wednesday makes it seem absorbingly short.

Anthony Boucher, "Reports on Criminals at Large," *New York Times Book Review*, 18 November 1956, p. 44

EARL F. BARGAINNIER   The biographical approach to any writer's work is a dangerous one, but it is difficult to think of the work of
any writer of mystery/detective fiction to which the approach seems so
appropriate as these eight novels of Ngaio Marsh ⟨involving the theatre⟩.
Her statements in *Black Beech and Honeydew* make clear that though her
detective novels have been her greatest success financially, she considers
her life in the theatre to have been the more personally satisfying. When
she decided to combine her two careers in these novels, she did not, as
⟨Julian⟩ Symons has noted, just use the theatre as a "puzzle box." Rather
her experiences as actress, director, and producer enabled her to create a fully
realized theatrical world, involving plot, characterization, and atmosphere, as

well as setting. They also allowed her—in her own voice or through her characters—to make statements on the personalities of actors, the nature of theatrical pain and joy, the necessary fantasizing process itself, and, most of all, her deep love of the theatre, in spite of her recognition of its jealousies, pretensions, and eccentricities. Whatever one may think of a particular novel, one must admit that Marsh has been generally able to use the theatre as an integral element of her detective fiction. (My own view is that in *Killer Dolphin* the theatrical story is better than the mystery; in *False Scent* the mystery is better than the theatrical story; and in *Enter a Murderer* the two are equally good.)

There is a passage of dialogue between Emily Dunne and Peregrine Jay in *Killer Dolphin* which, I think, expresses Marsh's feelings about the theatre:

> "I always think it feels so strange," she said, "after we've left it to itself. As if it's got a life of its own. Always waiting for us."
> "Another kind of reality?"
> "Yes. A more impressive kind. You can almost imagine it breathes."

Certainly, within Ngaio Marsh, the theatre breathes.

Earl F. Bargainnier, "Ngaio Marsh's 'Theatrical' Murders," *Armchair Detective* 10, No. 2 (April 1977): 179–80

NGAIO MARSH   ⟨Roderick Alleyn⟩ was born with the rank of Detective-Inspector, C.I.D., on a very wet Saturday afternoon in a basement flat off Sloane Square, in London. The year was 1931.

All day, rain splashed up from the feet of passersby going to and fro, at eye-level, outside my water-streaked windows. It fanned out from under the tires of cars, cascaded down the steps to my door and flooded the area: "remorseless" was the word for it and its sound was, beyond all expression, dreary. In view of what was about to take place, the setting was, in fact, almost too good to be true.

I read a detective story borrowed from a dim little lending library in a stationer's shop across the way. Either a Christie or a Sayers, I think it was. By four o'clock, when the afternoon was already darkening, I had finished it and still the rain came down. I remember that I made up the London coal-fire of those days and looked down at it, idly wondering if I had it in me to write something in the genre. That was the season, in England, when the Murder Game was popular at weekend parties. Someone was slipped a card saying he or she was the "murderer." He or she then chose a moment to select a "victim" and there was a subsequent "trial." I thought it might be an idea for a whodunit—they were already called that—if a real corpse was found instead of a phony one. Luckily for me, as it turned out, I wasn't aware until much later that a French practitioner had been struck with the same notion.

I played about with this idea. I tinkered with the fire and with an emergent character who might have been engendered in its sulky entrails: a solver of crimes.

The room had grown quite dark when I pulled on a mackintosh, took an umbrella, plunged up the basement steps, and beat my way through rain-fractured lamplight to the stationer's shop. It smelled of damp newsprint, cheap magazines, and wet people. I bought six twopenny exercise books, a pencil and pencil-sharpener and splashed back to the flat.

Then with an odd sensation of giving myself some sort of treat, I thought more specifically about the character who already had begun to take shape.

In the crime fiction of that time the solver was often a person of more-or-less eccentric habit with a collection of easily identifiable mannerisms. This, of course, was in the tradition of Sherlock Holmes. The splendid M. Poirot had his mustaches, his passion for orderly arrangements, his frequent references to "grey matter." Lord Peter Wimsey could be, as one now inclines to think, excruciatingly facetious. Nice Reggie Fortune said—and he said it very often—"My dear chap! Oh, my dear chap!" and across the Atlantic there was Philo Vance, who spoke a strange language that his author, I think I remember, had the nerve to attribute, in part, to Balliol College, Oxford.

Faced with this assembly of celebrated eccentrics, it seemed to me, on that long-distant wet afternoon, that my best chance lay in comparative normality—in the invention of a man with a background resembling that of the friends I had made in England—and that I had better not tie manner-isms, like labels, round his neck. (I can see now that with my earlier books I did not altogether succeed in this respect.)

I thought that my detective would be a professional policeman but, in some ways, atypical: an attractive, civilized man with whom it would be pleasant to talk but much less pleasant to fall out.

Ngaio Marsh, "Roderick Alleyn" (1977), *The Great Detectives*, ed. Otto Penzler (Boston: Little, Brown, 1978), pp. 3–5

LeROY PANEK   By creating unsavory situations and portraying people with credible motives for committing crimes Marsh, like other detective
writers in the thirties, created problems for herself which she could not
completely solve. By its very nature the Golden Age detective novel was
an entertainment; it was a puzzle, a game, with certain specific conventions
designed to engage readers in a guessing contest and to give them a surprise
at the close of the narrative. Within this framework it is difficult and often
undesirable to treat serious themes or to show a picture of the real world
of crime. A number of writers in the thirties, notably Sayers, Allingham,
and Cox as Francis Iles, tried to fuse the puzzle story with more serious
concerns. In each case this meant making certain adaptations of the conventional patterns. The same thing is true of Marsh: she wants to combine the
crime game with realism and needs to make certain adjustments. Marsh
knew, as Sayers did, that the chief impediment to making the puzzle story
into a realistic picture, or even a traditional narrative, was the convention
that the antagonist must be concealed in the detective story in order to
make the guessing game work. Without an identifiable antagonist, the writer
needs to modify the traditional way stories develop and has no character
upon whom to focus the negative side of the conflict of detective hero and
murderer-villain. Sayers solved this problem by making the identity of the
antagonists clear from the beginning of the plot, never cloaking them very
heavily, in order to communicate the various manifestations of evil. Marsh's
treatment of the antagonist, which is in some ways like Sayers', does not,
however, come from a pressing need to examine the nature of sin, but has
its beginnings in Marsh's grounding in the theater: it is important in a good
play to show a good deal of the antagonist. Consequently, Marsh does not
use plot devices like the least-likely-character or the character who is guilty
but only has a minimal role. Quite the opposite. In two of her novels of
the period she employs what can be called the most likely suspect formula:
that is, the person who is suspected of the murder actually is guilty. She is
most interested in showing murderers in all of their commonplace nastiness.
Even if Marsh gives in to convention in rigging up fancy ways of killing
people—like the gun in the piano trick in *Overture to Death*—the technical
means of murder is not as important as the people, not as important as the
time honored drama of confronting people with others and with themselves.

LeRoy Panek, "Ngaio Marsh," *Watteau's Shepards: The Detective Novel in Britain
1914–1940* (Bowling Green, OH: Bowling Green University Popular Press, 1979),
pp. 194–95

BRUCE HARDING   Although Marsh only set four novels in New Zealand, I would argue that at least three of them contribute something in their own distinctive way to the broader picture of life in this country. In making this claim I take issue with Randall Burdon's contention that 'in a literary sense Marsh was always below par when writing about her native land'; not with the view that London was her spiritual home, but with his idea that this fact 'may explain why Roderick Alleyn and his victims perform to greater advantage in a metropolitan than in a remote antipodean environment.' For this is tantamount to accepting the claim in a British newspaper that while it was true that Marsh was born in New Zealand, 'her first book was accepted while she was in England . . . so we are entitled to consider her as one of us.'

Marsh early resigned herself to the 'irreconcilable problem' of the expatriate and solved the dilemma of having two homelands by shuttling fairly frequently between them. In this sense she didn't fear Bill Pearson's view of the New Zealand artist who 'may pretend to be an exile in a hostile country: he knows it is better to stay at home as a big frog in a little pond than go abroad and be humble.' On the contrary, her supreme achievement as a New Zealand–born author was to combine the cosmopolitan outlook of an internationalist with a firm loyalty to her own people (Maori and Pakeha) and their respective traditions. The rub, was, of course, that in this process of oscillating between—in Gertrude Stein's terms—the country where she belonged (England) and the one in which she really lived (New Zealand), Ngaio Marsh appeared to some a misplaced Englishwoman. While one can argue that this geographical and emotional tension was a very fruitful one in generating all her artistic attainments, it meant that Marsh was misunderstood as a cultural prig by some of her own compatriots. ⟨. . .⟩ Marsh's pride in her own unique country is amply reflected in two books (both entitled *New Zealand*) which she has produced about it.   Dennis McEldowney was right to point out that in her stories Marsh 'always continued to write about New Zealand as though she were a visitor, while believing she was a native' but this need not diminish her national pride and loyalty. Indeed, it was precisely in maintaining this stance that Marsh's personal expression of loyalty consisted. Jessica Mann has written that Marsh's picture of England is rather an unreal one, adding suggestively: 'Perhaps it is because her view of England is inevitably one of a visitor, however devoted, that she retains this idealised view of life in the Northern hemisphere.' Can these two negatives of McEldowney's and Mann's create a positive? I think they can.

Bruce Harding, "The New Zealand Stories of Ngaio Marsh," *Landfall* 36, No. 4 (December 1982): 450–52

ALLAN C. DOOLEY and LINDA J. DOOLEY   One of the lasting pleasures of a Marsh mystery is the reader's entry into the world of the story. This world is a place, a time, a background, and more; it is a realm defined by an endeavour or a body of experiences that is inherently and immediately interesting. The novels do not usually take place in specific, identifiable locations. The street addresses in London are accurate enough, but Marsh's custom is to invent places that are distilled from real worlds. There is no Cloudyfold (*Overture to Death*) in the west of England, but its hills overlooking Pen Cuckoo are true to life. There is no Ottercombe (*Death at the Bar*), perhaps, but this isolated village with its dangerous and precipitious entrance is reminiscent of a dozen real villages in Dorset or Cornwall. Places in Marsh's fiction are clearly and vividly drawn, with a great deal of attention to appropriate detail. She takes care about the flora, the scenery, the architecture, and anything else about a place that can give us a concrete sense of place and time. Her most memorable descriptions are those of her native New Zealand (in *Colour Scheme, Died in the Wool,* and *Vintage Murder*); the manuka flowers, the hot springs, the mountains and unspoiled forests are rendered with loving detail. Marsh does not limit herself to evoking physical appearances; she captures the aura or atmosphere of the location she is building up in the mind. The lake island in *Photo Finish,* for example, is set down in a primeval wilderness that is in itself a harsh commentary on the artificial and corrupt lives of the people who invade it.

These settings are equally firmly located in time. Marsh always set her novels in the present (that is, the 'now' of the date of publication), and the speech of her characters (as well as their dress and manner) is true to prevailing fashions. Slang and catch-phrases change over the long course of her career, giving each novel a sense of belonging to a particular moment. Marsh's use of dialect is equally fine-tuned. Her characters speak the language of their place and station, and she had a fine ear for the varieties of English speech (including its Antipodean and American forms). With such details of time and place, Marsh's fictional settings establish what becomes for the reader an anchor in reality.

Allan C. Dooley and Linda J. Dooley, "Rereading Ngaio Marsh," *Art in Crime Writing: Essays on Detective Fiction*, ed. Bernard Benstock (New York: St. Martin's Press, 1983), pp. 33–34

JULIAN SYMONS   Ngaio Marsh never went so far as Allingham in attempting to write novels with a detective element, rather than detective stories. Her capacity for amused observation of the undercurrents beneath ordinary social interchanges was so good that one hoped for more than she ever tried to do. The first half of *Opening Night* (1951) gives a brilliant picture of the intrigues taking place before the opening of a new play. All this is, as it should be, preparation for the murder that takes place, and we hope that after the murder the book will remain in the same key and that the problems will be resolved as they began, in terms of character. To our disappointment, however, Marsh takes refuge from real emotional problems in the official investigation and interrogation of suspects. The temperature is lowered, the mood has been lost.

In later books like *When in Rome* (1971) and *Black as He's Painted* (1974) she similarly evaded the problems in terms of character suggested early in the books. Dame Ngaio defended her practice with modesty and charm, saying that she always began with two or three people about whom she wanted to write, and involved them in a crime of violence, but that 'the more deeply and honestly [a novelist] examines her characters, the more disquieting becomes the skullduggery that [she] is obliged to practise in respect to the guilty party'. To the suggestion that she avoided emotional problems she replied that this was 'almost a definition of one of the major limitations of the genre'. Well, not quite. Other writers managed to square this circle, and engaging though the books are, one is bound to regret that Ngaio Marsh did not take her fine talent more seriously.

Julian Symons, *Bloody Murder: From the Detective Story to the Crime Novel—A History* (1972; rev. ed. New York: Viking, 1985), pp. 141–42

MARGARET LEWIS   Her disarming description in 'Birth of a Sleuth' (1977) of how she embarked upon her first crime novel, *A Man*

Lay Dead, tends to obscure the fact that by this time she was already a very competent writer. From childhood her literary gifts had been encouraged, and through most of her life she had been transposing experience into prose. The travel essays she sent back to New Zealand newspapers were far more than mere descriptions of places and events; they were full of quirky observations and dramatically shaped vignettes that exactly capture the flavour of the moment. Looking back from a vantage point in the 1990s, when travel writing is a recognised genre, Ngaio's pieces rank high in any company. Their human interest makes the scene more immediate, and the novelist's essential curiosity about the hidden life behind the exterior is never absent. Ngaio was eminently qualified for her new task, and there was nothing amateur in her approach. She started as a professional and she remained one until she set down the manuscript of *Light Thickens,* her last novel, in December 1981, six weeks before her death. Having wasted ten years, as she recognised in a letter to Denys Rhodes written in the 1940s, she finally knew where she was heading.

Ngaio's fictional detective, Roderick Alleyn, was devised as a character who would be 'an attractive, civilised man with whom it would be pleasant to talk, but much less pleasant to fall out'. She tailored him to fit the country house society with which she had become familiar since arriving in England; his brother was a baronet and his mother Lady Alleyn of Danes Lodge, Bossicote, Buckinghamshire. He was a tall and good-looking: 'thin with an accidental elegance . . . fastidious . . . compassionate . . . with a cockeyed sense of humour, dependent largely upon understatement but, for all his unemphatic, rather apologetic ways, he could be a formidable person of considerable authority'. He is highly professional and successful in his field; we are told in *Vintage Murder* that his book *Principles and Practice of Criminal Investigation* (published by Sable and Murgatroyd at 21 shillings) is widely read throughout the world—'we've all been trained on your book', says the local Police Inspector in Middleton, New Zealand.

Interestingly, in view of the serious novel still in her mind at this time, the author found that when she started to develop the character of Roderick Alleyn he seemed familiar: 'if I had not fallen so casually into the practice of crime-writing and had taken to a more serious form, he would still have arrived and found himself in an altogether different setting'. Was Ngaio describing here the sort of man she had been hoping to meet for many years? Did she fall in love with her creation, as Dorothy Sayers did with Lord Peter Wimsey? She denied it firmly, but admitted to liking him very much: 'I've never got tired of the old boy'. And his eventual marriage to a successful painter, Troy, must represent a certain wish fulfilment on the part of a mature writer who was still not averse to the possibilities of romance.

Margaret Lewis, *Ngaio Marsh: A Life* (London: Chatto & Windus, 1991), pp. 55–56

KATHRYNE SLATE McDORMAN   Ngaio Marsh ultimately parted company with her contemporaries Christie, Sayers, and Allingham in her sensuous evocation of place and atmosphere and in the extent to which she analyzed character. Her challenge to the formulaic boundaries lifts her books from the limiting definition of predictable puzzle whodunits to the more complicated realm of novels of manners. No other detective fiction writer of this period painted external nature and internal space with such carefully crafted images. Whether the mystery occurs in the mud flats of New Zealand or in the country houses of the English gentry, Ngaio Marsh's lush prose painted them with broad and colorful strokes. Even when she set a winter scene with snow, ice, and the bitter wind, she filled it with smells and sounds that illuminate her themes of desperation and the chill of murder. In her three coldest novels, *Death and the Dancing Footman*, *Death of a Fool*, and *Tied Up in Tinsel*, the crimes are the most chilling: fratricide and patricide. Marsh wrote detective stories with careful attention to the elements and the physical surroundings, both of which reflect qualities of character and provide many twists to the already Byzantine plots. Marsh's theatrical experiences greatly enhance her ability to integrate sets, props, lighting, and character, thus providing her books with intricate texture and vivid color.

All of Marsh's novels are about more than the solution of crime. They are bursting with ideas and enthusiasm about a wide range of topics, from the future of the British Commonwealth to the passing of Victorian-Edwardian manners and morals. She explored a rather extensive sampling of Britons and New Zealanders to delineate not merely personal traits but national characteristics as well. As a social critic she deftly fileted England's class system, removing the skeleton still intact and exposing its shape and form to the last tiny bone. She accomplished this, not by digressive essays, but by the interaction of her characters in the throes of a murder investigation.

Kathryne Slate McDorman, *Ngaio Marsh* (Boston: Twayne, 1991), pp. 139–40

◈ Bibliography

A Man Lay Dead. 1934.

Enter a Murderer. 1935.

The Nursing-Home Murder (with H. Jellett). 1935.

Death in Ecstasy. 1936.

Vintage Murder. 1937.

Artists in Crime. 1938.

Death in a White Tie. 1938.

Overture to Death. 1939.

Death at the Bar. 1940.

Death of a Peer ⟨*Surfeit of Lampreys*⟩. 1940.

Death and the Dancing Footman. 1941.

New Zealand (with R. M. Burdon). 1942.

Colour Scheme. 1943.

Died in the Wool. 1945.

A Play Toward: A Note on Play Production. 1946.

Final Curtain. 1947.

Swing, Brother, Swing ⟨*A Wreath for Rivera*⟩. 1949.

Opening Night ⟨*Night at the Vulcan*⟩. 1951.

Spinsters in Jeopardy. 1953.

Scales of Justice. 1955.

Death of a Fool ⟨*Off with His Head*⟩. 1956.

Singing in the Shrouds. 1958.

False Scent. 1959.

Perspectives: The New Zealander and the Visual Arts. 1960.

Three-Act Special ⟨*A Wreath for Rivera, Spinsters in Jeopardy, Night at the Vulcan*⟩. 1960.

The Christmas Tree. 1962.

Another Three-Act Special ⟨*False Scent, Scales of Justice, Singing in the Shrouds*⟩. 1962.

Hand in Glove. 1962.

Dead Water. 1964.

New Zealand. 1964.

Black Beech and Honeydew: An Autobiography. 1965.

Killer Dolphin ⟨*Death at the Dolphin*⟩. 1966.

Curtain Calls ⟨*Enter a Murderer, Night at the Vulcan, Killer Dolphin*⟩. 1966.

Clutch of Constables. 1968.

When in Rome. 1970.

Tied Up in Tinsel. 1972.

Black as He's Painted. 1974.

Last Ditch. 1977.

Grave Mistake. 1978.

Grave Mistake and Two Other Great Mysteries ⟨*Spinsters in Jeopardy, Overture to Death*⟩. 1978.

Photo-Finish. 1980.

Photo-Finish and Two Other Great Mysteries ⟨*A Wreath for Rivera, Death and the Dancing Footman*⟩. 1980.

Light Thickens. 1982.

Five Complete Novels ⟨*Scales of Justice, Death of a Fool, Tied Up in Tinsel, Grave Mistake, Photo-Finish*⟩. 1983.

Collected Short Fiction. Ed. Douglas G. Greene. 1989.

⊞ ⊞ ⊞

Margaret Millar
1915–1994

MARGARET MILLAR was born Margaret Ellis Sturm on February 5, 1915, in Kitchener, Ontario, where her father was mayor. Margaret attended the local Kitchener-Waterloo Collegiate Institute, where she met Kenneth Millar, who would later become better known as the mystery novelist Ross Macdonald. She graduated from secondary school in 1933 and attended the University of Toronto, where she studied archeology. While reading in the public library in Toronto, Sturm spotted Kenneth Millar, whom she had not seen since secondary school. The two quickly became engaged, and Sturm dropped out of college and became Margaret Millar in June 1938.

For the next three years, the Millars lived in Toronto, where Kenneth taught high school while Margaret raised their daughter, Linda, and worked on her first novel, *The Invisible Worm* (1941), a mystery featuring the psychiatrist sleuth Dr. Paul Prye. The success of this novel and of the two following Prye books, *The Weak-Eyed Bat* and *The Devil Loves Me* (both 1942), enabled Kenneth to quit teaching, attend graduate school at the University of Michigan at Ann Arbor, and eventually publish his first novel in 1943.

In the mid-1940s Kenneth Millar left the university to serve in the navy; the Millars moved to Santa Barbara, where they made their permanent home. Margaret Millar continued to write prolifically, and in a career that spanned more than forty years she wrote twenty-one mystery novels (the most prominent of which are *The Iron Gates*, 1945; *Vanish in an Instant*, 1952; *Beast in View*, 1955; *The Listening Walls*, 1959; *A Stranger in My Grave*, 1960; and *Beyond This Point Are Monsters*, 1970) as well as four mainstream novels (*Experiment in Springtime*, 1947; *It's All in the Family*, 1948; *The Cannibal Heart*, 1949; and *Wives and Lovers*, 1954) and a study of the flora and fauna in the Santa Barbara area (*The Birds and Beasts Were There*, 1968).

The hallmark of Millar's work is a keen probing of psychological states, which often serve as more significant "clues" toward the solution of crimes than physical evidence. Many of her novels convey an air of brooding menace and depression that brings them close to the realm of horror. Millar received the Edgar Allan Poe Award from the Mystery Writers of America for *Beast in View*, served as president of that organization in 1957, and received its Grand Master award in 1982. Her novel *Rose's Last Summer* (1952) was made into a film by Alfred Hitchcock, and Millar was named Woman of the Year by the *Los Angeles Times* in 1965.

In addition to writing, the Millars became prominent environmental activists, spearheading efforts to preserve local wilderness areas and protesting oil spills. In 1970 their only daughter, Linda, died from a stroke; six years later Margaret Millar developed lung cancer and had to have part of a lung surgically removed (the Millars soon after became noted antismoking activists). In 1982 Millar lost her sight to an eye disease; her husband died the next year after a long bout with Alzheimer's disease. She continued writing, however, publishing her final novel, *Spider Webs*, in 1986. Margaret Millar died of heart failure in her home in Santa Barbara on March 26, 1994.

◈ *Critical Extracts*

WILL CUPPY   Now is the time for all good fans to realize that Margaret Millar is a humdinger, right up in the top rank of bafflers, including the British. We understand she used to live in Canada, but the main news is that she has followed up *The Invisible Worm* with an even better story ⟨*The Weak-Eyed Bat*⟩ about the sleuthing of Dr. Paul Prye, consulting psychiatrist, among some people who certainly needed his ministrations. You may not believe implicitly in Dr. Prye's brand of psychology—we do, ourself—but you're sure to get all worked up about the murderous proceedings at Muskoka, in Ontario, where three persons met violent ends in as pretty a puzzle as you'll be meeting. Miss Millar has a line of elegant semi-wacky fun, and it doesn't interfere with the excitement for one moment. Indeed, we're going overboard on this little number for its virtues in all branches of grown-up mystery. This department would not willingly hurt the feelings of any fellow creature, but this we do say: If you don't love *The Weak-Eyed Bat* it isn't Miss Millar's fault, really. Read it and see.

> Will Cuppy, [Review of *The Weak-Eyed Bat*], *New York Herald Tribune Books*, 22 February 1942, p. 18

JAMES MacBRIDE   No whodunit addict will pause for long over this smoothly written chiller ⟨*The Iron Gates*⟩, which has the shape of a detective novel and the style of a clinical report in abnormal (to put it mildly) psychology. Before he has turned to Page 2 the veteran will know just who dashed out the first Mrs. Morrow's brains with an axe in the snow-bound park; and even the rankest amateur can hardly get past the middle chapters without guessing who rubbed out the dope fiend with an overdose of morphine, drove the second Mrs. Morrow to madness by mailing her a dead man's finger, and polished off her old-maid sister-in-law when she asked one question too many. Of course none of this really matters, for the book is addressed to another type of addict, and relies on muted terror to keep up its tempo.

The psychothriller, or spook sonata played pianissimo, has had a mighty vogue these past years and the present author has won deserved plaudits as an expert in the field. But for this reviewer's money she has overreached herself in *The Iron Gates;* for him, at least, the book is too often grotesque rather than terrifying. Like many another writer fascinated by the psychoanalytic method, she has stayed too long in the clinic with her victims. The method is constantly getting in the way of the characters, reducing nearly all of them to stencils. ⟨. . .⟩ For all that, those who enjoy horror for its own sake will welcome her latest addition to the grisly shelf. Those who start reading after midnight have only themselves to blame if they wake up screaming.

> James MacBride, [Review of *The Iron Gates*], *New York Times Book Review*, 1 April 1945, p. 28

JAMES SANDOE   ⟨. . .⟩ Mrs. Margaret Millar ⟨. . .⟩ began a few years ago writing detective stories in which the sleuth was a psychiatrist, and ⟨. . .⟩ more recently has written two novels, both very highly praised, which attempt to combine the fascination of a clinical history with the charms of a detective story and its last minute surprise.

In *Wall of Eyes*, Mrs. Millar concerns herself with an oddly sorted household dominated by a blind and vindictive younger sister who holds her power by holding the family purse-strings. To be sure, this presumed an unsympathetic limpness on the part of her victims—the father, drained by his wife; the housekeeper-sister; the simple, hulking brother; the young and sensitive pianist—but Mrs. Millar's skill mitigated this in part. The blind tyrant is murdered and the ultimate object of the tale is the object of any detective story: to uncover the murderer.

But the method of the narrative is to present the tale through the perceptions of its characters and obviously, if she is to keep her murderer a secret, Mrs. Millar must at the same time lose her richest opportunity for exploring the murderer's mind. She must so sharply select his thought that she presents him piecemeal until, after all, it appears that what we have had is not a psychological study but some exceedingly adept sleight-of-hand. We have been in the fairly improbable position of sharing a murderer's mind fully, except for what after all must be occupying most of it—the matter of murder itself.

Mrs. Millar's latest novel, *The Iron Gates*, uses the same technique. Once more she is dealing with an uneasily ingrown family. At first the narrative is directed chiefly through the consciousness of Lucille Morrow, second wife of a distinguished gynecologist whose first wife has been hacked to death some years earlier while returning from an evening at her successor's house. The author establishes very deftly the pride of the second Mrs. Morrow in her possession of her husband, marks easily her humorous tyranny over him and the enmity felt toward her by her two stepchildren. And then, suddenly, after a ragged stranger's visit to deliver a box, Lucille disappears. Later she is found, raving. The second part of the novel describes her short stay behind the iron gates—the protecting gates—of Penwood asylum. But the gates are not impregnable, and Lucille's overwhelming fear that she will be murdered (why she fears we do not know; we share her fear but not its source) drives her to suicide. The third part of the novel is the unraveling, the diagnosis of madness and of murder's motive. Once more Mrs. Millar's concern has been to observe the workings of the terrified mind. But she has insisted, as well, upon hiding the causes of the terror so that she can surprise us at the last. And because of this, it would be a good deal more accurate to call her novel not a psychological novel but a tale of terror. For as a psychological study it is, by its own limitations, necessarily superficial.

James Sandoe, "Dagger of the Mind," in *The Art of the Mystery Story: A Collection of Critical Essays*, ed. Howard Haycraft (New York: Simon & Schuster, 1946), pp. 257–59

ANTHONY BOUCHER   The modern crime novel, at its highest peak, seeks to attain the values of the mainstream novel in its exploration of character and society, while retaining the elements of suspense, puzzlement and surprise which characterize the whodunit. It is a tricky proposition. When it comes off well, the results can be remarkable. Margaret Millar was one of the pioneers in this movement, with *Wall of Eyes* (1943), which she followed with many other books of unusual distinction, including the by-now-classic *Beast in View* (1955). But even by Mrs. Millar's unusually high standards, her latest, *The Fiend*, is something extraordinary. It may well be the finest example to date of the fusion of the novel of character and the puzzle of suspense.

The "fiend" is a borderline case who has served time for assaulting a little girl but who might yet be able to adjust himself to a normal life—if it were not for his obsessed attraction to 9-year-old Jessie. We come to know intimately poor Charlie and his problems, and Jessie (a delightful child) and the adults who surround her. When a crime finally occurs, the meticulously plotted puzzle and surprise serve to say something about these people (and about people, including us) that hardly any other device could have expressed so well. View *The Fiend* as a superb thriller, as a model of craftsmanship, or as a deeply disturbing psychological novel. From any viewpoint, it is a masterwork.

Anthony Boucher, [Review of *The Fiend*], *New York Times Book Review*, 21 June 1964, p. 20

JULIAN SYMONS   "Among the crime writers who have come into prominence since the war she has few peers, and no superior, in the art of bamboozlement. She presents us with a plausible criminal situation, builds it up to a climax of excitement, and then in the last few pages shakes the kaleidoscope and shows us an entirely different pattern from the one we have been so busily interpreting." I wrote these words about Margaret Millar more than a decade ago. They seem still perfectly true and yet to do her less than full justice, for Margaret (Sturm) Millar (1915–   ), the wife of Ross Macdonald, is also a most accomplished novelist, and it is this that should be mentioned first in any account of her writing. She is one of those novelists whose imagination is sparked off by the element of mystery, and the four "straight" novels which she published in the forties and early fifties are much less impressive as novels than her best mystery stories. As a mystery writer, too, her early books, which centered around a psychiatrist investigator called with infelicitous symbolism Dr. Paul Prye, were comparatively commonplace. It is the half-dozen books beginning with *Beast in View* (1955) that show the full scope of her skill as a novelist whose chosen theme is almost always a mystery with roots deeply hidden in the past.

This skill is shown at its finest in *How Like an Angel* (1962), which begins when Joe Quinn, a former casino cop at Reno who has lost his money gambling, lands up at the home of the True Believers in California, out in the bleak mountainous country forty-five miles from the nearest large town. The True Believers is a religious cult whose members believe that they are preparing for the ascension of a Tower which has five levels, of the earth, trees, mountains, sky, and at the top "the Tower of Heaven where the Master lives." A dotty cult, you might say, but nothing could better show the difference between the Golden Age story and the crime novel than the treatment given to similar groups by Allingham and Marsh. For them the cult serves merely as a background, ridiculous and slightly distasteful. Millar treats it seriously, describing its beliefs, physical situation, and adherents in detail. The practical good sense of Sister Blessing, the silence of Brother Tongue of Prophets, the excitement when a new convert arrives to join the slowly disintegrating group are conveyed with a powerful sense of pathos and absurdity joined to a respect for a way of life. The tension of the novel is partly created by the contrast between the simplicities of the group and the complexity of the investigation which Quinn undertakes on behalf of Sister Blessing into the background of Patrick O'Gorman, who apparently died five years earlier in a car accident. The puzzle is there all right, and its solution on the last page lives up to those phrases used about Millar's work, but by that time many readers will have become so much concerned with the fate of the characters that the problem itself is a secondary matter.

Julian Symons, *Mortal Consequences: A History—from the Detective Story to the Crime Novel* (New York: Harper & Row, 1972), pp. 191–93

DILYS WINN   ⟨. . .⟩ there are mystery readers who swear Mrs. Millar is more talented than, or at least as talented as, her husband Ross Macdonald (Kenneth Millar).

Mrs. Millar doesn't attract fans; she creates addicts. When her new hardcover comes out, they rush home to devour it. Dinner can wait. The dog can wait. They tell friends they'll call them back. That book gets finished in one sitting. And quoted from for months after.

Inevitably, a mind so trenchant arouses talk. And fantasies: *What do you think she's really like? Can you imagine the two of them in the same house? She's plotting to kill him, of course. And slowly, methodically, he's working toward a confrontation. Oh God, is it evil.*

Would you forgive them for being amiable and well-behaved?

Actually, Mr. and Mrs. Millar are shy people. He spaces each thought with a Pinteresque pause. She speaks a little too loud, a little too fast, in the manner of someone very timid who's trying to hide it. ⟨. . .⟩

She started writing when she was eight. Her first story concerned four sisters who were three months apart in age. "I was sixteen before I found out why everyone thought this was hilarious."

Her interest in mysteries piqued Ken's, though he preceded her in creating a private-eye sleuth: Lew Archer first appeared in '49; her Steve Pinata did not debut until 1960 (*A Stranger in My Grave*). Recently, in *Ask for Me Tomorrow* and *The Murder of Miranda*, she's featured Tom Aragon, a young lawyer protagonist.

Between the two books came a serious illness, in which Mrs. Millar underwent surgery for lung cancer. Though recovered, Mrs. Millar says: "Don't let anyone tell you you're not always looking over your shoulder after it. Because you are."

Miranda was finished during a violent attack of shingles. "It was a real test for her," says her husband. She says, "I wanted to see if I could do it. I remember sweating out that last page. I don't think anyone could tell from reading the book, though, what I was going through." True. Contrary to what you might expect, it happens to be very funny, with its maniacal poison-pen writer who cribs country club stationery for his efforts, its two meddlesome schoolgirls and its carefully preserved widow who views herself as if through a soft-focus lens. Says Margaret, "I used to write light books, then I got serious. I don't know why I'm funny again."

Actually, there has always been a bite to her work, an ability to nail a character so deftly, you think: Boy, I'm glad she's not *my* enemy. Her husband refers to this as "Margaret's somewhat sarcastic style." Her incisiveness is the result of hard work. "Some days, I'll write a sentence ten times. If I knew a lot of mystery writers who did that, then I think I'd read more of them. I can't stand sloppy writing and sloppy structure. I miss some of the older writers: Elizabeth Saxony-Holding, Helen McCloy, Charlotte Armstrong. I consider Christie an excellent plotter. When I read *Witness for the Prosecution,* I knew she really had a twisted little mind. I wished I had thought of it."

> Dilys Winn, "Margaret Millar and the Greatest Opening Lines Since 'In the Beginning . . .,' " *Murderess Ink: The Better Half of the Mystery* (New York: Workman Publishing Co., 1979), pp. 78–79

JOHN M. REILLY   *A Stranger in My Grave* and *Beyond This Point Are Monsters* use details of California race relations first of all to satisfy the requirement that the text should seem to refer to some reality other than itself. For that matter the appearance of conformity to extraliterary actuality is a basic explanation for the presence of all sorts of information about setting, the appearance of characters, and their behavior, not only in Millar's works but in all fiction within the broad boundaries of realism. On this level the aim is to create sufficient density to make the story seem plausible. The elemental appeal of believable detail makes it possible for some writers to lay into their texts well-researched data about the sights of distant localities and exotic behaviors, while other writers encourage imaginative participation in their tales by reporting the precise layout of the streets that typify the settings we ourselves live in. Somewhere in between lies Millar's creation of San Felice. At the beginning of her publishing career she specified her native Ontario, and the city of Toronto where she attended university, as the sites of her stories. These were adequate enough to provide the stories some place to happen without requiring Millar to give setting more than minimal attention. San Felice, however, represents an attempt to create a fictional setting for her more recent novels that will suggest relationship to other places of its type. San Felice seems to be located in the same part of California as Millar's home city of Santa Barbara, and the choice of its name that recalls the Spanish mission background of the state without specifying an actual city allows Millar to add a nearly symbolic dimension to her stories.

Readers can find the religious community in *How Like an Angel* or the evidence of California culture in other works intrinsically satisfying in the same way as Raymond Chandler's representation of the incongruous associations of sleaze and opulence in Los Angeles of the 1940s, or Ross Macdonald's revelation of meretricious contemporary Southern California. Still, social reference does not complete the function of Millar's detail, any more than it does Chandler's or Macdonald's. At their best the particulars of Millar's descriptions assume the function of units in a coded message from the character's inner being. For example, Lucille Morrow's estrangement from husband and family in *The Iron Gates* first becomes manifest through the description of a morning's routine in the household. Her husband's habitual inability to locate a scarf seems to reassure her of the household's normality. Gradually, though, the guilt symbolized in Lucille's dream of the night before arises in barely controlled anxiety when Andrew leaves the house without saying goodbye. She looks down at the memo pad she meant to use for planning menus and sees that she has drawn caricatures of Andrew's first wife. Absentmindedly she burns holes in the eyes with her cigarette. In this opening chapter the book's whole is adumbrated through concentration on details of mundane life that overlay the life beneath its surface like the ice on a Canadian lake. Similar illustrations can be found in each of Millar's novels; each shows the mark of her craft in providing the elemental appeal of a plausible reality at the same time as the characters, their manners, and their habitats unobtrusively reinforce the dynamics of plot.

John M. Reilly, "Margaret Millar," *10 Women of Mystery*, ed. Earl F. Bargainnier (Bowling Green, OH: Bowling Green University Popular Press, 1981), pp. 242–43

ROSS MACDONALD   My wife Margaret Millar keeps in a special box a copy of the Kitchener Collegiate Institute *Grumbler* in which ⟨my⟩ first story appeared. Her own first story, about a dying pianist in Spain, is in it, too. Elsewhere in that old school magazine, dogeared after nearly forty years, we can find more direct images of our adolescent lives. Margaret and I are there with the other members of the high school debating team, gazing confidently out of the picture on the page into eight more years of depression and six of war.

About six years later, in another city, I walked into the public library and found Margaret reading Thucydides in Greek. From then on, we saw each other nearly every day. I was just back from Europe, determined to become a writer. Margaret confessed she had the same ambition. We were married in June, 1938, the day after I graduated from college, and honeymooned at summer school in Ann Arbor. ⟨. . .⟩

We had a very Canadian eagerness to make something of ourselves. While I taught in our old high school in the winter, and studied at Ann Arbor in the summer, Margaret began to write mystery novels. Her books were humorous at first, then veered through the Gothic mode toward tragedy. Their success enabled me to leave high school teaching after two years and accept a full-time fellowship at the University of Michigan. Margaret's work was enabling to me in another way. By going on ahead and breaking trail, she helped to make it possible for me to become a novelist, as perhaps her life with me had helped to make it possible for her.

> Ross Macdonald, "Kenneth Millar/Ross MacDonald—A Checklist," *Self-Portrait: Ceaselessly into the Past* (Santa Barbara, CA: Capra Press, 1981), pp. 24–25

NICK KIMBERLEY   Margaret Millar's *Spider Webs* is a courtroom drama written with all the skill that 40 years of crime writing have given to Millar. Every character has an interest in the crime and putative criminal beyond the cause of simple justice. The defence lawyer, on the verge of admitting his gayness, wants his handsome black client as house-boy on his ranch. The court clerk, a fiercely independent woman, hopes that he'll be found innocent because she wants to marry him. Small wonder that the cocksure (and sure of his cock) Cully King demands to be found guilty: too many people want too much of a 'Not Guilty' verdict. By the end of this very funny novel, we don't know whether Cully's guilty or not, nor whether he'll survive for even ten seconds beyond the closing sentence. Millar tackles racism, sexuality, women's independence and a host of other 'problems', proving my point that the crime novel plays host to all our anxieties.

> Nick Kimberley, "Cops 'n' Proletarians," *New Statesman*, 6 March 1987, p. 39

MARILYN STASIO   Millar wrote her first novel, *The Invisible Worm*, in 1941; since then, she has written approximately thirty novels, most of them in the psychological-suspense genre. She is a subtle and, I think, genuinely original writer who creates suspenseful stories through her understanding of the pathology of crime. Her studies of the psychology of children are indeed extraordinary, and I direct you particularly to *Banshee*. Here she writes with exquisite sensitivity of a lonely child who invents playmates to console herself. The beauty of this portrait is its insistence on the child's honesty.

During an interview, I once asked her about her uncanny insights into the minds of her child characters. "Why is it that adults don't seem to take children seriously?" she asked me in return. I couldn't tell her, so she went on: "A kid will come home from school and tell his parents something important that happened; and the parents will say, 'Oh, the little bugger's lying again!' " This seemed to annoy her, because she said: "Adults always assume that the child is lying or having a fantasy. I, however, would always tend to believe the child and assume that the *adult* is having the fantasy."

I consider Millar one of the very few writers of suspense fiction who truly speaks for children's rights. Her young characters are always human beings, which is what makes her descriptions of childhood horrors so compelling. I think that Millar also understands that the essence of suspense involves the threat of evil to innocence—something which takes on extra *frisson* when the innocent is a child. There is also the drama, in suspense stories, when the victims are unable to communicate this threat of evil to those who might help them. With Millar's children, this becomes more poignant because they are doubly vulnerable, unable to communicate their fears to adults who either won't listen or won't believe them. That's genuine suspense—not those gory, pornographic, woman-loathing, slice-and-dice novels so often mislabeled "suspense" mysteries.

Marilyn Stasio, "A Sweep through the Subgenres," *The Sleuth and the Scholar: Origins, Evolution, and Current Trends in Detective Fiction*, ed. Barbara A. Rader and Howard G. Zettler (Westport, CT: Greenwood Press, 1988), p. 74

TONY HILFER   We can infer that the letter (quoted in *A Stranger in My Grave*) is from Daisy's father. But who is this? In chapter 4 Stan Fielding, alcoholic ex-husband of Daisy's mother, blows into town just long enough to get into trouble and is out again even before Daisy appears with the money to repay his bail bondsman, Stevens Pinata. This is how Daisy

happens on Pinata and launches her investigation. Fielding's voice is immediately recognizable to Daisy when she receives his call for help:

> "Hello, Daisy baby."
> Even if she hadn't recognized the voice she would have known
> who it was. No one ever called her Daisy baby except her father.

⟨. . . Fielding⟩ and Pinata talk as they await Daisy's money, even exchanging
confidences. Pinata is a foundling, so named because abandoned at a church
on Christmas Eve. He is not certain of his parents' ethnic identity. But
when Fielding commiserates—"Fancy that, not knowing who you are"—
he responds, "I know who *I* am . . . I just don't know who *they* were." But
by virtue of his name he has communally shared in discrimination against
Mexican-Americans. Fielding sees himself as opposite: "I know all about
my grandparents and great-grandparents and uncles and cousins, the whole
damn bunch of them. And it seems to me I got kind of lost in the shuffle.
My ex-wife was always telling me I had no ego, in a reproachful way, as if
an ego was something like a hat or pair of gloves which I'd carelessly lost
or misplaced." So we have two characters, Fielding and Daisy, who have
family but misplaced egos, and one, Pinata, who has a stable ego and a
misplaced family. He seems to have the best of it. ⟨. . .⟩

⟨. . .⟩ The reader will have realized before Pinata and Daisy that Camilla
has to be Daisy's biological father, author of the letter. Repudiated by
Mrs. Fielding out of sexual guilt and racial hysteria, killed, in ambiguous
circumstances, by Fielding on, of course, "The Day," Camilla is the absent
presence of this novel. Throughout the novel we have seen photos of
Camilla, have heard about him under his nickname of Curly, and, of course,
have been reading cumulatively the letter, sent to Daisy, intercepted and
hidden by her mother, and finally on the last two pages of the novel read
for the first time by Daisy and for the first time as a continuous, complete
discourse by the reader.

But Daisy does not, until the conclusion, know any of this. What she
discovered and subsequently repressed on "The Day" was that her husband
had had an affair culminating in illegitimate paternity. But the trick of it
is that there was no affair and no illegitimate child. Daisy was taken in by
an elaborate sham designed by her mother and husband to prove his potency
and her infertility, so as to divert her from the truth, which is that they
want her to be a child and not have one. As her mother sees it, a child
would be "marked by a stigma that must not be passed on." Paternity in

Sophocles' *Oedipus* is primarily a question of dynasty. In Millar's novel it is, in American fashion, a question of race. Daisy has been infantilized by husband, mother, and pseudofather to protect her from the realization of her blood relation to the racial other. Growing up, Daisy opts for the risks of realization against Pinata's advice that she not listen too hard or see too much. She is getting an idea of what she wants and Pinata is it. Pinata scrupulously reminds her of his lack of family or racial identity, but after her mother's overinvestment in these, she can feel the attraction in traveling light: family in this very American book (by an author of Canadian origin) can only impede identity; it is false consciousness institutionalized. The recognition scene to which she has been led by Camilla's ghost delivers her from the claustrophobic love and paranoiac pride of family. She cannot know what her children will look like or their precise racial mix, but to her they will be gifts and their name will of course be Pinata.

> Tony Hilfer, "Civilization and Its Discontents: Simenon, Millar, Highsmith, and Thompson," *The Crime Novel: A Deviant Genre* (Austin: University of Texas Press, 1990), pp. 114–16

CHARLES CHAMPLIN   In both 〈*A Beast in View* and *Beyond This Point Are Monsters*〉, the dark secrets of deeply disturbed psyches are carefully concealed until the very last stunning paragraphs. 〈Millar〉 had a magician's gift for misdirection, but she played fair and told no literary lies. Her books make being deceived a rare pleasure.

Millar's books are entertainments, but they are placed in a precisely observed and described world, most often Santa Barbara and Southern California generally. And she is no less convincing about the inner lives of migrant farm workers than of their well-heeled but not necessarily well-adjusted employers.

Her villains are monstrous indeed, innocuous as they may seem at first glance, and they are thrown into even sharper relief because they are surrounded by (or at least brush against) characters who represent the human decencies at their best. Pure good and pure evil were not really part of her equation, although the evil is undoubtedly high octane.

Her work reveals the author. In private, Maggie Millar was funny, feisty, a wickedly keen observer of the world she lived in, a fighter for the environment and other good causes, with a well-developed sense of outrage at injustices wherever she found them. And, not least, she was uncommonly brave in the face of a siege of medical problems. When she lost a lung to cancer, her complaint to a reporter was that it affected her buoyancy; the first time she resumed her daily swim at the Coral Casino, she sank to the bottom. ⟨. . .⟩

Maggie Millar can be imagined from her novels, which are full of clues to her intelligence, her compassion, her abiding concerns, her sly wit, her love of people and language. The novels we have are a handsome and enduring legacy, but it is a powerful sadness to think there will be no more.

Charles Champlin, "She Made Being Deceived a Pleasure," *Los Angeles Times Book Review*, 24 April 1994, p. 10

Bibliography

The Invisible Worm. 1941.

The Weak-Eyed Bat. 1942.

The Devil Loves Me. 1942.

Wall of Eyes. 1943.

Fire Will Freeze. 1944.

The Iron Gates: A Psychological Novel. 1945.

Experiment in Springtime. 1947.

It's All in the Family. 1948.

The Cannibal Heart. 1949.

Do Evil in Return. 1950.

Rose's Last Summer. 1952.

Vanish in an Instant. 1952.

Wives and Lovers. 1954.

Beast in View. 1955.

An Air That Kills ⟨The Soft Talkers⟩. 1957.

The Listening Walls. 1959.

A Stranger in My Grave. 1960.

How Like an Angel. 1962.

The Fiend. 1964.

The Birds and Beasts Were There. 1968.

Beyond This Point Are Monsters. 1970.

Ask for Me Tomorrow. 1976.

The Murder of Miranda. 1979.
Mermaid. 1982.
Early Millar: The First Stories of Ross Macdonald and Margaret Millar. 1982.
Banshee. 1983.
Spider Webs. 1986.

Ellery Queen

ELLERY QUEEN is the joint pseudonym of cousins Manfred Bennington Lee and Frederic Dannay. Lee was born Manford Lepofsky in Brooklyn, New York, on January 11, 1905, to middle-class Jewish parents. At an early age he developed a passion for reading as a refuge from his urban surroundings. Although he later showed an aptitude for music and briefly led a jazz combo, he determined to become a writer and nursed this interest through his college years at New York University.

Dannay was born Daniel Nathan on October 20, 1905, just five blocks from Lee's home. When he was less than a year old, his family moved to Elmira, in upstate New York, and until 1917 he knew his cousin only as a summertime visitor to his family's home. That year, however, Dannay's family returned to Brooklyn, and he began attending Boys' High School in Brooklyn with Lee. While recovering from an illness in the winter of 1917, Dannay read Conan Doyle's *Adventures of Sherlock Holmes*, an event that initiated his lifelong enthusiasm for mystery fiction and kindled his own ambition to write.

Lee was writing publicity material for a film company based in New York and Dannay was working as a copywriter and art editor for an advertising firm when, in the fall of 1928, they responded to a contest sponsored by *McClure's* magazine offering a $7,500 prize for a mystery novel. Over three months, the two worked together in their spare time to write *The Roman Hat Mystery*, a novel that featured a debonair and sophisticated amateur detective named Ellery Queen who assists his police inspector father in solving a sordid murder. The novel won first prize, but the magazine went bankrupt before the two could collect. When the book publisher that cosponsored the contest brought the book out in hardcover the following year, the cousins decided it should be issued under the pseudonym Ellery Queen, in the belief that readers would more likely remember a novel purportedly written by its hero. Acclaim for the first three Ellery Queen novels convinced the two to begin writing full-time in 1931. Lee and Dannay promoted further interest in their writings by keeping Queen's real identity a secret, and occasionally donning black masks to appear as Queen in public.

For much of the 1930s, Lee and Dannay featured Ellery Queen in a series of best-selling novels and stories written in the tradition of S. S. Van Dine's tales of Philo Vance. The Queen stories became known for their complex plots, rigorous logic, and formal challenges to the reader by the character Queen (whom Lee and Dannay depicted as a writer of mystery tales) to solve the mysteries through deductive reasoning. During the same period, Lee and Dannay wrote a quartet of novels under the pseudonym Barnaby Ross featuring Drury Lane, a former Shakespearean actor turned detective. In their erudition and elegance, the Queen and Ross novels contrasted sharply wtih the hard-boiled school of detective fiction then evolving in the popular fiction magazines. They were recognized as original variants on the classic tale of deduction and helped cement Lee and Dannay's reputation as the most literary mystery writers of the day.

Between 1939 and 1948 Lee and Dannay scripted the "Adventures of Ellery Queen" for radio and developed Queen's personality through a series of mature novels that increasingly reflected the changing social and political climate, as well the authors' own experiences in Hollywood and the publishing world. They were already prolific editors, collectors, and bibliographers of mystery fiction when, in 1941, they began editing *Ellery Queen's Mystery Magazine* (EQMM), a successful follow-up to their short-lived efforts as editors of *Mystery League* magazine between 1933 and 1934. Largely through Dannay's efforts, the magazine launched the careers of many writers and expanded the literary horizons of the mystery genre. Early in the 1940s the two also helped found the Mystery Writers of America.

By the end of World War II Ellery Queen had become a literary and publishing phenomenon. For the next thirty years, scores of volumes appeared under their name: novels (*Calamity Town*, 1942; *Ten Days' Wonder*, 1948; *The Glass Village*, 1954; *And on the Eighth Day*, 1964; *A Fine and Private Place*, 1971), short story collections (*The Case Book of Ellery Queen*, 1945; *Calendar of Crime*, 1952; *Queen's Bureau of Investigation*, 1954), critical studies (*Queen's Quorum*, 1951), and, especially, an enormous number of anthologies, many of them consisting of stories culled from EQMM. Ellery Queen also wrote a number of detective plays (most published in EQMM). Beginning in the 1940s, Ellery Queen leased out their pseudonym to other writers; in particular, a whole series of young adult volumes were published under the name Ellery Queen, Jr.

Lee married Kaye Brinker in 1942 and eventually moved to Roxbury, Connecticut, where he raised eight children. Dannay settled in Larchmont, New York, with his second wife, wrote a novel, *The Golden Summer*, under the name Daniel Nathan in 1953, and served as visiting professor of creative writing at the University of Texas at Austin in 1958–59. The two helped sustain the Ellery Queen industry until Lee's death from a heart attack on April 3, 1971. Dannay continued editing and writing but produced no other Ellery Queen tales before his death on September 3, 1982.

⊠ *Critical Extracts*

WILL CUPPY   To come right out and confess, in our time we have suffered over Ellery Queen in his great doubling act as author (pseudonymous) and hero (analytico-deductive detective) of some eight bestselling mysteries. We have deplored his Philo Vance-ish brandishing of culture and refinement and we have ached dully at the worst of his wit and humor; as for his picture on the blurb, complete with black mask (people don't do that, Mr. Queen!), you wouldn't believe how it used to infuriate us. It still does. In a word, we have been rather difficult about the whole matter.

Perhaps we're growing mellow. At least, we should like to record that our feelings about Ellery and his father and his books are fundamentally kind, in that we wouldn't bother to apply the sterner whips of our intellect to most detectives—it would be hitting below the belt. What is more, from the point of view of fandom, the virtues of Queen bafflers more than atone for the slight faults that happen to enrage this department, personally; they are meaty, thoroughly worked out as problems (whether you believe it or not) and generally way ahead of the average trade goods. After all, Mr. Queen's occasional highbrowism (and this includes the blue jokes) is only put in to impress the highbrows—and, by gosh, it sure does impress them. ("Brilliant, thrilling, ingenious."—William Lyon Phelps.)

The big news today ⟨in *The Chinese Orange Mystery*⟩ is the murder of a total stranger at the Hotel Chancellor while calling upon Donald Kirk, a philatelist—Donald even has an example of a rare Chung Hua Ming Kuo, the lucky devil. Means of death—blow on the head. Corpse's clothes put on backward and suspicion pointing more or less to a sizeable group of Kirk's friends. Who ate the second tangerine? Our author stirs up a really exciting case, which Ellery finally solves with a demonstration of the human intellect which we found too optimistic; it causes his father, dear old Inspector Queen, to exclaim, "Well, I'll be double-damned." Meanwhile you get generous quantities of stamp lore, tangerine lore, love and sundry.

We're not saying that Ellery, the hero, has totally reformed. The mere sight of a butler named Hubbell tempts him to say, "Hubbell, Hubbell, boil and bubble, or is it toil and trouble. . . . How does the witches' chant go?" Also, "I'm a bounder. That is I bound. Or perhaps I should say that I'm a rebounder, Hubbell. Yes, yes: I rebound after I'm thrown." And Ellery the author, in his challenge to the reader on page 252, remarks in the course of a friendly chat to us fans, "Longa dies non sedavit vulnera mentis, either, believe me." As we muffed that completely, it didn't help us in our determination to be nicer about Queens and Queenishness.

Will Cuppy, [Review of *The Chinese Orange Mystery*], *New York Herald Tribune Books*, 24 June 1934, p. 6

NICHOLAS BLAKE   Mr. Queen is another one who does us proud. *Half-Way House* is, I think, his best book since *The Roman Hat Mystery*. His style, which had lately tended to be rather too luscious for our sober English taste, is considerably more restrained; the plot is cunningly developed and apparently most complex, yet all hinges on one small obvious detail which Mr. Queen forces upon your attention time and again with the innocent expression of a poker player putting across a double-bluff. Joseph Wilson, a commercial traveller, is found murdered in a lonely shack. It soon becomes evident that he has been leading a double life: both Lucy Wilson and Mrs. Gimball, a New York Society woman, claim him for husband. Lucy, in whose favor Wilson had taken out a large insurance policy, is tried and convicted. But Mr. Queen finally convinces Andrea, Mrs. Gimball's attractive daughter, that honesty is the best policy and with the aid of the information she gives him manages to trap the real murderer in the nick of time. I would call your attention to the curious assortment of objects found in the same room as the corpse: a burnt cork, the stubs of a number of paper matches, a new writing-set, an empty fountain-pen, the precious stone out of a ring, and a complete absence of mud or tobacco. These are all important clues; but one of them, or perhaps two in conjunction, will give you the murderer. Mr. Queen has always been a bit of an exhibitionist in his final unmasking of the criminal; this time, at least, the convention justifies itself, for it produces a succession of thrills that will cause your spine to tingle pleasurably for a good quarter of an hour afterwards.

Nicholas Blake, "Leading You a Dance," Spectator, 25 September 1936, p. 514

DOROTHY PARKER   Though you may not have accounts of factual crimes every day, life can still be sweet. For fictional murders valiantly hold their own, from the stunning works of the mighty Dashiell Hammett, on down, down, down. And long before you get into the down, down, downs—tall among the very highest-ups, in fact—are the stories of Ellery Queen ⟨. . .⟩

Ellery Queen, the hero, is not a detective so much as a detector; that is he comes in when everything is thoroughly balled up and straightens it out, just for the love of justice. He is, I think, the most attractive of current investigators; though he must watch a nasty little habit of quoting from the classics and dropping into foreign tongues, which is creeping up on him. He is slightly built and a wearer, perpetually, of pince-nez, but quick and lethal with his fists, especially if he feels that something impolite has been said to his father, Inspector Queen of the New York Police Force. Women sigh and swoon for the young man, but he has yet to respond. His heart, so far as I can gather, belongs to Daddy. Not the least interesting passages in the Ellery Queen books are those that show glimpses of the home life of father and son, who live in a brownstone on the Upper West Side—I believe they have separate suites, but this has not been entirely clear—are served by a treasure of a sixteen-year-old houseboy named Djuna, and drink great pitchers of lemonade on hot nights. The reader would like to see more of this menage, perhaps, but, despite its fascination, it would hold up the rush of the story. And the rush of the story is, almost unfailingly, magnificent.

The latest Queen book is, actually, three books bound into one under the title of *The New York Murders*. (Ellery Queen deals entirely in murders; you are not fobbed off, as you are with Mr. Leslie Charteris's *Saint*, with pablum about the rape of the dowager's emeralds, or the theft of the blueprint of the newest submarine.) These three murder novels seem to me the best of the Queen stories, which, on the word of one who has watched closely for years, is serious praise. They have speed, ingenuity, and really brilliant examples of detection, and the ending consists more often of a double surprise than a single one.

Dorothy Parker, "Dorothy Parker on Books," *Esquire* 51, No. 1 (January 1959): 20–21

ANTHONY BOUCHER   Queen, one would gather, has had a marked influence on American mystery writers: almost every book of crime short stories in the past twenty years has been in whole or in part from E.Q.M.M., and such collections as the Mystery Writers of America's annual anthology are normally dominated by E.Q.M.M. stories. But he has yet to exert much influence on his fellow editors, who either fail to notice how he attains his success (his subscription list is some thirteen times as large as that of his nearest rival) or are just plain unable to emulate him.

This success of Queen's has not been solely with the reader of bookform mysteries. The quality of the fiction that he prints is such as to attract many admirers of the short story otherwise uninterested in crime. E.Q.M.M. stories appear regularly on Martha Foley's Roll of Honor and sometimes even in the contents of her annual *Best American Short Stories*. E.Q.M.M. has published every important crime writer who ever wrote a short story. (Well, there is one exception: Raymond Chandler; but a Chandler story is now in inventory awaiting publication.) It has also published an unbelievable number of Big Names from mainstream fiction not usually associated with crime, including twenty-seven Pulitzer and eight Nobel prize-winners.

Some of these are frequent E.Q.M.M. contributors—Mark Van Doren, for example, whose subtle and distinguished fiction usually appears either in some rarefied literary quarterly or in E.Q.M.M. Others, such as Sinclair Lewis, Arthur Miller or George Bernard Shaw, are fruits of Queen's indefatigable research.

For if Queen has a weakness, it is his crusading desire to prove that every significant writer who ever existed has written at least one story that can be subsumed into the crime-mystery category. An astonishing number, to be sure, really have; but Queen's Procrustean efforts to fit all writers to his deathbed threaten at times to turn E.Q.M.M. into a magazine of general fiction—and, on second thought, is this necessarily a bad thing?

Anthony Boucher, "There Was No Mystery in What the Crime Editor Was After," *New York Times Book Review*, 26 February 1961, p. 50

KINGSLEY AMIS   Hercule Poirot, Miss Marple, Ellery Queen, Inspector—later Assistant Commissioner Sir John—Appleby deserve, or at any rate will get, shorter shrift from me. I have never understood the fame of the two Agatha Christie characters, both of whom seem straight out of stock—Poirot the excitable but shrewd little foreigner, Marple the innocent, helpless-looking old lady with the keen blue eyes. And although some of the early Christies (*Why Didn't They Ask Evans?* for instance) had splendidly ingenious plots, the later Poirots and Marples have become thinned down, not surprising in a writer who has been hard at work for 45 years. Queen, who has been around just since 1929, has had his ingenuities, too, but he is too slight a figure to sustain more than a tiny corner of Holmes' mantle, acting mostly as a sounding board for the other characters, a camera for the story, and a mouthpiece when the author wants to chat things over with the reader. Ellery of the silver-colored eyes is seldom much more than an extension of the plot.

Kingsley Amis, "My Favorite Sleuths," *Playboy* 13, No. 12 (December 1966): 347

FRED ERISMAN   The plot of *And on the Eighth Day* is complex, with eerie overtones of "Young Goodman Brown." An exhausted Ellery Queen, returning to New York from a screen-writing stint in wartime Holly-wood (the story takes place in 1944), finds himself lost somewhere in California or Nevada—the exact location is never specified. He chances upon Otto Schmidt's "End-of-the-World Store," where he is given directions to lead him back to the main highway. The directions, however, lead Ellery not to civilization, but to the lost community of Quenan. Quenan, a Christian-communist society isolated since 1874, looks upon him as *Elroi Quenan*, the stranger whose coming has been foretold, and accepts him as an honored guest.

In Quenan, Ellery, though haunted by premonitions of impending disaster, soon comes to appreciate the organicism and innocence of the community. It is an agrarian-handicraft society, governed by a "Crownsil [sic] of Twelve," whose archetypal nature is emphasized by the members' always being referred to by their occupations: The Growther, The Miller, The Carpentersmith, and so on. The society's only contact with the outside world comes through the irregular treks of The Teacher and The Storesman to Otto Schmidt's store, where they buy such things as the community cannot produce for itself. Thus sealed off from the world for seventy years, innocent of all save the most rudimentary technology, Quenan has achieved utopia. As Ellery muses, "Where were art, and music, and literature, and science in this capsule in space-time? They were not here. But also not here—so far as he could tell—were discontent, and hatred, and vice, and greed, and war. The truth, it seemed to him, was that here in the lost valley, under the leadership of the all-wise patriarch, existed an earthly Eden whose simple guides were love of neighbours, obedience to the law, humility, mercy, and kindness."

Such perfection, however, cannot last. Ellery's premonitions come to fruition with the murder of the Storesman, and Quenan loses its innocence. Ellery investigates the murder, and accuses the one toward whom all the clues point. The Crownsil sits in judgment and condemns the accused to death, whereupon Ellery, reviewing the evidence, discovers a sophisticated frameup. His frantic arguments go unheeded; an innocent man is executed for the sins of another (and those of the community), and Ellery, heartsick, prepares to leave Quenan. As he leaves, he witnesses the crash of a crop-dusting airplane, whose pilot parachutes to safety.

In this man, literally dropping from the heavens, is the salvation of Quenan. He is Manuel Aquina, "a young man, tall and slender and dark, with curly black hair and aquiline features, quite handsome in an odd way; although he had obviously shaved that morning, his gaunt cheeks showed the foreshadows of a heavy beard. I've seen this fellow somewhere, Ellery thought. . . ." Aquina, a conscientious objector and obvious Christ-figure, goes to Quenan, presumably to be adopted as its leader. Ellery, purged of his horrors, continues his return to civilization, thinking, "It's more than reason can bear. . . . Too much, an infinite complexity beyond the grasp of man. Acknowledge. Acknowledge and depart." The interlocking relations of God and nature in the Southwest heal the sickened man from the East.

Although notable as a detective novel, *And on the Eighth Day* offers even greater riches for the student of utopias. It describes, obviously, a Christian utopia, staggered by its contacts with the outside world (the events leading to the murder begin at Schmidt's store). But more than that, it describes a uniquely Southwestern utopia, as Ellery Queen, the New Yorker who could not find salvation in the West, finds comfort and sustenance in a life closely attuned to the rhythm of Southwestern nature. That he must leave is Ellery's personal tragedy; that he has seen perfection is his salvation. He must return to the corrupt East, but he takes with him a new sense of proportion gained from the uncorrupted Southwest.

Fred Erisman, " 'Where We Plan to Go': The Southwest in Utopian Fiction," *Southwestern American Literature* 1, No. 3 (September 1971): 140–41

FRANCIS M. NEVINS, JR.   Not only is *The Origin of Evil* by far the best of Ellery Queen's Hollywood novels, it's one of his best books of the Fifties also. The plot is full of distinctively Queenian elements—murder by psychological shock as in *The Door Between,* a killer who uses another person as his living weapon as in *Ten Days' Wonder,* the solution within a solution, the "negative clue" device, and the series of seemingly absurd events connected by a hidden logic as in *Ten Days' Wonder, Cat of Many Tails* and *Double, Double.* The religious motifs of *Ten Days' Wonder* return in low-key with the appearance of not one but two Diedrich-like manipulators, each playing upon the other, one referred to as "the invisible god" and the other as "the god of events." As in *Ten Days' Wonder* the truth turns out to be devilishly complex; in fact my only serious objection to the story is that the murderer's plot *requires* the presence of a master detective to unravel certain complexities the killer wants to be discovered, although Ellery's entrance into the case is totally unexpected and accidental.

But, as usual since *Calamity Town,* Queen is up to more than just a good detective novel. The subject of *The Origin of Evil* is clearly stated in the title, and the answer to the title's implicit question is, quite simply, human nature. As in *The Cat of Many Tails,* Queen's meaning is most accessible in a scene wherein Ellery receives instruction. Near the end of Chapter VII he approaches Collier, the old retired naturalist-adventurer, and asks him bluntly: "Have you any idea what this is all about, Mr. Queen. . . . It's about corruption and wickedness. It's about greed and selfishness and guilt and violence and hatred and lack of self-control. It's about black secrets and black hearts, cruelty, confusion, fear. It's about not making the best of things, not being satisfied with what you have, and always wanting what you haven't. It's about envy and suspicion and malice and lust and nosiness and drunkenness and unholy excitement and a thirst for hot running blood. It's about man, Mr. Queen."

Of course this speech is not the only indication of Queen's intent. It's no accident that every major character in the novel except Ellery and his nemesis is compared over and over again to various animals, nor that the imagery of the jungle recurs every few pages. Both the killer's adopted name and his plot are grounded in Darwinian biology with its themes of endless struggle for survival and of "nature red in tooth and claw." The player on the other side turns out to be quite literally "the old Adam," and at the end of the novel the old Adam is not only unbeaten but has become the intimate and familiar of Ellery himself. This union of apparent opposites seems especially apt when we recall Ellery's all-too-human reaction of moralistic outrage and contempt when he learned of Delia's sexual habits, despite his very clear desire to have her himself. No man can call another animal, for the same nature stains us all. Or, in the words of old Collier, "People mean trouble.... There's too much trouble in this world."

But the major trouble with this book is that Queen's treatment of the Korean war and of impending nuclear holocaust is completely at odds with his grim view of man. The conflict in Korea is portrayed not as one more monument to man's power-hunger and blood-lust but in the standard propaganda terms of the filthy Commies from the North attacking their peaceful democratic neighbors in the South. And the threat of World War III is presented literally as a hoax, a publicity gimmick dreamed up by a young would-be actor to get himself into the movies (the actor quite fittingly winds up volunteering for the crusade against evil in Korea). We must remember, of course, that in those days when Joe McCarthy ruled the land, thousands of Americans had their careers ruined for raising doubts about matters such as these; and it seems clear that in 1951 Queen was not yet ready to put his body on the line. So if *The Origin of Evil* fails to cohere thematically, the reign of terror is more to blame than Queen.

Francis M. Nevins, Jr., *Royal Bloodline: Ellery Queen, Author and Detective* (Bowling Green, OH: Bowling Green University Popular Press, 1974), pp. 147–51

STEFANO BENVENUTI and GIANNI RIZZONI   The discovery of the real name of Ellery Queen's creators sheds light on some of the famous investigator's psychological characteristics and explains, in part, the reason for his massive success in America. The detective Ellery Queen provides an example of the American dream, a success story to which all aspire. His father, Richard Queen, is a self-made, middle-class citizen who has fought to improve his social status throughout his life. He has succeeded,

but only by killing himself with work and sacrificing any other aspiration
on the altar of fundamental needs: a house, a secure job, his family needs,
a little money in the bank. In short, Richard Queen is a first-generation
American struggling for dignity and a sense of well-being. Ellery Queen,
on the other hand, is of the second generation, completely Americanized
in character and at ease in the American metropolis. His father has handed
down all his own intellectual aspirations: a cultivated upbringing, a university
education, a good social position, a comfortable life, personal elegance,
refinement, and distinguished manners. Ellery Queen seems, in European
eyes, rather affected, clumsy, and ridiculous rather than elegant, refined, or
distinguished. However, to the middle-class American he is the ideal refined
man, and as such is the personification of middle-class aspirations.

> Stefano Benvenuti and Gianni Rizzoni, *The Whodunit: An Informal History of Detective
> Fiction* (1979), tr. Anthony Eyre (1980; rpt. New York: Collier, 1981), pp. 97–98

ANTHONY J. MAZELLA   Where has Ellery Queen gone? Perhaps
an examination of *The French Powder Mystery* may offer some clues. This
is the second Ellery Queen novel. It is set in Manhattan—the major scene
of the crime being French's department store on Fifth Avenue and 39th
St. And it deals with several murders, those of Mrs. Winifred French and
her daughter Bernice Carmody, both of whom were ensnared in the deadly
machinations of a notorious drug ring. The novel has an "annotated" cast
of characters, a map, and the familiar "Challenge to the Reader" ⟨. . .⟩ It
also plays scrupulously fair with the reader. And that may be the chief
problem. When I worked with this novel in my "Mystery Story" course
during a recent semester, every student in class had deduced the identity
of the killer, some having done so fairly early in the novel, whereas virtually
no one had been as successful with Agatha Christie's classic, *The Murder
of Roger Ackroyd*. The clues, the action of the novel, the progression of the
plot, the details of characterization—all led to one person. Indeed, some
students cited merely a single piece of evidence as conclusive, evidence
pointedly alluded to in the title. If the revelation at the end of the novel
is to prove anticlimactic (the very last words are the name of the killer), then
the rest of the novel must consequently be rewarding. Students, however, felt
that the novel was padded, a criticism they also leveled at Dorothy Sayers'
Clouds of Witness. If the denouement isn't startling, and the novel feels
padded, perhaps a redeeming feature is its style, much as Raymond Chandler's

use of words, described as having a "raw richness of simile seldom seen in a detective yarn" by Will Cuppy in the *Encyclopedia of Mystery and Detection*, helped readers through his convoluted plots, so convoluted that not even Chandler knew who killed Owen Taylor, the Sternwoods' chauffeur, in *The Big Sleep*.

An analysis of several sections of *The French Powder Mystery* reveals a weakness in style as well. Consider the discovery of the corpse of Mrs. French in the store's window on Fifth Avenue:

> What they [the onlookers] saw was a marvel indeed—so unexpected, so horrible, so grotesque that at the instant of its occurrence faces froze into masks of stunned incredulity. It was like a moment snatched out of an unbelievable nightmare . . . For, as the model pushed the ivory button, a section of the wall slid outward and downward with a swift noiseless movement, two small wooden legs unfolded and shot out of the forepart of the bedstead, the bed settled to a horizontal position—and the body of a woman, pale-faced, crumpled, distorted, her clothes bloody in two places, fell from the silken sheet to the floor at the model's feet.

The unexpected setting for the murder is a brilliant stroke, but the adjectives in triplicate vitiate the excitement: "unexpected," "horrible," "grotesque"; "two," "small," "wooden"; "pale-faced," "crumpled," "distorted." The cliches, "unbelievable nightmare," "faces froze into masks," detract as well. ⟨. . .⟩

Similarly disturbing for a contemporary audience may be *The Roman Hat Mystery*. In this novel about the murder of a noisome blackmailer in the middle of a performance at the Roman Theatre in New York, a novel dominated by Inspector Queen, who is endearing but comes across as doddering, the murderer's history is described at the climax of the novel as "a sordid story . . . to make it short and ugly, [the killer] has a strain of negroid blood in his veins."

Anthony J. Mazella, "Whatever Happened to Ellery Queen?" *Columbia Library Columns* 35, No. 2 (February 1986): 29–31, 33

◈ *Bibliography*

Works by Dannay and Lee:
The Roman Hat Mystery. 1929.

The French Powder Mystery. 1930.

The Dutch Shoe Mystery. 1931.

The Greek Coffin Mystery. 1932.

The Tragedy of X. 1932.

The Egyptian Cross Mystery. 1932.

The Tragedy of Y. 1932.

The American Gun Mystery ⟨*Death at the Rodeo*⟩. 1933.

The Tragedy of Z. 1933.

The Siamese Twin Mystery. 1933.

Drury Lane's Last Case: The Tragedy of 1599. 1933.

The Chinese Orange Mystery. 1934.

The Adventures of Ellery Queen. 1934.

The Ellery Queen Omnibus ⟨*The French Powder Mystery, The Dutch Shoe Mystery, The Greek Coffin Mystery*⟩. 1934.

The Spanish Cape Mystery. 1935.

Halfway House. 1936.

The Ellery Queen Omnibus ⟨*The Roman Hat Mystery, The French Powder Mystery, The Egyptian Cross Mystery*⟩. 1936.

The Door Between. 1937.

The Devil to Pay. 1938.

Ellery Queen's Challenge to the Reader (editor). 1938.

E. Q.'s Big Book ⟨*The Siamese Twin Mystery, The Greek Coffin Mystery*⟩. 1938, 1944 (as *Ellery Queen's Mystery Parade*).

The Four of Hearts. 1938.

The Dragon's Teeth. 1939.

The New Adventures of Ellery Queen. 1940, 1940 (as *More Adventures of Ellery Queen*).

101 Years' Entertainment: The Great Detective Stories 1841–1941 (editor). 1941, 1946.

Ellery Queen's Adventure Omnibus ⟨*The Adventures of Ellery Queen, The New Adventures of Ellery Queen*⟩. 1941, 1949 (as *The Case Book of Ellery Queen*).

Calamity Town. 1942.

Sporting Blood: The Great Sports Detective Stories (editor). 1942.

The Detective Short Story: A Bibliography. 1942.

The Female of the Species: The Great Women Detectives and Criminals ⟨*Ladies in Crime*⟩ (editor). 1943.

There Was an Old Woman. 1944.

The Misadventures of Sherlock Holmes (editor). 1944.

Best Stories from Ellery Queen's Mystery Magazine (editor). 1944.

The Adventures of Sam Spade and Other Stories by Dashiell Hammett (editor). 1944.

The Case Book of Ellery Queen. 1945.

Rogues' Gallery: The Great Criminals of Modern Fiction (editor). 1945.

The Murderer Is a Fox. 1945.

The Continental Op by Dashiell Hammett (editor). 1945.

To the Queen's Taste: The First Supplement to 101 Years' Entertainment, *Consisting of the Best Stories Published in the First Five Years of* Ellery Queen's Mystery Magazine (editor). 1946.

Hammett Homicides by Dashiell Hammett (editor). 1946.

The Queen's Awards (editor). 1946–57. 12 vols.

Murder by Experts (editor). 1947.

Dead Yellow Women by Dashiell Hammett (editor). 1947.

The Riddles of Hildegarde Withers by Stuart Palmer (editor). 1947.

Dr. Fell, Detective, and Other Stories by John Dickson Carr (editor). 1947.

The Department of Dead Ends by Roy Vickers (editor). 1947.

The Case Book of Mr. Campion by Margery Allingham (editor). 1947.

Ten Days' Wonder. 1948.

Twentieth Century Detective Stories (editor). 1948, 1964.

Nightmare Town by Dashiell Hammett (editor). 1948.

Cops and Robbers by O. Henry (editor). 1948.

Cat of Many Tails. 1949.

Double, Double: A New Novel of Wrightsville. 1950.

The Literature of Crime: Stories by World-Famous Authors (editor). 1950.

The Creeping Siamese by Dashiell Hammett (editor). 1950.

The Monkey Murder and Other Hildegarde Withers Stories by Stuart Palmer (editor). 1950.

Queen's Quorum: A History of the Detective-Crime Short Story as Revealed by the 106 Most Important Books Published in This Field Since 1845. 1951, 1969.

The Origin of Evil. 1951.

The King Is Dead. 1952.

Calendar of Crime. 1952.

The Scarlet Letters. 1953.

The Glass Village. 1954.

Queen's Bureau of Investigation. 1954.

Inspector Queen's Own Case: November Song. 1956.

Wrightsville Murders ⟨*Calamity Town, The Murderer Is a Fox, Ten Days' Wonder*⟩. 1956.

The Hollywood Murders ⟨*The Devil to Pay, The Four of Hearts, The Origin of Evil*⟩. 1957.

In the Queen's Parlor and Other Leaves from the Editors' Notebook. 1957.

The Finishing Stroke. 1958.

The New York Murders ⟨*Cat of Many Tails, The Scarlet Letters, The American Gun Mystery*⟩. 1958.

Ellery Queen's Mystery Annual (editor). 1958–61. 4 vols.

Ellery Queen's Anthology (editor). 1959–71. 13 vols.

The XYZ Murders ⟨*The Tragedy of X, The Tragedy of Y, The Tragedy of Z*⟩. 1961.

The Bizarre Murders ⟨*The Siamese Twin Mystery, The Chinese Orange Mystery, The Spanish Cape Mystery*⟩. 1961.

A Man Named Thin and Other Stories by Dashiell Hammett (editor). 1962.

Ellery Queen's To Be Read Before Midnight (editor). 1962.

Ellery Queen's Mystery Mix (editor). 1963.

The Player on the Other Side. 1963.

Ellery Queen's Anthology: Mid-Year Edition (editor). 1963–70. 8 vols.

And on the Eighth Day. 1964.

Ellery Queen's 12 (editor). 1964.

Ellery Queen's Double Dozen (editor). 1964.

Ellery Queen's International Case Book. 1964.

Ellery Queen's 20th Anniversary Annual (editor). 1965.

Ellery Queen's Lethal Black Book (editor). 1965.

The Fourth Side of the Triangle. 1965.

Queens Full: 3 Novelets and a Pair of Short Shorts. 1965.

A Study in Terror ⟨*Sherlock Holmes versus Jack the Ripper*⟩. 1966.

Ellery Queen's Crime Carousel (editor). 1966.

The Woman in the Case ⟨*Deadlier Than the Male*⟩. 1966.

Ellery Queen's All-Star Lineup (editor). 1966.

Face to Face. 1967.

Ellery Queen's Poetic Justice: 23 Stories of Crime, Mystery and Detection by World-Famous Poets from Geoffrey Chaucer to Dylan Thomas (editor). 1967.

The House of Brass. 1968.

QED: Queen's Experiments in Detection. 1968.

Ellery Queen's Mystery Parade (editor). 1968.

Cop Out. 1969.

The Case of the Murderer's Bride and Other Stories by Erle Stanley Gardner (editor). 1969.

Ellery Queen's Minimysteries: 70 Short-Short Stories of Crime, Mystery and Detection (editor). 1969.

Ellery Queen's Murder—in Spades! (editor). 1969.

Ellery Queen's Shoot the Works! (editor). 1969.

Ellery Queen's Murder Menu (editor). 1969.

The Last Woman in His Life. 1970.

Ellery Queen's Mystery Jackpot (editor). 1970.

Ellery Queen's Grand Slam (editor). 1970.

P as in Police by Lawrence Treat (editor). 1970.

A Fine and Private Place. 1971.

Ellery Queen's The Golden 13: 13 First Prize Winners from Ellery Queen's Mystery Magazine (editor). 1971.

The Spy and the Thief by Edward D. Hoch (editor). 1971.

Ellery Queen's Anthology: Spring–Summer Edition (editor). 1971–73. 3 vols.

Ellery Queen's Headliners (editor). 1971.

Ellery Queen's Anthology: Fall–Winter Edition (editor). 1971–73. 3 vols.

Ellery Queen's Best Bets (editor). 1972.

Ellery Queen's Mystery Bag (editor). 1972.

Amateur in Violence by Michael Gilbert (editor). 1973.

Ellery Queen's Crookbook (editor). 1974.

Ellery Queen's Christmas Hamper (editor). 1974.

Ellery Queen's Murdercade (editor). 1975.

Kindly Dig Your Grave and Other Wicked Stories by Stanley Ellin (editor). 1975.

Ellery Queen's Aces of Mystery (editor). 1975.

Ellery Queen's Masters of Mystery (editor). 1975.

Ellery Queen's Crime Wave (editor). 1976.

The Prizewinners (editor). 1976.

Ellery Queen's Giants of Mystery (editor). 1976.

The Grand Masters (editor). 1976.

Ellery Queen's Magicians of Mystery (editor). 1976.

Ellery Queen's Searches and Seizures (editor). 1977.

How to Trap a Crook and 12 Other Mysteries by Julian Symons (editor). 1977.

The Golden Age (editor). 1977. 2 vols.

Ellery Queen's Champions of Mystery (editor). 1977.

Ellery Queen's X Marks the Plot (editor). 1977.

Ellery Queen's Crimes and Consequences (editor). 1977.

Ellery Queen's Faces of Mystery (editor). 1977.

Ellery Queen's Who's Who of Whodunits (editor). 1977.

Detective Directory (editor). 1977–78. 2 vols.

Ellery Queen's Masks of Mystery (editor). 1978.

Ellery Queen's A Multitude of Sins (editor). 1978.

Ellery Queen's Napoleons of Mystery (editor). 1978.

Japanese Golden Dozen: The Detective Story World in Japan (editor). 1978.

Cherished Classics (editor). 1978.

The Old Masters (editor). 1978.

The Supersleuths (editor). 1978.

Stories Not to Be Missed (editor). 1978.

Amateurs and Professionals (editor). 1978.

The Forties (editor). 1978.

The Fifties (editor). 1978.

The Sixties (editor). 1978.

The Seventies (editor). 1979.

Ellery Queen's Wings of Mystery (editor). 1979.

Ellery Queen's Scenes of the Crime (editor). 1979.

The Supersleuths Revisited (editor). 1979.

The Grand Masters Up to Date (editor). 1979.

Choice Cuts (editor). 1979.

Ellery Queen's Secrets of Mystery (editor). 1979.

Ellery Queen's Windows of Mystery (editor). 1980.

Ellery Queen's Circumstantial Evidence (editor). 1980.

Ellery Queen's Veils of Mystery (editor). 1980.

The Amazing Adventures of Lester Leith by Erle Stanley Gardner (editor). 1980.

The Best of Suspense (editor). 1980.

Ellery Queen's Crime Cruise round the World (editor). 1981.

Ellery Queen's Doors to Mystery (editor). 1981.

Ellery Queen's Eyes of Mystery (editor). 1981.

Ellery Queen's Eyewitnesses (editor). 1982.

Ellery Queen's Maze of Mysteries (editor). 1982.

Ellery Queen's Book of First Appearances (editor; with Eleanor Sullivan). 1982.

Five Complete Novels ⟨*And on the Eighth Day, The Player on the Other Side, Inspector Queen's Last Case, Cat of Many Tails, Double, Double*⟩. 1982.

Ellery Queen's Lost Ladies (editor; with Eleanor Sullivan). 1983.

The Best of Ellery Queen (editor). 1983.

Ellery Queen's Memorable Characters (editor; with Eleanor Sullivan and Karen
     A. Prince). 1984.

The Best of Ellery Queen: Four Decades of Stories from the Mystery Masters.
     Ed. Francis M. Nevins, Jr., and Martin H. Greenberg. 1985.

Classic Crime (editor). 1987.

Six of the Best: Short Novels by Masters of Mystery (editor). 1989.

The Omnibus of Modern Crime Stories (editor; with Eleanor Sullivan). 1991.

Masters of Suspense (editor; with Eleanor Sullivan). 1992.

Works by Dannay:
The Golden Summer. 1953.

Works Attributed to Ellery Queen but Not by Dannay or Lee:
The Last Man Club. 1940.

Ellery Queen, Master Detective. 1941.

The Penthouse Mystery. 1941.

The Black Dog Mystery. 1941.

The Perfect Crime. 1942.

The Murdered Millionaire. 1942.

The Golden Eagle Mystery. 1942.

The Green Turtle Mystery. 1942.

The Red Chipmunk Mystery. 1946.

The Brown Fox Mystery. 1948.

The White Elephant Mystery. 1950.

The Yellow Cat Mystery. 1952.

The Blue Herring Mystery. 1954.

Dead Man's Tale. 1961.

Quintin Chivas. 1961.

The Mystery of the Merry Magician. 1961.

Death Spins the Platter. 1962.

The Scrolls of Lysis. 1962.

The Mystery of the Vanished Victim. 1962.

Murder with a Past. 1963.

Wife or Death. 1963.

Kill as Directed. 1963.

The Golden Goose. 1964.

The Four Johns. 1964.
The Duke of Chaos. 1964.
Blow Hot, Blow Cold. 1964.
The Last Score. 1964.
Beware the Young Stranger. 1965.
The Copper Frame. 1965.
A Room to Die In. 1965.
The Cree from Minataree. 1965.
The Killer Touch. 1965.
The Devil's Cook. 1966.
The Purple Bird Mystery. 1966.
The Madman Theory. 1966.
The Passionate Queen. 1966.
Where Is Bianca? 1966.
Who Spies, Who Kills? 1966.
Why So Dead? 1966.
Losers, Weepers. 1966.
Shoot the Scene. 1966.
How Goes the Murder? 1967.
Which Way to Die? 1967.
What's in the Dark? 1968.
Guess Who's Coming to Kill You? 1968.
Kiss and Kill. 1969.
The Campus Murders. 1969.
The Black Hearts Murders. 1970.
The Blue Movie Murders. 1972.

✦ ✦ ✦

Rex Stout
1886–1975

REX TODHUNTER STOUT, the son of John Wallace and Lucetta Todhunter Stout, was born on December 1, 1886, in Noblesville, Indiana. Less than a year after his birth his parents moved to a farm near Wakarusa, Kansas, where Rex performed chores with his three brothers and five sisters and also read voraciously. After graduating from Topeka High School in 1903, Stout entered the University of Kansas but left after a few weeks. In 1905 he joined the navy, traveling throughout the eastern seaboard and the West Indies. He received his discharge in 1907.

After working a variety of jobs in the Midwest, Stout moved to New York City in 1908 and became a bookkeeper. He remained restless, however, and in 1911 he lived in twelve different states, from Louisiana to Washington, before returning to New York. In 1912, having published a few poems and articles, Stout decided to attempt a career in writing. Over the next five years he wrote four novels and dozens of short stories for *All-Story*, a pulp magazine of the Munsey chain (one of these, *Under the Andes*, was published in book form in 1985). Most of these stories were tales of adventure and romance, although a few involved crime and suspense.

Stout married Fay Kennedy in 1916, the same year he and his brother Bob established the Educational Thrift Service, an agency that encouraged schoolchildren to open savings accounts. The agency proved very successful, allowing Stout more time for writing and other pursuits. He worked for the American Civil Liberties Union, became president of the Vanguard Press, and developed friendships with the New York intelligentsia, including John Dos Passos and Dorothy Parker.

In 1926 Stout, now financially secure, left the Educational Thrift Service, spending the next year traveling in Europe. In 1929 he returned to the United States, building a house in Brewster, New York, where he would live for the rest of his life. In that year he published the first of five mainstream novels. Although well received, these works did not establish Stout as a major American writer. After divorcing his wife in 1931 and marrying Pola Weinbach in 1932, Stout began work on a detective novel, *Fer-de-Lance*, which was published in 1934. This is the first novel to feature the huge detective Nero Wolfe, who never leaves his Manhattan apartment but instead practices armchair detection based upon the information gathered by his assistant, Archie Goodwin. Over the next decade Stout wrote many novels about Wolfe and a few about another detective, Tecumseh Fox (the first of which was *Double for Death*, 1939).

The Nero Wolfe novels conform generally to the tradition of the fairplay detective story, where all clues are made available to the reader. Stout, however, produced an amalgam of the pure detective story and the hardboiled crime novel by having Wolfe play the role of the infallible logician and Goodwin act as a vigorous pursuer of clues and criminals. The Nero Wolfe novels are more than intellectual puzzles: they feature Stout's deeply felt beliefs on morality, society, and justice; for Stout, the capturing of a criminal (who is often allowed or pressured to commit suicide) represents the restoration of social order from chaos or anarchy.

World War II interrupted Stout's writing, as he worked for a number of organizations, including the Fight for Freedom Committee and Freedom House, that supported American entry into the war and attacked Nazi propaganda. He also helped to found the Writer's War Board, which produced radio dramas supporting the war. Stout came under criticism for his ferocious anti-Germanism, since he blamed not only Hitler but the whole German people for the war. After the war, however, Stout became devoted to the cause of world government.

By 1946 Stout had returned to writing Nero Wolfe novels and novelettes, producing at least one or two books every year until 1969. One late novel, *The Doorbell Rang* (1965), provoked controversy by its attack on the FBI and J. Edgar Hoover. Shortly thereafter, Stout achieved notoriety of a different sort by his outspoken support of the Vietnam War. His health began to fail in his later years, and Stout died on October 27, 1975, shortly after finishing his final novel, *A Family Affair* (1975). His biographer John McAleer has assembled a collection of his early pulp writings, *Justice Ends at Home and Other Stories* (1977).

◈ Critical Extracts

ISAAC ANDERSON   Several times in the course of this story ⟨Fer-de-Lance⟩ Nero Wolfe is called a genius. The term is painfully inadequate, but it is the best that the dictionary offers, so it will have to do, unless one prefers to call him a miracle man. Without stirring from his chair, Wolfe senses a connection between the disappearance of an Italian metal worker from his lodgings in New York and the sudden death of a college president on the links of a Westchester County golf club. Furthermore, although there has been no suspicion of foul play in the case of the college president, Wolfe offers to bet the District Attorney of Westchester County that an autopsy will show a poisoned needle or dart in the body. The District Attorney does not take the bet, but he does order an exhumation and an autopsy, which shows that Wolfe is right. The clues from which Wolfe draws his conclusions are so slight that to an ordinary person they appear to be negligible, and yet the genius is able to deduce from them not only that murder has been done but the precise manner in which it was done. The only thing he does not know at the very beginning is the identity of the murderer. That he is to learn later, and the method he chooses for revealing his knowledge to the authorities provides a sensational concluding chapter for a story which abounds in surprises.

Nero Wolfe is so fat that locomotion is next to impossible for him. For his fact-finding he depends upon his secretary, Archie, and it is the latter who tells the tale. The author has done a clever bit of work in making the narrative style employed by Archie correspond so exactly to his character and attainments as they are revealed in little touches here and there throughout the book.

> Isaac Anderson, "New Mystery Stories," *New York Times Book Review*, 28 October 1934, p. 18

EDMUND WILSON   Here ⟨in *Not Quite Dead Enough*⟩ was simply the old Sherlock Holmes formula reproduced with a fidelity even more complete than it had been by Jacques Futrelle almost forty years ago. Here was the incomparable private detective, ironic and ceremonious, with a superior mind and eccentric habits, addicted to overeating and orchid-raising, as Holmes had his enervated indulgence in his cocaine and his violin, yet always prepared to revive for prodigies of intellectual alertness; and here were the admiring stooge, adoring and slightly dense, and Inspector Lestrade of Scotland Yard, energetic but entirely at sea, under the new name of Inspector Cramer of Police Headquarters. Almost the only difference was that Nero Wolfe was fat and lethargic instead of lean and active like Holmes, and that he liked to make the villains commit suicide instead of handing them over to justice. But I rather enjoyed Wolfe himself, with his rich dinners and quiet evenings in his house in farthest West Thirty-fifth Street, where he savors an armchair sadism that is always accompanied by beer. The two stories that made up this new book—"Not Quite Dead Enough" and "Booby Trap"—I found rather disappointing; but, as they were both under the usual length and presented the great detective partly distracted from his regular profession by a rigorous course of training for the Army, I concluded that they might not be first-rate examples of what the author could do in this line and read also *The Nero Wolfe Omnibus*, which contains two earlier book-length stories: *The Red Box* and *The League of Frightened Men*. But neither did these supply the excitement I was hoping for. If the later stories were sketchy and skimpy, these seemed to have been somewhat padded, for they were full of long episodes that led nowhere and had no real business in the story. It was only when I looked up Sherlock Holmes that I realized how much Nero Wolfe was a dim and distant copy of an original.

Edmund Wilson, "Why Do People Read Detective Stories?" (1944), *Classics and Commercials: A Literary Chronicle of the Forties* (New York: Farrar, Straus, 1950), pp. 232–33

REX STOUT   It is more difficult to write a good story—or anyhow an exciting story—about a child catching a butterfly than one about a man catching a murderer. Some judges of the art of writing, both professional and amateur, seem, therefore, to think that it is more commendable for a storyteller to tell about catching butterflies than about catching murderers. That line of reasoning is over my head. The greatest commendation does not necessarily go to the greatest overcomer of difficulties. It is harder to eat soup with a fork than with a spoon, but not ergo more praiseworthy.

A good deal of the current irritation in certain quarters with writers of mysteries (or detective stories or murder tales) appears to be based on a resentment of the fact that they do not instead try their hands at another

Hamlet or *Divine Comedy* or a novel by Henry James. Surely that is asking for trouble. It would be just as sensible to interrupt a man digging a ditch with the angry demand, "Why the devil aren't you repairing watches or painting murals?" Should he, incredibly, accept the criticism as valid and start to do a mural or fix a watch, the result would be painful. It would be similarly painful should a murder story writer attempt a Henry James; and more painful still should a Henry James undertake to write a detective story. He wouldn't have what it takes.

What it takes is more than the simple faculty of getting excited about a corpse and a man hunt, though that is essential. A poet or a philosopher can write about life and death, but only a storyteller can write about *this* life and *this* death. Not only is there no occasion for comparison; there is no basis for one. The poet or philosopher stirs your soul; the storyteller makes you sit on the edge of your chair. It all depends, not on some transcendental scheme of ultimate values, nor on the slow pronouncement of the tribunal of time, but on what you are after at the moment.

Rex Stout, "Introduction," *Rue Morgue No. 1*, ed. Rex Stout and Louis Greenfield (New York: Creative Age Press, 1946), pp. ix–x

---

ALVA JOHNSTON   Nero Wolfe, the fat detective of Rex Stout's novels, towers over his rivals in one respect: he is a superman who talks like a superman. It is a very tough literary trick to make a mastermind sound like a mastermind. Most of the storybook detectives are too much like the new ultra-scientific calculating machines, which have gorgeous electronic brains for solving problems but no particular talent for dialogue. Genius is the curse of the mystery story. It tends to destroy individuality and drag everybody down to the same level. It is harder to tell intellectual giants apart than Hollywood blondes. Nero, however, is an exceptional character creation—a genius who rises above mediocrity.

Circulating-library detectives can generally be traced to distinguished antecedents—Napoleon, Robin Hood, Frank Merriwell, Jehovah, Howe & Hummel, Galahad, Houdini, Sam Spade. Nero is different. He has no resemblance to any of the eminent men of action. His specialty is fallacy-detecting; he solves mysteries by spotting bad logic and exposing it in choice English. He is a born debater, a distant cousin of Parliamentary fighting cocks like Pitt, who ran men out of public life for uttering fallacies in his presence. He is a curiously elegant and luminous talker for a foul-play investigator. His outbursts have a faint flavor of the great days of word-bandying when men paid thirty guineas a seat to hear the metaphors whistle past Warren Hastings. ⟨. . .⟩

Rex Stout himself has been accused of being the original of Nero Wolfe. At first sight, he is an unlikely candidate, for he bears no physical resemblance to his hero. Stout is a sort of dual personage. He has one public consisting of Nero Wolfe fans; he also has a public of his own, developed by his activities as a platform orator and radio debater, as chairman of the Writers' War Board, president of the Authors' Guild, and leader of many causes, particularly that of world federation. He is the head of the recently formed Writers Board for World Government. Mystery readers generally assume that Rex Stout looks like Nero Wolfe, and they are sometimes much taken aback when they confront the author in person. It is on record that Nero Wolfe weighs two hundred and eighty-two pounds; Stout weighs a hundred and fifty. The detective is smooth-shaven; Stout has a square-trimmed grayish beard of moderate length. The beard, however, happens to be a bit of evidence that the author and the character are fundamentally alike. The ruling principle with Nero Wolfe is economy of effort; Stout's beard is a protest against wasting time and energy on shaving.

Alva Johnston, "Alias Nero Wolfe—I," *New Yorker*, 16 July 1949, p. 26

KINGSLEY AMIS   Wolfe gets about as far as a human being can, much further than Sherlock Holmes, in his suspicion, fear, almost hatred of humanity. We all have such moods, and Wolfe is there to reassure us that these feelings are quite proper for an intelligent, learned, humane and humorous man. This is perhaps the secret of his attraction, for attractive he abundantly is. Along with this goes a marked formidable quality, such that one would, on meeting Wolfe in the flesh, feel grateful for his approval and daunted by his contempt. All really great detectives inspire this reaction, perhaps by acting as some version of a father figure. ⟨Father⟩ Brown does it to us, Dr Fell does; even, granted the shift in general outlook since late-Victorian times, Holmes does. Any kind of real policeman does not, and anybody Mike Hammer took a liking to ought to feel a twinge of alarm.

Another part of Wolfe's appeal is his addiction to views and attitudes that seem both outdated and sensible, reactionary and right, the sort of thing you and I ought to think and feel, and probably would if we had Wolfe's leisure and obstinacy. Who has not wanted to insist on never going out, living to an unshakable routine, distrusting all machines more complicated than a wheelbarrow and having to be heavily pressured each time before getting into a car, allowing hardly anybody to use one's first name, keeping television out and reading all the time, reacting so little in conversation that an eighth-of-an-inch shake of the head becomes a frenzy of negation, using an inflexible courtesy such that proven murderers are still referred to as 'Mr' and an eighteenth-century style of speech that throws off stuff like: 'Afraid? I can dodge folly without backing into fear' and: 'Madam, I am neither a thaumaturge nor a dunce'? Wolfe is every man's Tory, a contemporary Dr Johnson. The original Dr Johnson was a moralist before everything else, and so at heart is Wolfe. This, I suppose, makes him even more of an antique.

Kingsley Amis, "Unreal Policemen" (1966), *What Became of Jane Austen? and Other Questions* (London: Jonathan Cape, 1970), pp. 122–23

WILLIAM S. BARING-GOULD   "I have no talents. I have genius or nothing," Nero Wolfe is fond of saying. "But all genius is distorted," he is prepared to admit, "even my own."

In his own view, Wolfe is also "a philosopher," "an artist," and "a born actor with a weakness for dramatic statements." "I was born romantic," he adds, "and I shall never recover from it." And again: "I need a lot of money and ordinarily my clients get soaked. But I am also an incurable romantic."

Among other things, Wolfe is a man of honor, although he does not approve of that word. "It has been employed too much by objectionable people and has been badly soiled," he says in *Some Buried Caesar*. "I rarely offer pledges, because I would redeem one, tritely, with my life," he tells Howard Bronson in that same adventure. "What the tongue has promised the body must submit to," he says in *Too Many Cooks*, perhaps quoting an East European folk saying. To Rudolf Faber in *Over My Dead Body* he says, "I can give you my word, but I know what it's worth and you don't." And: "No man alive can say that I ever dishonored my word," he says in *The Doorbell Rang*.

Wolfe is also admirably free of prejudice: he despises the word "nigger" and insists on "Ethiope." "The ideal human arrangement," he told the cooks, waiters, and busboys at Kanawha Spa in West Virginia, "is one in which distinctions of race and color and religion are totally disregarded."

Wolfe further regards himself as one of the "only three or four" men in the world who can be depended upon to base their decisions on reason—"and even we will bear watching."

His colossal conceit aside, Wolfe's "only serious flaw" is his lethargy, and he tolerates Archie Goodwin and "even pays him" to help him circumvent it.

> William S. Baring-Gould, *Nero Wolfe of West Thirty-fifth Street: The Life and Times of America's Largest Private Detective* (New York: Viking Press, 1969), pp. 3–4

ARNOLD JAFFE   Wolfe could ⟨. . .⟩ justify his assults upon murderers from a ⟨. . .⟩ philosophical angle. A murder might be seen as a violation of individual freedom, as a unilateral declaration of war upon the ethic of Wolfe's relativistic world view. As far as Wolfe was concerned a search for personal vengeance "would be accepting the intolerable doctrine that man's responsibility is to his ego." That, he exclaimed, was the policy of Malenkov, Tito, Franco, and Joseph McCarthy and Hitler before them. It masqueraded "as a basis for freedom, [but] it is the oldest toughest of the enemies of freedom." Wolfe declared in *The Black Mountain* (1954) that the essence of humanity was freedom, without which it lost its identity. Without freedom, humans lacked choice, and without choice, in Wolfe's scheme of things, life was neither absurd nor living.

Of course, the ultimate denial of choice was its termination through death. As a solution to the issue of which option to choose, Wolfe considered death perfect:

> A man's time is his own only by sufferance. There are many ways in which he may be dispossessed: flood, famine, war, marriage—not to speak of death which is the most satisfactory of all because it closes the question finally. (*Fer-de-Lance*)

Yet, death was not equivalent to murder, which he considered both melodrama and tragedy. Therein lay the nub of Wolfe's conceit. When he set out to ensnare a murderer he could see himself not merely as a worker, not even solely as an artist, but as a representative of modern civilized morality. Throughout his career Wolfe emphasized the importance of saving lives, preventing unnecessary violence and accepting the limitations imposed by civilization on murderous urges. Wolfe's interpretation of his art, and its role in society, raised detection beyond the level of either intellectual or sordid puzzle solving. With Wolfe as its spokesperson, fictional detectives emerged as preservers of individual freedom in a world where interdependence and interference had grown commonplace and normal.

Arnold Jaffe, "Murder with Dignity: Rex Stout," *New Republic*, 30 July 1977, p. 43

JOHN McALEER   Between 1929 and 1933, before embarking on his career as a detective story writer, Rex Stout wrote four psychological novels, which he hoped would establish him as a serious writer. While the critics did indeed allow that he showed some potential as an *avant-garde* novelist, they also reported sighting an orthodox storyteller riding amid the billows of psychological upheaval. Rex saw that being a storyteller was not a deplorable fate. He could be one and still say what he had to say. He never regretted that decision. At the end of his life, when he reflected that his books had received generous critical acclaim and had, as well, sold more than a hundred million copies, he concluded that he had not blundered in taking the road he had traveled on. ⟨. . .⟩

The work of those early years constitutes, in fact, an honorable record of preparation. Yet, writing for the pulps, Rex had to produce on demand and produce quickly. At times he was, he acknowledged, "a goddamn fiction factory." Despite that, he did a variety of things well. His dialogue was terse, witty, reliable, and alive. He avoided stereotypes. He did not overplot. He was neither preachy nor pretentious. Here and there a debt to Chekhov, O. Henry, Stephen Crane, and Alfred Lewis is discernible. But he was not glaringly derivative. He was too adequate a person for that. Nor did he flaunt his surprising erudition. Even when Culp lectures Leg on Montaigne he does so with becoming reluctance.

Rex's names fit his characters. They always did. He prided himself on that. His characters fit the situations they find themselves in. Rex provided for that too. Even though Culp insists that it is easier to look into the mirror that Montaigne held up to nature than to hold up one's own mirror, Rex's comments on human nature were founded mostly on his own observations. Yet he was not tied to his experiences. Some he utilized; more often he transcended them. Without propagandistic effect, a therapeutic intent suffuses the entertainment. For him facts were the foundation of higher, wider truths. He instructed as he amused. He rebuked bureaucracy, the law, lagging prison reform, Puritanism, the Protestant ethic, racial prejudice, inherited wealth, social and intellectual arrogance, pride, avarice, and pedantry. He was confident and merry, but behind the façade of fun, Rex Stout, a man of many causes, conspired to bring about a better, wiser humanity. The young writer had not found a single advocate through whom he could speak, an oracle to lift facts above the platform of common life and confer on them universal significance. No Wolfe stood then at his door, but just around the corner Wolfe lay waiting. And by the howls he would raise, giving voice to Rex Stout's passionate commitment to a just, well-ordered society, he would buy time for free men everywhere so that they might set their houses in order and put to rout whatever fiends lay in wait to devour them.

John McAleer, "Introduction," *Justice Ends at Home and Other Stories* by Rex Stout (New York: Viking Press, 1977), pp. xxvi–xxvii

---

P. G. WODEHOUSE   Nobody who claims to be a competent critic can say that Rex Stout does not write well. His narrative and dialogue could not be improved, and he passes the supreme test of being rereadable. I don't know how many times I have reread the Nero Wolfe stories, but plenty. I know exactly what is coming and how it is all going to end, but it doesn't matter. That's *writing*.

Does the ordinary reader realize how exactly right those Nero Wolfe stories are? There are no loose ends. One could wonder why Sherlock Holmes, fawned on by kings and prime ministers, was not able to afford rooms in Baker Street—price at the turn of the century thirty bob a week including breakfast—unless he got Doctor Watson to put up half the money, but in Nero Wolfe, a professional detective charging huge fees, you can believe. Those orchids, perfectly understandable. He liked orchids and was in a financial position to collect them. He liked food, too. Again perfectly understandable. He refused to leave his house on business, and very sensible of him if his wealth and reputation were such that he could get away with it. In other words, there was nothing contrived about his eccentricities, purely because Stout knew his job.

P. G. Wodehouse, "Foreword," *Rex Stout: A Biography* by John McAleer (Boston: Little, Brown, 1977), p. xv

DAVID R. ANDERSON   In significant fiction, themes imply values. Out of the Wolfe cycle grows a world imbued with values; indeed, the most striking thing about Wolfe as a character is his continuous and emphatic insistence on values in everything from quality of food to quality of thought. Archie, too, lives in a world of clearly defined values—as clearly defined as the routine of their household. Some of the values are comic; others reflect the themes of the Wolfe cycle, its pattern, and its roots in Rex Stout's concept of crime fiction.

The Wolfe novels value truth. Of course, both Wolfe and Archie lie routinely to the police and others in their search for murderers, but that is irrelevant. The crucial fact is that they are devoted to finding murderers, to finding out the truth. Lies committed in pursuit of that goal merely serve the truth which is their goal. But Wolfe's intellect thrives on other kinds of truth as well. He removed Sir Thomas More's *Utopia* from his bookshelves upon discovering that More had framed Richard III to flatter Henry. He despises advertising for its commitment to ignoring truth when it will not help sales. Madeline Fraser sells Hi-Spot, a soft drink, with great success, yet the taste of it makes her ill. "She is a dangerous woman," Wolfe comments. He will not permit flummery, flattery, or self-deception from clients, from victims, from Archie, or even from himself.

The Wolfe novels also value order. Wolfe's rigid daily schedule, his fondness for the routine he shares with Archie, his contempt for international intrigue and domestic corruption, but most of all his crusade to unmask the violators of social order—murderers—all these attest to his respect for order. The haphazard, the unexpected, and the unpredictable offend Wolfe not because he is small-minded but because he values the stability and security of order. It is tempting to link his value of truth with his value of order, to find a metaphysical ground where they merge, so that truth becomes order and order truth. But this is not Wolfe either. These novels value not so much a particular form of order as order in the abstract, order as opposed to destructive disorder. They value the kind of order affirmed in "Jack and the Beanstalk" and "St. George and the Dragon." They value the order that gives sense to human community and finally to civilization itself.

Finally, the Wolfe novels value reason. They dramatize the pursuit of crime by reason as embodied in Nero Wolfe. Amidst a world, like the real one, dominated by unpredictable, uncontrollable passion, Wolfe personifies reason, which controls his thought, illuminates his inquiries, brings down his game. In doing so it upholds order, hence the cycle's approval of it.

Reason is not valuable strictly in itself; its value derives from its service to human organization. Yet reason is not merely utilitarian. Wolfe's rationality is hard-won. Bloodless rationality is the property of an Arnold Zeck, not a Nero Wolfe. The value of reason in this sense is that it is the product of a struggle. Upholders of order are our romantic heroes, and Wolfe qualifies under that category. His daily schedule is as much an insistence on order as a tribute to it; similarly, Wolfe's fat, his gruffness, and his seclusion betray his struggle to insulate himself from emotions, to harness them, to grant them a place, but a smaller one than they claim. Reason then is a goal; it is also a process, a struggle. The Wolfe novels value it as both.

> David R. Anderson, *Rex Stout* (New York: Frederick Ungar Publishing Co., 1984), pp. 19–23

NORMAN E. STAFFORD   Innovation was a hallmark of Stout's business and artistic life. Not surprisingly, it also became evident when he began writing mystery fiction. Although probably unintentional, his creativity in the Nero Wolfe tales altered significantly the long-established classical detective formula. Nero Wolfe the character conforms perfectly to the model of the classical detective, standing beside Hercule Poirot as a direct descendant of C. Auguste Dupin and Sherlock Holmes. Like them— eccentric, aloof, detached from the concerns of ordinary people—he is a genius, with awe-inspiring mental powers, living in a world he has created. The Nero Wolfe fiction differs significantly from other works in the classical formula, however, because of the greatly expanded role of the narrator, Archie Goodwin, Wolfe's principal investigator. The formula of the hard-boiled detective was in its nascent stage at the time that Stout began exploring its possibilities. Stout's elevation of the narrator merges the two detective story formulas, creating a "hybrid" in which the progeny possesses the strengths of both parents. The combination of formulas in the Wolfe story line, which adheres to the classical tradition in emphasizing the solution, either masks shortcomings in plot or reinforces plot elements. The Archie story line follows the hardboiled tradition in concentrating on the protagonist's actions, and Stout's unique blending of conventions mitigates the tragic implications inherent in the formula. 〈. . .〉

Paradoxically, by including elements of the hardboiled, Stout also establishes the limits of the classical formula. Although Peter Wimsey and Hercule

Poirot often do their own legwork, Archie does virtually all of Wolfe's. When Wolfe is on stage, therefore, his performance as a master of ratiocination is the focus, not the way in which he gathered the facts that he analyzes.

The classical formula, however, also ameliorates the hardboiled, creating a less tragic protagonist. Because the Wolfe fiction conforms primarily to the classical formula, with Wolfe as the protagonist, the cases always conclude on the Wolfe story line, when Wolfe solves the mystery. The reader is usually unaware of the effect on Archie of the quest for the solution. Although he moves through the same chaotic world of violence, murder, and other forms of lawlessness as do Travis McGee, Lew Archer, Philip Marlowe, and Sam Spade, Archie's psychic scars are always hidden by the gigantic shadow of Wolfe. Robert B. Parker's Spenser novels mark a return to this element of the Wolfe fiction. Susan Silverman's love provides Spenser solace and protection from an otherwise meaningless world. Archie is also a marginal man, an ironic loner seeking a retreat from the real world, not in a houseboat nor in a dingy office, but in a single room distinctly separate from the rest of the Wolfe household.

Norman E. Stafford, "Partners in Crime," *Armchair Detective* 23, No. 3 (Summer 1990): 349–50, 353

Bibliography

How Like a God. 1929.

Seed on the Wind. 1930.

Golden Remedy. 1931.

Forest Fire. 1933.

The President Vanishes. 1934.

Fer-de-Lance. 1934.

The League of Frightened Men. 1935.

O Careless Love! 1935.

The Rubber Band. 1936.

The Red Box. 1937.

The Hand in the Glove ⟨*Crime on Her Hands*⟩. 1937.

Too Many Cooks. 1938.

Mr. Cinderella. 1938.

Some Buried Caesar. 1939.

Mountain Cat. 1939.

Double for Death. 1939.

Over My Dead Body. 1940.

Where There's a Will. 1940.

The Broken Vase. 1941.

Red Threads. 1941.

Alphabet Hicks. 1941.

Black Orchids. 1942.

The Illustrious Dunderheads (editor). 1942.

The Nero Wolfe Omnibus ⟨*The League of Frightened Men, The Red Box*⟩. 1944.

Not Quite Dead Enough. 1944.

Bad for Business. 1945.

The Silent Speaker. 1946.

Rue Morgue No. 1 (editor; with Louis Greenfield). 1946.

Too Many Women. 1947.

And Be a Villain ⟨*More Deaths Than One*⟩. 1948.

Trouble in Triplicate. 1949.

The Second Confession. 1949.

Three Doors to Death. 1950.

In the Best Families. 1950.

Curtains for Three. 1951.

Murder by the Book. 1951.

Triple Jeopardy. 1952.

Prisoner's Base ⟨*Out Goes She*⟩. 1952.

The Golden Spiders. 1953.

Three Men Out. 1954.

The Black Mountain. 1954.

Full House: A Nero Wolfe Omnibus ⟨*The League of Frightened Men, And Be a Villain, Curtains for Three*⟩. 1955.

Before Midnight. 1955.

Three Witnesses. 1956.

Might as Well Be Dead. 1956.

Eat, Drink, and Be Buried ⟨*For Tomorrow We Die*⟩ (editor). 1956.

Three for the Chair. 1957.

If Death Ever Slept. 1957.

And Four to Go ⟨*Crime and Again*⟩. 1958.

All Aces: A Nero Wolfe Omnibus ⟨*Some Buried Caesar, Too Many Women, Trouble in Triplicate*⟩. 1958.

Champagne for One. 1958.

Plot It Yourself ⟨*Murder in Style*⟩. 1959.

Three at Wolfe's Door. 1960.

Too Many Clients. 1960.

Five of a Kind: The Third Nero Wolfe Omnibus ⟨*The Rubber Band, In the Best of Families, Three Doors to Death*⟩. 1961.

The Final Deduction. 1961.

Homicide Trinity. 1962.

Gambit. 1962.

The Mother Hunt. 1963.

Trio for Blunt Instruments. 1964.

A Right to Die. 1964.

Royal Flush: The Fourth Nero Wolfe Omnibus ⟨*Fer-de-Lance, Murder by the Book, Three Witnesses*⟩. 1965.

The Doorbell Rang. 1965.

Death of a Doxy. 1966.

The Father Hunt. 1968.

Kings Full of Aces ⟨*Too Many Cooks, Plot It Yourself, Triple Jeopardy*⟩. 1969.

Death of a Dude. 1969.

Three Aces: A Nero Wolfe Omnibus ⟨*Too Many Clients, Might as Well Be Dead, The Final Deduction*⟩. 1971.

Three Trumps ⟨*The Black Mountain, If Death Ever Slept, Before Midnight*⟩. 1973.

Please Pass the Guilt. 1973.

The Nero Wolfe Cook Book (with the editors of the Viking Press). 1973.

Triple Zeck ⟨*And Be a Villain, The Second Confession, In the Best of Families*⟩. 1974.

A Family Affair. 1975.

The First Rex Stout Omnibus ⟨*The Doorbell Rang, The Second Confession, More Deaths Than One*⟩. 1976.

Corsage: A Bouquet of Rex Stout and Nero Wolfe. Ed. Michael Bourne. 1977.

Justice Ends at Home and Other Stories. Ed. John McAleer. 1977.

Under the Andes. 1985.

Josephine Tey
1896–1952

JOSEPHINE TEY is the pseudonym of Elizabeth Mackintosh, who was born in Inverness, Scotland, on June 25, 1896. Her parents, Colin and Josephine Horne Mackintosh, were working-class people devoted to their Scottish heritage; her father was a native Gaelic speaker who learned English only in school. Elizabeth, the oldest of three daughters, attended the local Inverness Academy and the Anstey Physical Training College in Birmingham. After graduating from college, Mackintosh worked in a physiotherapy clinic and a number of schools until she was called back home in 1923 to nurse her ailing mother. After her mother died, Mackintosh remained in Inverness to look after her father.

In 1925 Mackintosh began to publish poetry and short stories under the name Gordon Daviot. Her first novel, *Kif: An Unvarnished History*, appeared in 1929 and was followed by her first mystery novel, *The Man in the Queue*, published later that same year. Despite the fact that it was written in under three weeks, *The Man in the Queue*, introducing the character of Scotland Yard Inspector Alan Grant, was a critical success and won the Dutton Mystery Prize when it was published in the United States. Mackintosh did not especially enjoy writing mysteries, which she felt were limited in structure, and abandoned the genre in favor of writing plays. The early 1930s saw three of her plays produced in London, most notably *Richard of Bordeaux* (produced 1932; published 1933), starring John Gielgud. Other plays include *The Laughing Woman* (produced and published 1934), *Queen of Scots* (produced and published 1934), and *The Stars Bow Down* (produced and published 1939). She also wrote a biography, *Claverhouse* (1937). During this time her pronounced shyness and distrust of the press became well known; throughout her life she refused interviews of any kind, and many personal details of her life remain obscure.

Mackintosh produced her second mystery novel, *A Shilling for Candles*, in 1936 under the pseudonym Josephine Tey (the name of a great-great-grandmother). Mackintosh then abandoned the mystery genre for more than a decade, writing plays and a biography of John Graham as Gordon Daviot. After World War II, Mackintosh returned to both mysteries and the Tey pseudonym with a vengeance, publishing six mysteries in as many years. She began in 1946 with *Miss Pym Disposes*, a murder mystery that takes place in a girls' academy and is solved by a Miss Marple–like amateur detective. It was followed by *The Franchise Affair* (1948), a contemporary retelling of a famous eighteenth-century case involving a false allegation of kidnapping, then by *Brat Farrar* (1949), a story of a charming criminal impostor who uncovers an old murder. In 1950, the year of her father's death, she published *To Love and Be Wise*, an intricate mystery involving a female transvestite.

Around the time of the publication of *To Love and Be Wise* Mackintosh discovered that she was fatally ill. The nature of her illness is unknown; Mackintosh apparently ceased her associations with the outside world in order to prevent her ailment from becoming general knowledge. Nonetheless she continued to write, publishing a historical mystery featuring Inspector Grant, *The Daughter of Time* (1951), shortly before she died on February 13, 1952, during a trip to London. Two other novels were published posthumously that year: *The Privateer*, an historical novel about the pirate Harry Morgan, which appeared under the name Gordon Daviot, and *The Singing Sands*, the final Inspector Grant mystery, which appeared under the name Josephine Tey. Her collected plays were issued in three volumes in 1953–54.

▓ *Critical Extracts*

UNSIGNED   This story ⟨*The Man in the Queue*⟩ has a promising beginning, even though it is a bit preposterous. In a queue of people waiting to secure tickets for a musical comedy a man suddenly drops to the ground and is found to be dead from a stab in the back. The persons who were near him are questioned but with no success. No one knows the man, no one remembers seeing any one leave the line, and no one knows when he was stabbed, for he was so tightly wedged in the line that he might have been held upright for several minutes after his death. There is the possibility, of course, that some one in the queue has guilty knowledge of the murder, but if so the police are unable to discover it. Inspector Grant of Scotland

Yard, who is assigned to the case, does some clever sleuthing and has some exciting adventures before he learns the identity of the murdered man and his slayer, and the story might have been rather better than the average detective yarn if the author had only refrained from revealing to us at great length the mental processes of the detective. Judicious pruning would have made the story much more readable.

Unsigned, "New Mystery Stories," New York Times Book Review, 28 July 1929, p. 13

JAMES SANDOE   Any reader unwary enough to mistake ⟨Tey's⟩ leisure for slowness or the digressions for padding is probably a bird who reads digests of Dickens and Dostoevski or chews up a hamburger because roast beef takes longer to cook. Certainly Miss Tey does not stint her readers. There is a richness of delineation even among the minor players (Dora Siggins in *To Love and Be Wise*, for instance) that is particularly contenting. There is savour too in the setting and in the characters' responses to it. This is most integrally apparent in *Brat Farrar* but it is present in all of them.

Then of course there is Grant, the least insistently genteel of detectives (a cousin of E. C. R. Lorac's Inspector Macdonald, one would guess) and the most satisfyingly human even in the private adversities which enter the latest novels. One has only to recall some of Grant's older contemporaries (Lord Peter Wimsey, Mr. Campion, Roderick Alleyn) in a *crise de nerfs* to measure the accomplishment.

Grant himself was absent from the third of the mysteries, *Miss Pym Disposes* (1947) ⟨. . .⟩ For a mystery it is made up of most unpromising stuffs: the students and staff of a girls' physical education college, observed by a visiting "popular psychologist," wound in an all but plotless succession of incident which has as its apparent climax the nomination of one of the girls for "the Arlinghurst job." Save for one premonitory brush there is no mystery, much less murder, until the novel has run four-fifths of its course. The fact of murder thereafter is, to be sure, the more shocking on that account.

But meanwhile, and observing through Miss Pym's alert, sardonic-compassionate perceptions, we have been altered (as she is) from perhaps casual observers to fierce advocates. This is due only in part to Miss Pym herself, admirable companion though she is. It is the consequence of meeting a lively and provoking company from the coolly gaudy Nut Tart to the shifty Miss Rouse. In a day when one opens the first page of a detective story to be blasted at once by a tommygun, the skill of sustaining human interest in itself seems as rich as it is certainly rare.

> James Sandoe, "Introduction," *Three by Tey: Miss Pym Disposes, The Franchise Affair, Brat Farrar* by Josephine Tey (New York: Macmillan, 1954), pp. vi–vii

---

DOROTHY SALISBURY DAVIS   It has been said that Hammett took the mystery out of the vicar's garden and put it in the hands of those who knew what murder was about. Allowing the too apparent truth of where the pseudo-Hammetts dragged this body of fiction, I wonder if it cannot be said that Josephine Tey spirited it back to the vicar's garden. And there, I submit, it is neither more nor less seemly, and possibly a bit more newsworthy.

A cadaver is a cadaver in any morgue, a corpse a corpse in any coffin. The difference lies not in the dead, but in the living; not in the sightless but in the viewers. Brutality is not necessarily realism any more than compassion is necessarily sentimentality. What fouls us up, and I use the word "foul" in its more offensive sense, is getting sentimental over brutality.

The vicar's garden may seem to imply a small world. It is small only if the vicar is small minded, and of course my allusion is meant only to imply the pleasantness of the company of the late Josephine Tey. She knew her share of vicars: it is quite as impossible to ignore the vicar in England as it is to miss teatime. And as foolish. There was practically no stratum of English society with which she was not conversant, and if any one characteristic most distinguished Miss Tey's work it was her power to evoke character, atmosphere, mores by conversation. Her people talk as though speech comes natural to them. It is good talk as well as story propelling. Indeed it makes one nostalgic for the art of conversation. ⟨. . .⟩

⟨. . .⟩ All Miss Tey's plots could have been written on the back of a match box. But her characters have the diversity of flame, and the sum of their impact is as irresistible. ⟨. . .⟩

Alan Grant, Miss Tey's Scotland Yard man, and himself the most reluctant of heroes, is present ⟨in *Three by Tey*⟩ only in *The Franchise Affair*, and in that he is the antagonist, bringing the case against the women of the Franchise. This is a truly remarkable putting of a detective in his proper place! It must have given Miss Tey a great deal of pleasure to relegate him now and then. So many of her esteemed colleagues in the field have become slaves to their detectives. Grant is perilously human for a detective of fiction: he sometimes sniffles, as who could escape it in the English clime; in one book he needed to go off to Scotland because of an impending breakdown; and in what I believe is a classic use of the detection technique he pursues that wiliest of demons, history, until it yields an amazingly convincing confession about Richard III, the purported murderer of the princes in the Tower—this while Grant is strung up like a plucked fowl, with a broken leg.

> Dorothy Salisbury Davis, "On Josephine Tey," *New Republic*, 20 September 1954, p. 17

HANNA CHARNEY   The crime ⟨in *The Daughter of Time*⟩ concerns only the past, the mystery of the murders of the princes in the Tower of London, which were supposedly instigated by King Richard III. This novel presents a fascinating experiment. The suspense produced by our interest in the future (the fate of the characters affected by the consequences of the crime or the charge) is missing. It is replaced by our general familiarity with this historical episode and its versions in literature, especially Shakespeare's *Richard III*. As Grant, with the help of a student, investigates the mystery, he concludes that King Henry VII and not King Richard III was guilty of the crimes. This reconstruction of the past, this shifting of focus as in a stereograph image, is made all the more effective by the final irony: the theory is not new. Detection has reconstituted an old theory. The truth remains poised in the present, which has buried the past.

Why then does it matter? ⟨. . .⟩ The historical paradigm has its literary counterpart. Why do we care if one or another fictive character killed an imaginary victim, or a victim who is irremediably dead, the murderer having also died long ago? The answer given by detective fiction is that it obviously matters *now*, since we and the detective and other characters are the ones who are presently engaged in the question. Even when it is totally oriented toward a past event, the detective novel reaffirms the process of its motion in time: forward or backward, in whatever segment of the process it is moving. The detective novel thus confirms another crucial concept in contemporary fiction: the acts of writing and reading are in themselves the substance of the book while it is being written or read.

This self-consciousness, which constantly equilibrates time, level of reality, and style, is a key to the form of the detective novel. To overlook this aspect of the detective novel leads to basic misunderstandings. Julian Symons, who has an obvious distaste for detection, thus misinterprets *The Daughter of Time* in *Mortal Consequences*:

> These is nothing new about this theory, as the student discovers
> at the end of their research, and Grant's almost total ignorance of
> history is the most remarkable thing about the book. The pleasure
> taken by critics in the very slow unfolding of a thesis already well
> known suggests a similar ignorance on their part.

This is a perfect way to miss the boat.

Tey's novel is not a piece of historical research, although it is ironically cast in that mold. It describes a full circle and returns to the beginning: one theory against another; this is part of its "message." Symons unwittingly states another part of the "message," "the pleasure taken by critics in the very slow unfolding of a thesis already well known." But then again—once more the balance is redressed—the thesis is not only a thesis; it deals with historical fact, which has deep roots and also branches reaching out into the future. A fact established by history can be taken to be real. Yet the questions posed by its interpretations and an evaluation of its consequences are comparable to those raised by imaginary events: possible analogies are persuasively presented in 〈Robin W.〉 Winks's *The Historian as Detective*. History does not write itself; both the past and the future fully engage human responsibility.

Hanna Charney, *The Detective Novel of Manners: Hedonism, Morality, and the Life of Reason* (Rutherford, NJ: Fairleigh Dickinson University Press, 1980), pp. 18–20

SANDRA ROY   Tey, like most authors, reiterates a limited number of themes in her novels. The most pervading of all is that of deception—things are not what they seem. Appearances are deceiving, the author feels. A man who looks guilty is in fact innocent, while an innocent-appearing person is guilty. Individuals seem to be what they are not; Brat Farrar seems to be the long missing and presumed dead Patrick Ashby while Leslie Searle appears as a strikingly handsome man when she is in fact a woman. No one is as reliable as they seem. The ever-faithful Liz Garrowby could be lured away from her fiancé Walter by Searle. Those who make a big display of religion are especially untrustworthy. Albert Ellis, for example, in *Expensive Halo* is a part-time preacher, full-time Bible quoter and thief. The world must have seemed an extremely deceptive place to the author.

A second theme frequently occurring in the Tey novels is that of mistaken identity or "in place of another." Kenrick in *The Singing Sands* is at first identified as Charles Martin, a Frenchman. Brat Farrar and Leslie Searle impersonate non-living individuals. Brat, as the result of Simon's death, ultimately replaces him in the family's affections. In this novel too, Aunt Bee replaces the mother for Brat and Uncle Charles replaces Brat's unreliable father, Walter.

Thirdly, most of the characters are unable to form significant relationships. Most are isolated due to their chronic inability to respond freely. When Grant himself is tempted to fall in love with Zoë Kentallen in *The Singing Sands*, he is at first frightened and then deeply relieved when his job calls him away from her siren song. He never feels threatened by Marta Hallard, for whom acting supersedes personal emotion. The author herself tended to be remote and distant, having few if any friends and no one close to her. Only in *The Privateer*, her last novel, are close friends portrayed. Here Harry Morgan is seen as willing to lose his own life to protect or avenge a friend. Since Tey spent her last year of life dying painfully alone, the reader might see this as a mute protest against an empty existence.

Sandra Roy, Josephine Tey (Boston: Twayne, 1980), p. 180

JESSICA MANN   After the end of World War II, Josephine Tey published six crime novels. The best, and the one on which her reputation rests, is *The Franchise Affair* (1948). It is a modern reconstruction of a case which has fascinated criminologists since the eighteenth century, the disappearance of Elizabeth Canning. Tey's explanation is less memorable than the exposure of the characters in the story and the convincing detail of the setting in a small English town. This was her first mystery without murder, and it is the better for it. Tey is one of the few writers who can make other crimes equally interesting. *To Love and Be Wise* is about transvestism and revenge, and *Brat Farrar* about impersonation. Although the plotting of these stories is good and the characterisation of a very much higher standard than that found in other contemporary mystery novels, the chief charm, and what lingers longest in the reader's memory, is the style in which Josephine Tey wrote. It is not always perfectly grammatical—she over-used the short, verbless, dramatic sentence—but her wry wit has a very personal flavour, and the acid clarity, almost cattiness, with which she dissects some of her characters and their pretensions may not appeal at all to some readers, but it is attractive to others. Several times she strips the pretensions from actresses, not only in *The Man in the Queue,* which was written before she could have met many, but also in *A Shilling for Candles* and *To Love and Be Wise,* which were both written after her experiences as a successful playwright and give the impression that she knew what she was talking about. She also took an unenthusiastic view of reporters and of the sentimental viciousness of cheap scandal rags. In *To Love and Be Wise* she exposed the pretensions of the arty and the crafty, and especially of the arty writer. The author's own voice is very audible in these novels. She always felt as a writer that her characters' emotions, whether virtuous or malign, were projections of her own complicated self. ⟨. . .⟩

In *The Daughter of Time* Josephine Tey defined a belief which had already appeared *obiter dicta* in all her earlier work: that the face is the mirror of the soul. Inspector Grant always uses his reading of features as a potent clue. In *The Singing Sands,* a brief glimpse of the dead man's 'reckless eyebrows' convinces Grant that the face could not have been that of a French criminal. Not for Tey the remark which Ngaio Marsh puts into the mouth of one of her characters in *False Scent:* 'People talk about eyes and mouths as if they had something to do with the way other people think and behave. Only bits of the body, aren't they? Like navels and knees and toenails. Arrangements.'

To Tey, these arrangements of the bodies were of paramount importance. 'Faces are my business,' Inspector Grant says. ⟨. . .⟩ The quest in *The Daughter of Time* arises because Grant, looking at the anonymous portrait of Richard III, sees a conscientious and perfectionist magnate rather than a murderer. In *The Franchise Affair* the colour of eyes is a clue. The girl who claims to have been kidnapped is called oversexed: 'I have never known anyone, man or woman, with that colour of eyes, who wasn't. That opaque dark blue, like a very faded navy, it's infallible,' says the accused woman, who is later to be proved right.

Jessica Mann, "Josephine Tey," *Deadlier Than the Male: Why Are Respectable English Women So Good at Murder?* (New York: Macmillan, 1981), pp. 215–17

NANCY ELLEN TALBURT   Standard mystery fiction does exist to produce suspense, to display suspicion of the innocent and the apparent innocence of the guilty until the conclusion, and to depict ill-treated victim and suspects. Tey's practice, on the other hand, is to extend the number of the sufferers, to extend the range of sufferings, and, more important, to reveal the character of her detectives by their participation in the sufferings of others, some of which they cause. Most important, these trials of the innocent raise questions concerning the nature of the world where the innocent suffer so regularly, and so much, and in many novels, no resolution is possible of the sort which regularly dispenses happiness to the innocent and punishment to the guilty at the conclusion of the classic detective novel.

The sufferings of Tey's characters go much beyond the social discomfort of being avoided by one's suspicious acquaintances or having to answer the sharply put questions of the Yard. Innocent sufferers represent every class of character: victim, suspect, criminal and detective. Some victims are wholly innocent (Patrick in *Brat Farrar*, the princes in *The Daughter of Time*, Christine Clay in *A Shilling for Candles*). This is often not the case in detective fiction, where the sorrow for the death of the victim must not be allowed to detract from the interest in the investigation of the murder. Thus Roger Ackroyd is stingy, Philip Boyes is self-centered, and the King of Bohemia is a fool, though neither of the two former deserve being murdered. Even when innocent, the victim suffers off-stage, and death is instantaneous in most classic mysteries.

Tey employs two imaginative suffering-but-innocent criminals. Mrs. Wallis (*The Man in the Queue*) is the technical criminal, but the prey of her "innocent" daughter. Brat Farrar is a criminal imposter but suffers three murderous attacks. An innocent suspect is hounded into a fall which results in a severe head injury. Another faints, suffers from exhaustion, and develops near pneumonia as a result of attempting to evade wrongful arrest. The detective suffers in conscience and in reputation for his persecution of a wrong suspect, and, later, spends a week in a hospital bed, and finally develops acute claustrophobia as a result of overwork. In Tey's third novel the treatment of the innocent sufferer achieves a high point. No one who reads the novel will be likely to forget the sufferings of Mary Innes (*Miss Pym Disposes*), whom the detective sentences to an extra-legal lifetime of restitution. Mary is first denied her deserved professional appointment by a prejudiced head mistress. Then she discovers that her best friend has committed murder on her behalf. The resolution of this novel is far from the return to innocence and order of the typical detective novel. The resolution of the fourth novel (*The Franchise Affair*), though less harsh, is similar. The innocent women lose their peaceful life and the means, their house and possessions, to an independence which they had only lately received and had much prized. The lightness of treatment and their strength and ability to cope do not detract from the resolution of this novel in which the regaining of their good name cannot begin to compensate them for their wholly undeserved losses. As Marion Sharpe says: "I suppose tomorrow life will begin again and be just the usual mixture of good and bad. But tonight it is just a place where dreadful things can happen to one." ⟨. . .⟩

There are other uses of the suffering of the innocent in Tey, and it becomes one of her most consistent motifs, even when it is not the central theme of a novel. The regular appearance of this situation lessens the distance usually maintained between reader and what are often rather two-dimensional characters in much of detective fiction, and it is their ability to feel and their vulnerability to suffering which distinguish Tey's detectives.

Nancy Ellen Talburt, "Josephine Tey," *10 Women of Mystery*, ed. Earl F. Bargainnier (Bowling Green, OH: Bowling Green University Popular Press, 1981), pp. 48–50

VICTORIA NICHOLS and SUSAN THOMPSON   Alan Grant is a gentleman. An inheritance has made it unnecessary for him to work for a living. The work he does, however, is what he loves and that for which he is well suited. Little is known about Grant's origins. He describes a grandfather as a renegade Scot and never speaks of his parents. He lives in a comfortable flat and is cared for by devoted housekeepers (Field and Tinker). Most of his life is lived among his colleagues and through his investigations. Grant is well thought of by both his superiors and his subordinates. He and Sergeant Williams, Grant's faithful Watson in all cases, provide a balance for each other and share a high, mutual regard.

Along with the advantage of not looking like a policeman, Grant possesses "flair." Like Tibbett's nose, this flair is an intuitive grasp of information beyond the normal limits of conscious thinking. However, what Grant knows intuitively is not always borne out by the evidence in a case. At times, his colleagues and his own professionalism force him to disregard his flair. It is a powerful force of its own though and worries away at Grant's thinking until he is compelled to do something to acknowledge its significance. In *The Man in the Queue*, his flair acts as a double-edged sword, first leading Grant to the discovery and capture of a fleeing suspect, then acting preconsciously to make him uncomfortable with a too neatly concluded case.

Grant was introduced in 1929 as a developed personality, and over the twenty-three years the series spans, this remains consistent. In the third book, *The Franchise Affair*, written twelve years after the second, Grant makes only a token appearance as Scotland Yard personified, yet even in this brief role, his flair is mentioned. Grant is in charge again in *To Love and Be Wise*, and continues to grow in stature (quite literally from medium height in 1929 to six-foot-plus in 1950).

The Singing Sands, published the year Tey died, is, in every sense, the last book in the series. On leave from his job, Grant is feeling the effects of overwork manifested by severe claustrophobia. Leaving the train which has taken him to the Scots Highlands, where he has gone to recuperate, Grant is confronted with the dead body of a young man in a sleeping compartment. Something in the young man's countenance and the few lines of poetry scribbled in the margin of a newspaper compel Grant to investigate what evidence and authority declare to be an accident. The ex officio investigation is at once Grant's salvation and the means to bring his career at the Yard to an end.

⟨. . .⟩ The success of Tey's novels do not lie in the presence of a dead body and the detection of the perpetrator of murder. She effectively demonstrates, through the perceptions of her main character, that what seems one thing is often, in reality, quite another, and that the other is not necessarily less a crime than the act of murder. Tey's mastery is the ability to use character and setting to subtly guide the reader to precisely the conclusion she has drawn, while keeping the reader unaware of being led. These books can be read as good, escapist mystery stuff. Don't be surprised, however, to know more after you've read a Tey novel than you thought you had learned.

Victoria Nichols and Susan Thompson, *Silk Stalkings: When Women Write of Murder* (Berkeley, CA: Black Lizard Books, 1988), pp. 49–50.

RALPH STEWART   Arguing that ⟨King⟩ Richard ⟨III⟩ was not the murderer of the princes entails, at least in a detective story, showing who the real murderer was: Tey's candidate ⟨in *The Daughter of Time*⟩ is Richard's successor as king, Henry VII. While reading the novel, one has the sense of a detailed and wide-ranging case being built up, but when the arguments are finally made explicit, in a one-page "summing up," they are surprisingly weak and limited. The case against Henry is essentially that he had reason to kill the princes—if they were still alive—and probably had the necessary unscrupulousness to do so; but this is very far from showing that he was actually responsible for their deaths. ⟨. . .⟩

Yet, despite their lack of substance, Tey's arguments remain persuasive, a generation after the original publication of her novel. ⟨. . .⟩ One might say that the weaker the book is as history, the more impressive it is as rhetoric. Tey unobtrusively establishes a set of contexts that controls the reader's impressions, adroitly maintains some very shaky arguments, and is particularly skillful at neutralizing evidence that works against her thesis. Many of the rhetorical techniques used are characteristic of detective fiction but are modified for the extra-literary purpose.

In the first place, the novel is guided by the usual conventions of a detective story: one expects the detective to begin afresh, without much reliance on previous investigations; the obvious suspect is not usually the murderer; the detective's judgments have considerable authority, and in general are to be accepted unless actually shown to be mistaken. In consequence, Inspector Grant's cavalier dismissal of most of the historians of the past four centuries seems unexceptionable, Richard's villainous reputation becomes almost a point in his favour, and Grant's opinions—on, for example, whether someone has behaved suspiciously or not—are soon assumed as fact. ⟨. . .⟩ The vacuum created by the expulsion of the historians is filled partly by assuming that the past was rather like the present—a major point against the historians' Richard III is that Grant has not met anyone like that—and the assumption helps with some details of the book's case. The tower was a royal residence and therefore "not a prison at all." Parliament is treated as if it were like a modern one, independently powerful, and even capable of "giving Richard the title to the crown."

More positively, a new background is built up by Grant's musings on the "green, green England" of the Wars of the Roses, and by lengthy quotations from the novel *Rose of Raby*. The former suggests a simple, orderly world where no one comes to much harm—the war is like a private party or football game (Grant's analogies). The quotations from *Rose of Raby* present the Yorkists as a large, happy family with Richard especially devoted to

Edward, the princes' father. With this idealized view of England and the Yorkists established, the accusations made against Richard's character seem grossly unlikely. ⟨. . .⟩

If *Daughter of Time* relied entirely on pronouncements of this kind, it would be fairly obviously irrelevant to the historical Richard; and it would also be rather flat as a novel—some more fundamental opposition and conflict is necessary for literary vitality. In fact, the novel does include a great deal of historical evidence that tells against Richard—perhaps even all that Tey was aware of—but it is absorbed so skillfully that the central theme remains intact. Tey's techniques for dealing with awkward facts can be studied in microcosm in the report of Richard's clash with Earl Rivers, the princes' maternal uncle. It is not disputed that Rivers and three others were detained and then killed by Richard's orders between Edward IV's death (early April) and Richard's assumption of the crown (late June). ⟨. . .⟩

The account of what happened to Rivers would fill only about a page if assembled in one place, but it is dispersed in six different parts with much unconnected information in between. ⟨. . .⟩ The impression made by the event is dissipated simply because it is related in such an interrupted way: by the time the reader is told that Rivers and his companions have been executed as conspirators, he is unlikely to remember that neither the charge of conspiracy nor the circumstances of Rivers' arrest have been explained.

Ralph Stewart, "Richard III, Josephine Tey, and Some Uses of Rhetoric," Clues 12,
No. 1 (Spring–Summer 1991): 93–95

▨ *Bibliography*

Kif: An Unvarnished History. 1929.

The Man in the Queue. 1929.

The Expensive Halo: A Fable without a Moral. 1931.

Richard of Bordeaux. 1933.

The Laughing Woman. 1934.

Queen of Scots. 1934.

A Shilling for Candles: The Story of a Crime. 1936.

Claverhouse. 1937.

The Stars Bow Down. 1939.

Leith Sands and Other Short Plays. 1946.

Miss Pym Disposes. 1946.
The Franchise Affair. 1948.
Brat Farrar. 1949.
To Love and Be Wise. 1950.
The Daughter of Time. 1951.
The Singing Sands. 1952.
The Privateer. 1952.
Plays. 1953–54. 3 vols.
Three by Tey: Miss Pym Disposes; The Franchise Affair; Brat Farrar. 1954.